Hushed Voices

Unacknowledged Atrocities of the 20th Century

Edited by

Heribert Adam

BERKSHIRE ACADEMIC PRESS

HUSHED VOICES
Unacknowledged Atrocities of the 20th Century

Published by
Berkshire Academic Press Limited
The Barn
Milestone Cottage
Highclere
Berkshire
RG20 9QA
UK
www.berkshireacademicpress.co.uk

First Edition

Cased ISBN-13: 978-1-907784-00-2
Paperback ISBN-13: 978-1-907784-03-3

British Library Cataloguing-in-Publication Data
A catalogue record for this book is available from the British Library

Cover photograph reproduced courtesy of iStockphoto/asterix0597.

Printed in UK by Good News Digital Books

Contents

	Foreword *Alex Boraine, Founding President and Chair of the International Center for Transitional Justice, New York*	v
	Acknowledgements	ix
	About the Contributors	xi
	Introduction *Heribert Adam*	xv
1	Robert Mugabe's Gukurahundi *Sheila Paoli*	1
2	Nightmare in Paradise: The 1964 Zanzibar Revolution and Genocide *Sandra Lockwood*	13
3	Unpacking the "Mau Mau" Rebellion *Salima Charnia*	27
4	The Biafran War for Independence: Nigeria in the 1960s *Patricia Kelly*	41
5	The Algerian Harkis: Témoignages d'une Histoire Cachée *Dylan van der Schyff*	51
6	Unmarked Graves and Old Wounds: The Spanish Civil War *Michael Donovan*	61
7	Blind Spot: The Allied Bombing of Dresden *Scott-Ryan Abt*	75

8 Broken Promises and Blind Eyes: The Expulsion of Ethnic Germans from Czechoslovakia and Poland after World War II 89
Lianna Laberge

9 No One Else to Ask: Investigating the Ukrainian Holodomor 101
Jean Kosar

10 The G-Word: Why Turks and Armenians Can't Talk 113
Karen DeVito

11 Syria: Hama Massacre 125
Omar Ilsley

12 Israel: Stillborn Nation 137
Dale Darychuk

13 The 2002 Massacre of Gujarati Muslims: The Violent Face of Hindu Nationalism 149
Vinit Khosla

14 Shadow Play: Political Mass Murder and the 1965 Indonesian Coup 163
Elaine Brière

15 Comfort Women: Sexual Slaves of the Imperial Japanese Military 177
Linda Elaine Vogt Turner

Conclusions 187
Heribert Adam

Selected Bibliography 203

Index 215

FOREWORD

Alex Boraine, Founding President and Chair of the International Center for Transitional Justice, New York

✧

The Rule of Law is fundamental to the existence of a free, democratic society. It separates us from anarchy. It follows that to maintain the rule of law, accountability for transgressions against the law is imperative. The rule of law and the fair administration of justice deserve the greatest respect by individual countries and the international community alike. No society can claim to be free or democratic without strict adherence to the rule of law. Dictators and authoritarian regimes abandon the rule of law at the first opportunity and resort to brazen power politics, leading to all manner of excesses. It is of central importance, therefore, that, as far as possible, those who violate the law, who violate fundamental human rights, are punished.

In the past 15 years the prosecution of war criminals has featured very prominently. International criminal law has moved from the single most important example, Nuremberg, to a much wider legal response to most crimes. It is this shift from impunity to accountability in terms of prosecutions which has become the defining feature of the international human rights movement. The world has witnessed the birth of very important tribunals such as the Hague Tribunal, the Rwanda Tribunal, the Sierre Leone Special Court and most importantly the advent of the International Criminal Court. This Court makes possible the prosecution of war criminals in countries which are unable or unwilling to prosecute.

It is understandable, therefore, that these steps to halt impunity have been hailed not only by the human rights community, but also by victims in many parts of the world. To victims whose hands and arms were amputated in Sierra Leone, to HIV-positive rape victims in Rwanda, to families burnt out of their homes in East Timor and Bosnia, the day of reckoning for perpetrators brings enormous comfort.

It was soon recognized, however, that it is impossible to prosecute all perpetrators. There are clearly limits to retributive justice and wherever there are human rights violations on a massive scale, such as in the former Yugoslavia, Rwanda, Sierra Leone or the Democratic Republic of Congo, it is impossible to prosecute everyone. So the law becomes selective and the focus is on those who are judged to be the most responsible for human rights violations.

There was recognition that whilst International Law offers a measure of personal culpability in the face of grotesque crimes, there are limits to what it can achieve. Not only is it impossible to prosecute all perpetrators but there are also considerable political restraints. Examples of this include the Extraordinary Chambers of Cambodia which will examine only the crimes of the Khmer Rouge committed between 1975 and 1979. The Iraqi Special Tribunal has no jurisdiction to judge crimes committed since the invasion of that country by the United States and its allies. The International Criminal Court is severely hampered in its work by the well-known opposition of the United States and cannot begin to apply universal rules to fully half the world's countries, including Russia and China.

Clearly, societies in transition need other instruments and other models in order to supplement one form of justice. Transitional justice is not a contradiction of criminal justice, rather it seeks to complement retributive justice with restorative justice. Its approach is holistic, giving due accord to context and political circumstances. It recognizes that justice is the art of the possible and a holistic approach can help to create a just society. It requires more than just punishment to achieve a just society. Documentation of justice and the truth about the past, restoring dignity to victims and embarking on the process of reconciliation are vital elements of a just society. Equally important is the need to begin transforming institutions so that old structures do not impede progress toward the consolidation of democracy and the establishment of a culture of human rights.

It is in this context that Truth Commissions came into being, first in Latin America and then in many parts of the world. There are close to thirty such commissions world wide, and it is generally recognized that the South African model should be a referral point for all commissions that followed. These commissions have had varied success in dealing with the past, publishing the truth, achieving limited accountability and acknowledgement. They are all imperfect instruments but at their best have given victims and societies considerable access to truth and an awareness of the need for accountability.

The emphasis on retributive justice and the growth of transitional justice models is cause for celebration. As this book of *Hushed Voices* makes strikingly clear, there should also be room for remorse and regret that so many thousands of victims have not been heard. There were no trials, no truth commissions, no acknowledgement, no accountability for so many people in many parts of the world. Where were the voices raised in the Genocide in Zanzibar, why has the Japanese government got away with a half-hearted apology concerning the so-called Korean sex slaves? How easily were the victims of the Biafran War of Independence in the 1960s forgotten? Will the Turkish government be allowed to join the European Union without acknowledging once and for all the committing of Genocide against the Armenians? The list of *Hushed Voices* is long and is a devastating commentary on the lack of accountability for many hundreds of thousands of people. But the list could even be longer: what about the Stalinist purges where millions were starved to death, as the essay on the Ukrainian famine (Holodomor) makes clear? How concerned is the human rights community about the thousands of people wrongly incarcerated or executed in China? Is justice only possible in less powerful countries? And who cares about the Russian atrocities in Chechnya? Both today and yesterday nations get away with mass murder.

Is there anything that can be done so that *Hushed Voices* can be heard? It is easy to be cynical and to reply in the negative. There are so many modern injustices that cry out for attention: Sudan, Sri Lanka, Zimbabwe, Israel and Palestine to mention but a few. But it is important to take a nation's past seriously. Every life is precious. The moral imperative for dealing with the past can be summed up in the commandment from the Jewish tradition "to remember is the secret of redemption", and it is to be hoped that modern Israel will take heed of this age old tradition. The psychological argument reminds us that "It is as bad for nations as it is for individual people to suppress the memory of evil or mournful experience." And the political argument is summed up in the famous statement by George Santayana, "Those who forget the past are doomed to repeat it." There is good reason therefore to bring to life *Hushed Voices* not only for the sake of the victims but also because it is the wise and right thing to do.

So what can be done? First, nations and communities need to be reminded of the atrocities which are listed in *Hushed Voices*. Second, at least some may be persuaded to apologize for their direct involvement or their participation in the conspiracy of silence. There are many examples of apologies which have really counted for something. Willy Brandt, the Chancellor of West Germany, both symbolically and practically apologized to the Polish people who had suffered so grievously as a result of the Nazi occupation. Many will recall Brandt kneeling silently at the Warsaw Memorial Museum as an act of confession and repentance for offences against the Polish people.

Another example can be taken from the United States of America. A year after the Japanese air force attacked Pearl Harbor in 1941 the American government ordered the internment of 120,000 Americans of Japanese descent. They were summarily rounded up, lost their homes and property and were subjected to humiliation and persecution. It took the United States 40 years to apologize and offer compensation. In 1976 Gerald Ford issued an official apology to Japanese-Americans and their families who had been unjustly incarcerated. The Canadian government followed a similar process of late recognition of its injustices to Japanese-Canadians. In Australia, when the theft of aboriginal children by the state and the church became a public issue, the then Prime Minister John Howard refused point blank to apologize. Fortunately his successor, Prime Minister Ken Rudd, issued an unqualified apology to the Aboriginal people.

Who then should be called upon to apologize today? Certainly the Turkish government should not only apologize but accept accountability for the murderous treatment of Armenians in 1915. The Japanese government should fully accept that Korean women were used as sex slaves by their soldiers in World War II. The United Kingdom should refrain from boasting about the successful bombing of civilians in Dresden and acknowledge that this was conduct unbecoming and a war crime. We can add to the list but the point is made. We owe it to all those whose voice was silenced to give back to them and their descendants their human dignity and for those responsible to accept their accountability for committing grave atrocities. It is hoped that this innovative volume of "Unacknowledged Atrocities" can at least further the emerging awareness about such shortcomings.

ACKNOWLEDGEMENTS

✧

As with most edited volumes, a diverse group of contributors with various political orientations inevitably differ in style and interpretation of controversial events. We have not tried to impose a uniform line of political correctness on authors who individually bear responsibility for the veracity and quality of their research. However, an editorial committee, Karen DeVito, Vinit Khosla and Elaine Briere, ensured uniform readability by correcting academic jargon. Their painstaking diligence and editorial professionalism in suggesting elaboration and clarification is much appreciated.

My Introduction and Conclusion received valuable feedback from friends and colleagues on different continents: Denis Beckett, Andre du Toit, Hermann Gilliomee, Norman Levy, Ken Owen, Milton Shain, Laura Stovel, Gary Teeple, John Torpey, Pierre van den Berghe, Stanley Uys and Jerry Zaslove. Harvey Weinstein, editor of the prestigious journal *Transitional Justice* and fellow summer resident of Pender Island, insisted on useful clarifications in several discussions. A March 2009 seminar on the topic at the Center for African Studies at the University of Cape Town as well as a three-session lecture series at the University's 2010 Summer School proved helpful, as did many conversations with a long-time friend, Alex Boraine, who not only was the moving spirit behind the celebrated South African Truth and Reconciliation Commission and subsequently founded the International Center for Transitional Justice, but also kindly agreed to write the Foreword to this volume.

Thanks is owed to the contributors who conscientiously followed the guidelines and conceptual frameworks developed in our study group, but often went imaginatively beyond what was expected in regular research. Respectful but frank mutual criticism in our weekly encounters also sharpened our arguments and exposed hidden biases. This book therefore represents a collective effort which hopefully testifies to a stimulating endeavour.

About the Contributors

✧

All contributors are affiliated with the Graduate Liberal Studies Program at Simon Fraser University in Vancouver and are involved with diverse research projects in the Social Sciences and Humanities. In addition to these academic interests, most also pursue other professional careers, are human rights activists or associated with community endeavours which are outlined below.

Heribert Adam, a Fellow of the Royal Society of Canada, is the author, co-author or editor of 11 books on ethnic conflict and peacemaking. He is Professor Emeritus of Sociology at Simon Fraser University and the recipient of several awards, including the 1998 Adenauer Prize of the German Humboldt Foundation, the 2006 Outstanding Achievement Award of the Canadian Sociology Association, and the 2008 Sterling Prize.

Scott-Ryan Abt is a graduate of Simon Fraser University (B.A.) and the University of British Columbia (B.Ed.). He teaches senior history and comparative politics at York House in Vancouver. He is fascinated by the creation of national myths. In particular, he is intrigued by the question of who holds the power of myth-making and how events are remembered or forgotten in the process.

Elaine Brière is an award-winning filmmaker and photojournalist. *Testimony, Photographs of East Timor* was published in 2004 by Between the Lines. *Bitter Paradise: The Sell-out of East Timor*, won Best Political Documentary at the 1997 HOT DOCS film festival.

Salima Charania is a researcher and community organizer. Her academic interests include critical studies in immigration, multicultural policies, race and gender. Of South Asian heritage, she was born in Kenya and immigrated to Canada.

Dale Darychuk has been a practising litigation lawyer for over 25 years. He holds a B.A. in Linguistics from the University of Chicago and a J.D. from the University of Toronto.

Karen DeVito, B.Sc. University of Dayton, M.A. Simon Fraser University, has been an educator and community leader in Vancouver. During a two-year residence in Iowa she worked as a precinct captain and organizer for now-Vice President Joe Biden.

Michael Donovan, born in Manchester, England, and brought up in British Columbia, holds a B.Sc. in physics from Simon Fraser University. He subsequently studied robotics and co-authored academic conference papers in the field. Mike worked in automation and software development before his involvement in Graduate Liberal Studies.

Omar Ilsley holds a B.A. in Religion from Concordia University in Montréal. His interest in Islam and human rights in the Arab world originated from working for twelve years in Saudi Arabia. He was a commercial pilot on Canada's west coast prior to his involvement in graduate studies.

Patricia Kelly, born in northern British Columbia, teaches in the Adult Education system of Greater Vancouver. She has been a human rights activist since the 1990s, primarily with Amnesty International, and is also involved in raising public awareness of rights abuses through documentaries and community television.

Vinit Khosla was born and raised in India. After receiving a B.A. from Swarthmore College in Pennsylvania, he moved to Vancouver, where he trained as an instructor of English as a second language at the University of British Columbia. He taught English to adult immigrants for many years at Vancouver Community College. He is keenly interested in political and social developments, including those in the country of his birth.

Jean Kosar holds a B.A. from the University of Regina and her teaching degree from Simon Fraser University. Her grandparents left Ukraine in the early part of the last century and homesteaded in Saskatchewan, raising a family of ten on a small farm. Kosar, a former actor, now teaches drama at Steveston London Secondary School.

Lianna Laberge holds a degree in Education from the University of Alberta. As a teacher, she became interested in community development. She is a family program coordinator for a Vancouver neighbourhood house in a multicultural community, where she develops programs and support services for families with language, economic and social barriers.

Sandra Lockwood holds a B.A. from the University of Toronto (Asian Studies), a B.F.A. from Emily Carr University (Film/Video major), and a post-graduate diploma from Sheridan Institute of Technology (Computer Graphics). She also attended Nara Women's University in Japan as a research student in classical Japanese literature. She is currently a graphic/web designer in Vancouver.

Sheila Paoli, B.A., University of British Columbia in Religious Studies, has worked for 20 years in mental health, the last 10 years as a counsellor in the treatment of eating disorders. She is especially interested in the religions of the Ancient Near East, and the interface between religion and psychology.

Dylan van der Schyff, born in Johannesburg, South Africa, presently tutors in Classical Mythology at Simon Fraser University. He has been involved in creative music for the past twenty years and has appeared on over 50 recordings. He works, as both musician and producer, with international ensembles and artists, and collaborates in theatre, dance and film projects. Articles about his work have been published in *Downbeat*, *The Globe and Mail*, *The New York Times*, *The Village Voice*, *The Chicago Reader*, and *The Wire*.

Linda Elaine Vogt Turner, B.A., Simon Fraser University, has worked in social justice programs sponsored by the United Church of Canada. In June 2008, she presented her paper, *Protecting the Priceless Environment: Lessons from the Magdalene Stories*, at a conference on Ecology and Environmental Ethics held in Crete. Her paper entitled *The Comfort Women* which is included in this book, was presented at the 4th International Social Science conference in Athens in July, 2009.

Introduction

✧

"Unacknowledged Atrocities" denotes the deliberate outright killing or uprooting with deadly consequences of thousands of people by state actors who deny, minimize or rationalize the event. It also includes tolerating massacres when the authorities in charge could have prevented them. Under the principle of "command responsibility" those bystanders should be held accountable. In cases of unacknowledged atrocities, no compensation has been offered to victims, though in a few instances subsequent governments have issued carefully worded expressions of regret without incurring legal liability.

Unlike widely reported genocides (Nazi Germany, Cambodia, Rwanda, Darfur), unacknowledged atrocities are more or less forgotten, not officially memorialized and not taught in history classes. Yet the focus on this buried past is important, because perpetrators of gross human rights violations should be held accountable and because victims or their descendants remember and warrant recognition. Victims who remain unacknowledged are killed a second time. They have died in the collective memory. Unacknowledged atrocities breed resentment and may prevent reconciliation until a society honestly comes to terms with the crimes of its past. Unrecognized atrocities taint the collective identity of a nation; they cause future divisions when subsequent generations challenge the sanitized versions of history. Above all, non-acknowledgement prevents learning from past injustices that may help to avoid future repetitions. At the very least, one can hope that a society does not condone past crimes. Official silence about past misdeeds suggests complicity and promotes impunity.

The UN "Convention on the Prevention and Punishment of the Crime of Genocide" defines genocide as "acts committed with intent to destroy, in whole or in part, a national, ethnical, racial or religious group". Our meaning of atrocities goes beyond genocide. The massacres and slaughters discussed here are not necessarily based on intent to annihilate entire groups. The bombing of civilians, the starvation of prisoners or the displacement and expulsion of people – in what is nowadays euphemistically referred to as "transfer" or "ethnic cleansing" – does not fit the legal genocide category, but constitutes atrocities or at least gross human rights violations.

Several of our case studies, especially the Armenian genocide, the *Nakba*, the Mau Mau rebellion or the crimes of the Japanese imperial army have already generated a vast scholarly literature. We rely on those sources and do not claim novel insights, but aim at highlighting under-explored or misrepresented aspects in those disputed events. Most of the contributors give more voice to the victims while others focus more on the motivation of perpetrators or the role of bystanders. All eschew glib analogies which often skew our understanding of the causes of massacres. By highlighting several forgotten or less familiar episodes of mass murder, we not only want to fill an astounding gap, but aim at understanding antecedents and grasping the agonies of people whose claim to our attention has, for various reasons, been less compelling than the usual templates. Since our case studies span different continents, they may also allow some tentative conclusions about controversial cultural or national preconditions for ethno-political violence, as discussed in the concluding chapter by the editor.

"Atrocity" in this text is not meant to refer to random violence, perpetrated by some misguided individuals or even state agencies. Tiananmen Square-like army/police massacres occur almost monthly in different parts of the world. Rather, most of our cases analysed comprise systemic violence, built into the ongoing strife, which should not be individualized. In other words, the violence flows from the very system and ideology that it was meant to uphold, regardless of the intention of persons. This focus is not meant to exonerate perpetrators and encourage a culture of impunity through the popular therapeutic discourse of healing and forgiving. Reconciliation, whatever that is, through confessions, forgiveness or repentance carries a high price, though carefully devised amnesties can play a useful role in social reconstruction. In short, we do not want to downplay the important role of instigating leaders; we equally want to avoid losing sight of the social forces that brought those leaders to power. What made followers susceptible to the calls of demagogues or the ideology of nationalism is the more challenging sociological question.

The book deals with fifteen cases of unacknowledged atrocities around the world. While such events happened throughout human history, this collection is confined to 20th-century occurrences, i.e. to the "living memory" of survivors and their descendants.

It is difficult to establish clear, let alone consensual, criteria as to when a crime is acknowledged or not. Acknowledged by whom? The Turkish government vehemently denies the Armenian genocide while academic opinion and even some Western legislatures affirm it. The Palestinian narrative is founded on the *Nakba*, while the Israeli government forbade any reference to it in schoolbooks in July 2009. Can memory be outlawed? As a rough guide, we consider crimes unacknowledged when the current or past authority of the state in which it happened does not recognize it and does not mourn it. Common knowledge of atrocities differs from official acknowledgement. Only when victims are affirmed and their fate is honoured, does a society heed the lessons of its past. Therefore, "acknowledgement" in our definition does not mean a mere pro forma apology without assuming responsibility. A sordid history is "acknowledged" only when it becomes part of the identity and collective memory of a society, which entails soul-searching on why the atrocity happened. In this respect our book draws attention to an important deficit in public memory, without wanting to detract from the major widely acknowledged crimes of the 20th century, especially the Holocaust.

There exists a problematic sentiment, particularly in Israel, that the Holocaust is diluted by comparing it with other genocides. Such enlargement, it is said, deprives the Holocaust of its distinct character. Yehuda Bauer in his book *Rethinking the Holocaust* talks of the Holocaust as unprecedented. Yet what precisely is "unprecedented"? The industrialized killing in gas chambers? We now know that almost as many victims were killed in mass executions by Eastern European auxiliary forces and German army units than in Auschuitz Birkenau.[1] In the 1994 Rwandan slaughter more persons were butchered with machetes during three months than the Nazis managed in their industrialized death camps in similar periods. Was the indiscriminate targeting of all group members, including women and children, unique in the history of genocide? Certainly not, although in some historical eliminationist events, the lives of women or children were spared, or they were forced to convert or compelled to incorporate themselves into the dominant group. While details of mass slaughters are always unique, there is one aspect that stands out in the Nazi case: the perpetrators' drive to annihilate Jews worldwide, had Germany conquered more territory or won the war. No other genocide intended to erase an entire group from the face of the earth, instead remaining confined to the state that initiated it.

Making such comparisons or drawing attention to other than Jewish victims does not diminish the Nazi infamy. On the contrary, comparative analysis deepens the historical understanding and context. Above all, it allows lessons to be drawn, demonstrating how current and future atrocities can be prevented. The late activist historian Howard Zinn has advocated that the Holocaust memory be universalized rather than ghettoized as the monopoly of Jews only. "If the Holocaust was to have any meaning, I thought, we must transfer our anger to the brutalities of our time. We must atone for our allowing the Jewish Holocaust to happen by refusing to allow similar atrocities to take place now – yes, to use the Day of Atonement not to pray for the dead but to act for the living, to rescue those about to die."[2] Such a universalization of the Nazi atrocities would increasingly seem to pervade Holocaust studies the world over. It is also the intent of this collection of unacknowledged atrocities.

Instrumentalizing the Holocaust mainly for legitimating Zionism, or uncritically celebrating Israeli policies as the natural right of survivors or descendants, narrows the true meaning of the tragedy and betrays its educational implications. Glorifying an exclusive ethnic Jewish state not only makes the 20 percent non-Jewish residents second-class citizens, but mirrors the same exclusive nationalism that fed anti-Semitism in Europe. An inclusive cosmopolitanism in a multicultural Israel could guarantee security for fearful minorities much better than the hostility engendered by an exclusive ethnocracy. That ideal, of course, would have to apply to both sides in the conflict. It is unattainable as long as minority Islamists insist on the same ethnocentric designs as their Jewish counterparts, or worse, proclaim the elimination of Jews from sacred soil.

The current volume originates from a study group at Simon Fraser University that met weekly during the Fall of 2008, discussing all fifteen cases in depth. The discussions raised related questions such as when and how colonial settlers become natives; how indigenous people should be compensated for their conquest; whether immigrants should be expected to assimilate rather than maintain their identity of origin; and what "reasonable accommodation" means. Readings on multiculturalism and peacemaking in ethnic conflicts alternated with reflections on transitional justice, Truth Commissions, and memorialization. The South African and Israeli/Palestinian conflicts served as major test cases for successful or elusive conflict resolution. The editor's long standing familiarity with these areas accounts for the frequent references to African and Middle Eastern examples.

Each author revised her or his chapter in light of these wide-ranging weekly discussions. Finally, an editorial committee coordinated the articles, which encompass most regions of the globe without claiming to be comprehensive. Sandra Lockwood provided the graphics.

Three chapters cover cases from the Middle East (*Nakba*, Hama, Armenia), three deal with Asian events (Suharto, Gujarat, Japan) and four probe European incidents (Holodomor, Spanish civil war, Dresden, postwar Eastern Europe). Africa is represented through four case studies (Zanzibar, Algerian Harkis, Mau Mau and Gukurahundi in Zimbabwe).

The cases were selected on the bases of the interests and expertise of its fifteen authors. Many other potential cases were discussed, but could not be included because of such constraints. For example, we would have preferred to include the first genocide of the 20th century, the almost total elimination of the rebellious Hereroes and Namas by the German colonizers in current-day Namibia in 1904; or the equally brutal Belgian atrocities under King Leopold in the Congo; or the first large-scale bombing of civilians in the Basque town of Guernica in 1936; or the Soviet massacre of 15,000 Polish officers in Katyn in 1940 which was acknowledged by Gorbachev only in 1989; or the incredible brutalities of the Russian army in separatist Chechnya well into the 21st century.

This collection is designed as a model for further exploration. The neglected atrocities of Mao's cultural revolution and the Chinese repression of Tibet, as well as unrecognized colonial crimes in the Americas, also warrant detailed analysis. The original twin sins of America – the near extermination of the native population and the enslavement of Africans – have been barely acknowledged. No Latin American cases are included, because the major Latin American countries pioneered Truth Commissions in response to the crimes of military dictatorships during the 1970s and 1980s. In addition, there are unacknowledged crimes of more recent US administrations through support of proxies in various countries (Guatemala, Angola) during the Cold War period. These periods of Western colonialism, as well as the equally heinous crimes of Soviet imperialism, were long stretches of domination, while our book focuses on specific incidents within their historical contexts.

Excluded from this volume is also the vast topic of indirect fatalities, caused by misguided policies. For example, the South African HIV/Aids denialism under President Thabo Mbeki's watch has been rightly described as "silent genocide". According to a Harvard study, 365,000 lives could have been saved had the South African state not blocked the distribution of freely available anti-retrovirals before a policy reversal in 2007. No truth commission has held a compliant cabinet and the ANC leadership accountable.[3] Although the rhetoric and policies changed in subsequent administrations, the male chauvinism and enduring notions of a domineering masculinity in a deeply patriarchal African tradition continued. One only has to probe the impact of President Jacob Zuma's polygamous and extra-marital affairs on young males to gauge the challenge of overcoming the HIV risks. In short, while the South African HIV/Aids denialism, stigmatization and ignorance lacked the malicious intent usually associated with genocide, the outcome was the same.

The category of indirect mass murder also comprises the estimated daily 50,000 deaths due to poverty-related illnesses worldwide. Yet hunger, slums, water pollution, child labour and infectious diseases can no longer be considered natural phenomena in a world where $300 billion annually (or 0.6 percent of world income) could guarantee 30 percent of the world population better survival chances and lift them out of extreme misery. More is spent on US military expenditure alone. Despite an absolute decline of global poverty, international inequality has increased so that 10 percent of the wealthiest section now command 85 percent of global income, compared with 0.03 percent of humanity at the bottom. Our focus on the neglected direct and intentional killing ought not obscure the ongoing preventable indirect mass murder by the unjust rules of global trade and the callous greed or indifference of national and international elites.

More gender-conscious informed readers could also ask why the sexual death of tens of thousands of raped and mutilated women, girls and babies in the war zones of the Eastern Congo and elsewhere has been overlooked, as almost all of these crimes go unpunished and destroy a society from within by scarring its ostracized victims for life. The *New*

York Times columnist Nicholas D. Kristof (*New York Times*, January 31, 2010) has pointed out that the civil war in eastern Congo has claimed at least 30 times as many lives as the Haiti earthquake which received huge publicity at the time, yet no humanitarian crisis generates so little attention as the ongoing Congo massacres. Again, the ills of humanity span a wide spectrum and we could only focus an a few specific events, such as the case of the "comfort women" of the Japanese imperial army.

Dale Darychuk discusses why the story of the *Nakba* – the Palestinian term for the "catastrophe" of their expulsion from current-day Israel in 1948 – has been "so slow in coming and why, even when the stories are told, their full moral weight is either ignored or marginalized". Omar Ilsley describes how the minority Alawite regime in Syria ensured collective amnesia for the past 25 years by massacring the population of the rebelling city of Hama, dominated by the Muslim Brotherhood, in 1982. The mutual myth-making of Turks and Armenians is investigated by Karen DeVito, who outlines the 1915 Armenian genocide, but above all reflects on how both nations can be reconciled through an acknowledgement of a shared history rather than criminalizing any discussion of the events as "insulting Turkishness".

Elaine Brière details the murder of up to one million Indonesians by the Suharto dictatorship in 1965 under the guise of rescuing the country from communism. Western governments and media supported or downplayed the crimes of this repressive regime. What is often so lightly dismissed as inter-communal rioting has discernible causes, instigators, perpetrators and bystanders. Vinit Khosla highlights the unrecognized state complicity of the regional authorities as well as the bystander role of the Indian central government in the 2002 massacres of thousands of Muslims in the Gujarat province. Linda Turner tells the painful story of the abuse of "comfort women" by the Japanese imperial army for which the Tokyo government still has not accepted legal responsibility.

Jean Kosar movingly sketches the Holodomor, the death by starving of 7 million Ukrainian peasants under Stalin's direction. Russia still refuses to accept responsibility and prefers to stay "hostage to the lies of the past". Mike Donavan portrays vividly the atmosphere of the 1936–39 Spanish Civil War, the official "Pact of Forgetting" after Franco's death and the renewed attempts to unearth the graves of half a million victims on both sides. Lea Laberge chronicles the expulsion of 15 million ethnic Germans from Czechoslovakia and Poland after the end of World War II, a widely approved collective punishment for alleged Nazi sympathies and an experiment in ethnic cleansing resulting in two million unrecognized deaths. In a similar vein, Scott-Ryan Abt reflects on just and unjust behaviour in war by analyzing the 1945 counter-productive Allied bombing of Dresden. Reminding us that the victors often write history, the author focuses on why it happened, why it has been forgotten and why it should be remembered.

Dylan van der Schyff explores the fate of the Harkis, Muslim Algerians who supported France. In 1962, at the end of the Algerian war, more than 50,000 Harkis were killed by the victorious FLN, and Harkis in France were isolated in concentration camps – "a distant nightmare that both the Algerian and French government would have preferred to let disperse into the fog of time". Salima Charania records the British suppression of the anti-colonial Mau Mau movement in Kenya and its Eurocentric justification that still permeates much of the literature. Sheila Paoli probes the deadly activities of "Gukurahundi", the North Korean-trained Fifth Brigade, used in Robert Mugabe's subjugation of the minority Ndebele between 1980 and 1990, never officially acknowledged inside and forgotten outside the tortured country. Patricia Kelly looks at the attacks against Ibos, preceding the Biafra war of independence in 1966, in which 3 million Nigerians died. Sandra Lockwood outlines a similar story of a forgotten African atrocity, resulting largely from British colonial policy: the 1964 mass murder of Zanzibaris of Arab and Indian origin, shortly before the island was incorporated into the newly independent Tanzania.

The concluding chapter by the editor draws out commonalities and deals with such diverse issues as the reasons why some atrocities remain unacknowledged, the causes of mass massacres, theories of ethnocentrism and what is to be done to avoid repetition. While only touching on the expanding transitional justice debate in this volume, valuable further reading on how to deal with crimes of the past can be found in Rosalinda Shaw et al, eds, *Transitional Justice: Interventions and Priorities after Mass Violence* (Stanford University Press, 2010) and Tricia D. Olsen et al, eds, *Transitional Justice in Balance: Comparing Processes, Weighing Efficacy* (Washington: USIP Press, 2010).

NOTES

1 See T. Snider, "Holocaust: the ignored reality", *The New York Review of Books*, July 16, 2009.

2 "A Larger Consciousness", http://www.zmag.org/zspace/commentaries/128.

3 A growing literature documents the scandal of the South African HIV denialism. Two books stand out in exposing the charlatans who exploited the confusion with pseudo-science. Nathan Geffen's *Debunking Delusions* (Johannesburg: Jacana, 2009) is the account of a leading activist who focuses on the evolution of the most effective civil society movement which forced the government to change course. The book *The Virus, Vitamins and Vegetables*, edited by Kerry Cullinan and Anso Thom (Johannesburg: Jacana, 2009) chronicles comprehensively the intrigues, the paranoia about multinational pharmaceuticals, the sheer ignorance about the scientific evidence and the embracing of untested remedies of the lunatic fringe by the political leadership that led to the unfolding tragedies. An insightful account by James Myburg focuses on the ANC's connection to the industrial solvent Virodene that led to the denial of the link between HIV and Aids which was openly challenged by only one brave former ANC MP, Pregs Govender. Everybody else kowtowed to the conformity pressure emanating from an intimidating President, for whom racist stereotypes about black male sexuality were an additional weapon to silence critics.

Unacknowledged Atrocities of the 20th Century

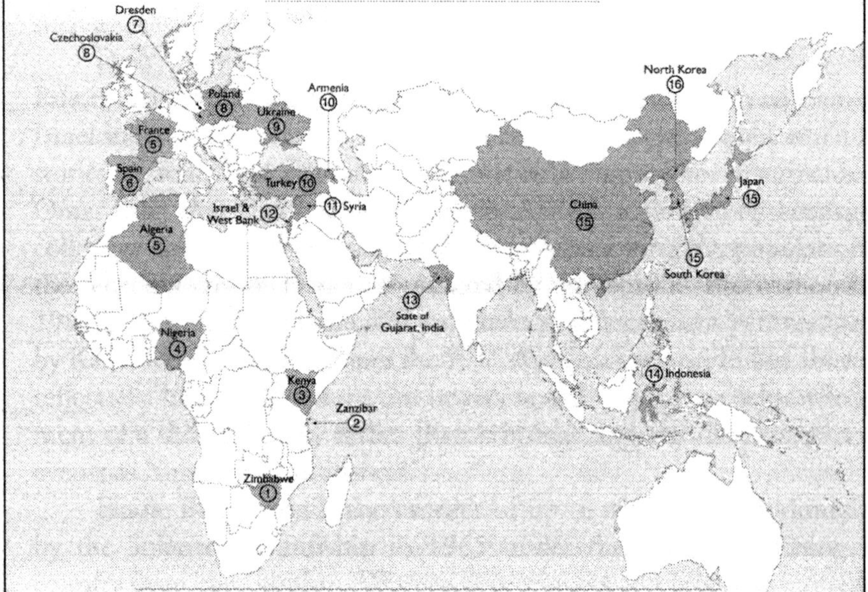

1. Robert Mugabe's Gukurahundi in Zimbabwe
2. Nightmare in Paradise: The 1964 Revolution and Genocide in Zanzibar
3. Unpacking the 'Mau Mau' Rebellion in Kenya
4. The Biafran War for Independence: Nigeria in the 1960s
5. The Algerian Harkis: Témoignages d'une Histoire Cachée
6. Unmarked Graves and Old Wounds: The Spanish Civil War
7. Blind Spot: The Allied Bombing of Dresden
8. Broken Promises and Blind Eyes – The Expulsion of Ethnic Germans from Czechoslovakia and Poland after World War II
9. No One Else to Ask – Investigating the Ukrainian Holdomor
10. The G-Word: Why Turks and Armenians Can't Talk
11. Hama Massacre in Syria
12. Israel: Stillborn Nation
13. The 2002 Massacre of Gujarati Muslims: The Violent Face of Hindu Nationalism
14. Shadow Play: Political Mass Murder and the 1965 Indonesian Coup
15. Comfort Women: Sexual Slaves of the Imperial Japanese Military

1

Robert Mugabe's Gukurahundi

Sheila Paoli

✧

We are a traumatised nation that needs slow but intensive rehabilitation. We have been turned into beggars, robbers, thieves, liars, killers, murderers, sorcerers, hoodlum and destitute. We are now what we were never meant to be and never wanted to be. While the people get rehabilitated, Mugabe has to face the fullest wrath of the people.

Masola Wa Dabu, *The Standard*, Zimbabwe

Armed conflict did not end with Zimbabwe's independence in April 1980. By 1983 Prime Minister Robert Mugabe had launched a campaign of terror in Matabeleland and the Midland provinces of Zimbabwe, meant to squelch opposition to his leadership and maintain primacy of his ZANU party. From 1980 to 1990 it is estimated that Mugabe's various military forces, especially his North Korean-trained Fifth Brigade, were responsible for the massacre of 20,000 Ndebele Zimbabweans.[1] A detailed report of the atrocities, written jointly by the Catholic Commission for Justice and Peace and the Legal Resources Foundation, exposed Mugabe's crime to the world in 1997. Despite this report, Mugabe and his forces have not accepted responsibility for the atrocity, and Ndebele Zimbabweans continue to experience personal pain and government-sanctioned violence.

Zimbabwe's Fight for Freedom

The leaders of the black majority of Rhodesia fought for decades to win independence – first from British rule then, after 1965, from the white settler government that had unilaterally declared independence under

Ian Smith. Joshua Nkomo, a popular black leader in Southern Rhodesia, founded the Zimbabwe's African People's Union (ZAPU) in 1961. Prominent members of ZAPU, including Robert Mugabe, became disenchanted with Nkomo's leadership and formed a splinter group, the Zimbabwe African National Union (ZANU), in 1963. The early infighting and political rivalry between ZAPU and ZANU became a longstanding pattern of conflict as the two parties vied for primacy in black Zimbabwe's fight for freedom and were aligned with the rival superpowers the Soviet Union and China. This conflict set the stage for Robert Mugabe's ruthless massacre of the Ndebele people some twenty years later.

An important aspect of the split in the political parties was the ethnic allegiance of each. Nkomo had long been active in the black freedom struggle and considered himself a leader across ethnic lines. This did not prove to be the case. Nkomo was from the Matabeleland area and drew allegiance almost exclusively from the Ndebele population after the ZANU–ZAPU split. Mugabe, on the other hand, hailed from the Shona-speaking majority outside of Matabeleland and garnered his support from the Shona people. Much has been made regarding this ethnic bifurcation, and Mugabe's later actions against the Ndebele are often minimized as a natural continuation of a historical animosity between the two groups. However, this superficial analysis obscures the political motives behind Mugabe's later targeted violence. While it is the case that each leader was supported mainly by his respective ethnic group, both ZANU and ZAPU incorporated people of both ethnicities (sometimes holding key positions). Even beyond the political realm, segregation between these groups was not absolute; intermarriage between Ndebele- and Shona-speaking people was not uncommon, and the general populace of Zimbabwe had no reason to harbour grudges against each other.

The animosity between the two groups was exacerbated by Nkomo and Mugabe's longstanding personal dislike of each other. Mugabe thought Nkomo far too willing to compromise his ideals by entering into negotiations with Ian Smith prior to Zimbabwe's independence in 1980. Further, Mugabe was also a strong believer in a one party state – Nkomo's ZAPU party was therefore a de facto threat to his political philosophy and leadership. And neither party was above using violence to increase its status, as each coerced people to become members and intimidated political opponents.

In the eyes of the Rhodesian government, ZAPU and ZANU were illegal organizations. Nkomo and Mugabe, along with their key party members, were frequently jailed, often for long periods of time. In order to remain free to direct their party's operations, Mugabe and Nkomo sought asylum in neighbouring countries that had been recently liberated from colonial rule and therefore sympathetic to the ideals of ZAPU and ZANU. Nkomo used Zambia as his base, and formed the armed unit ZIPRA (Zimbabwe People's Revolutionary Army), funded by the Soviet Union and East Germany. Mugabe found refuge in Mozambique, funding his army, ZANLA (Zimbabwe African National Liberation Army), with the support of Communist China.

Party Conflict

Though briefly uniting in a final effort to liberate Zimbabwe from Rhodesia, ZANU and ZAPU reverted to mutual distrust and political competition following Zimbabwe's independence and the subsequent election of Mugabe as Prime Minister in 1980. After conflicts between the two rival parties escalated, Mugabe declared a state of emergency which was maintained until 1990. Within six months of his election, Mugabe had entered into negotiations with North Korea with the intention of training a specialized military unit, the Fifth Brigade, whose authority was to lie outside of the army and would be answerable only to Mugabe himself. Nkomo expressed his concern at this series of events. Little was he, his party, or the Ndebele people prepared for what was to transpire.

Mugabe unfolded his brutal plan under the guise of preventing civil strife. Zimbabwean newspaper articles in the early 1980s reported a continuous stream of dissident violence in Matabeleland. The details of these reports have been disputed, as the Mugabe government had seized control of the media, appointed its editors, and banned foreign journalists from Matabeleland. Observers in Matabeleland, and the disenfranchised ex-ZIPRA dissidents themselves, believe that dissident numbers were relatively small. While not the political threat that ZANU feared, the dissidents did disrupt peace in Matabeleland by looting stores, raping women, and murdering white farmers. To counter this activity, the government sent various army, police, and intelligence organizations to the area. In early 1982, a large weapons cache was found in Matabeleland, which prompted Mugabe to charge ZAPU with plotting a coup against him. Later, Nkomo was expelled from his government post. His response to this expulsion, and charges of treason against his ZAPU colleagues, was, "I've never done anything wrong, and Robert knows it. I tell you, this is for personal power."[2] Later that year, members of a tourist group were kidnapped and killed near Victoria Falls. Mugabe blamed ZAPU/ZIPRA dissidents for the attack and in January 1983 sent his newly trained, but not newly planned, Fifth Brigade into Matabeleland.

Gukurahundi

The Fifth Brigade came to be known as Gukurahundi, "the first rain that washes away the chaff of the last harvest before the spring rains".[3] Enos Nkala (of Ndebele origin himself), the ZANU Minister of Home Affairs, led the offence against the Matabeleland people, under the guise of quelling dissident violence. But the North Korean-trained Fifth Brigade was not meant to target the dissident problem – it was trained specifically to murder Mugabe's political opponents and terrorize the Ndebele into compliance. In a detailed study of Zimbabwe's dissidents during this period, Jocelyn Alexander quotes a former dissident:

> The Gukurahundi wasn't a good fighting unit. It was trained to reduce the Matabeleland population, it was just killing civilians. The Gukurahundi weren't soldiers—where do you see soldiers who sing when on patrol? They were looking for civilians, not other soldiers, so we would come across them singing and we would just take cover. Soon after, you'd hear people crying in their homes.... [W]e'd clash with them, but instead of following us they'd call for the villagers. That's where they'd take revenge, that's where you'd hear bazookas and AKs firing into homes.[4]

If it were not for the efforts of Catholic missions, lawyers working in the area, and the Ndebele people themselves, knowledge of the Fifth Brigade massacres of the Ndebele might now be lost to history. People living in Zimbabwe but outside Matabeleland and the Midlands were not aware of events within their own country. In March 1983, after the first round of violence by the Fifth Brigade, two Catholic organizations met with Mugabe to discuss what they had witnessed and asked Mugabe to investigate the actions of the Fifth Brigade. According to the participants,

Mugabe feigned innocence of the events in Matabeleland; immediately after the discussion, Mugabe dismissed the Catholic representatives as "sanctimonious prelates".[5] A government investigation was commissioned shortly after this discussion, but the results have never been made public. Later, detailed records were reviewed, cross-checked and verified, and hundreds of Ndebele people were interviewed in a joint effort by the Catholic Commission for Justice and Peace and the Legal Resources Foundation in Zimbabwe. The result of their effort, *Breaking the Silence, Building True Peace: A Report on the Disturbances in Matabeleland and the Midlands 1980–1990* (*BSBTP*), first published in 1997, exposed to the world the atrocities committed at the hand of the Gukurahundi. According to the report,

> ...one of the saddest outcomes of the violence in the 1980s is that many people have come to see the conflict during this time as ethnic in nature. It has been misinterpreted as a civil war between Shonas and Ndebele. This is not accurate... It is important to remember the conflict was really more about politics than ethnicity; it was about creating a one-party state in Zimbabwe.[6]

Exact numbers of people killed, tortured, or missing are hard to verify. All too frequently whole extended families were killed and complete villages destroyed; no survivors therefore remained to account for missing members of the community or their family. In a conservative estimate outlined in *BSBTP*, the Fifth Brigade was responsible for 5,734 human rights violations in two case study areas alone, compared to 142 violations by dissidents in the same areas and time period (1982–1987).[7] The Fifth Brigade was not the only perpetrator of violence against the Ndebele; concurrent with their campaign was the additional violence inflicted by the army, the Central Intelligence Organization, and the ZANU-PF Youth. At the time of information gathering for *BSBTP* its "very low" estimates for all areas on file were 10,000 detained, 7,000 tortured, and "...almost certain dead number between 3,000 and 4,000: possible dead could be double this or more".[8] A number of later reports confirmed that these figures were indeed conservative. According to the US State Department, 20,000 people died during the Gukurahundi.[9]

Case Studies

While statistics point to the enormity of the atrocity against the Ndebele, they do not provide an accurate depiction of the horror that took place. In order to grasp the ferociousness of the violence the Ndebele suffered, *BSBTP* offered case studies as part of the report. One such study recounted the events of February 13, 1983, in the village of Gulakabili:

> Whole village abducted from nearby to the Pumula Mission area, where they were beaten. Some were then forced to dig a mass grave, made to climb in, and were shot. They were buried while still moving, and villagers were made to dance on the grave and sing songs in praise of ZANU-PF. Number of dead given as 12... One victim locked in a hut and burned to death."[10]

The Fifth Brigade operated a type of concentration camp in southern Matabeleland. According to *BSBTP*:

> Bhalagwe Camp was originally a military camp. In 1982 the mainly ZIPRA army unit there were accused of being dissidents. The camp was shut down and not used much. It became a feared place in 1984, when thousands of civilians from all over Matabeleland South were trucked in and detained there. They were brutally tortured and many were killed. People were kept in very bad conditions. They were overcrowded and beaten daily.
>
> CIO as well as Fifth Brigade also gave people electric shocks, submarine and other forms of torture. There was a lot of sexual torture at Bhalagwe. Women were raped and had sticks forced into them. Men had their genitals tied in rubber and beaten. People had to dig graves for those killed. Later, these bodies were removed and those who died were thrown down mine shafts in the region.[11]

In 1984, Mugabe inflicted another form of misery upon the Ndebele – starvation. In the midst of a prolonged drought, Mugabe's forces began a policy of controlling food supplies into Matabeleland. The Ndebele had come to rely on food donations and their ability to feed themselves greatly diminished in this period. *BSBTP* estimates that 400,000 people were "brought to the brink of complete starvation".[12] Mugabe's blueprint for the subjugation of the Matabeleland's ZAPU-supporting population crystallized at this time; tortured, starved and murdered, the Ndebele were physically and psychologically crippled.

Response and Responsibility

During Zimbabwe's 1985 elections, intimidation and violence in Matabeleland increased to an even greater degree. In the fall of 1987, ZAPU was officially banned. Due to the number of Ndebele lives lost or destroyed and in the face of continued persecution, Nkomo could no longer justify ZAPU political opposition to ZANU. In December 1987, the Unity Accord was signed between Nkomo and Mugabe; ZANU absorbed ZAPU and became ZANU-PF (Zimbabwe African National Union-Patriotic Front) and so became the one-party state which Mugabe had always longed for.

Mugabe has never admitted responsibility for the atrocities that he instigated against the Ndebele. In the mid-1980s, Amnesty International spoke out against Mugabe's human rights abuses; Mugabe in turn went on the attack, and accused Amnesty of lying. Two Zimbabwean government-sponsored inquiries into the events in Matabeleland have never been released. The report *Breaking the Silence, Building True Peace,* originally a more thoroughly documented account in book form, was not acknowledged by Mugabe or his government. Mugabe minimized the need for accountability by calling the massacre of tens of thousands of Ndebele "a moment of madness".[13]

The world at large would have been informed had foreign government representatives cared to share what they had known. For example, the British High Commissioner in Zimbabwe during the Gukurahundi was told to "steer clear of it" by London; he states that "We were extremely interested that Zimbabwe should be a success story..."[14] Australian Prime Minister Malcolm Fraser, who was also aware of events in Matabeleland, "...declined to comment".[15] India and Sweden also supported Mugabe, though aware of his human rights abuses; they supported the anti-colonial movement in Africa and did not want to interfere in its development.[16] The United States also had an embassy in Zimbabwe, which was established in 1980; it is unlikely that the United States was unaware of unfolding events in Matabeleland. It was not until 2000, however, that the United States took "...a leading role in condemning the Zimbabwean Government's increasing assault on human rights and the rule of law..."[17] In effect, the world stood by while Mugabe created a living hell for the Ndebele.

Aftermath

The Ndebele continue to suffer from the ramifications of past violence. As documented by *BSBTP*, individuals show signs and symptoms consistent with post-traumatic stress disorder which disrupts their daily lives and general psychological health. Torture, with its associated long-term physical disabilities, has also left its mark on its victims.[18] The Ndebele cannot properly mourn their missing and presumed dead family members, and the manner in which murdered bodies were disposed of by the Gukurahundi creates spiritual distress for a people who have specific ceremonies in regard to proper burial. Thus, the aftereffects of the Gukurahundi encompass all realms of the Ndebeles' lives: physical, psychological, spiritual, and social. A general amnesty for all parties involved (the few dissidents and the many government forces, including the Fifth Brigade) was granted in 1988; Mugabe renewed this amnesty for perpetrators of political violence in 2000. This amnesty, of course, served to further demoralize the Ndebele, as any possible legal recourse to justice was blocked. In addition, the UN Refugee Agency reported in 2003 that the Ndebele also "...encounter low-grade economic and political discrimination by the Shona majority... that they are second-class citizens... and that their culture is at risk".[19]

Understandably reticent to publicly voice their opinion or actively participate in politics, the Ndebele nevertheless, and without fail, vote against ZANU-PF in all elections. This "way of keeping faith with their dead"[20] has come at a high price. ZANU-PF-instigated violence against the Ndebele peaks in the months leading up to an election, which in turn re-traumatizes the population of Matabeleland. Clearly, the time has come for the suffering of the Ndebele to be addressed.

Mugabe's refusal to acknowledge his seminal role in the violence in Matabeleland allows the persecution to continue. ZANU-PF party officials and cabinet ministers who sanctioned Mugabe's attacks (both past and present) against the Ndebele remain in positions of power, conducting business as usual, while the Ndebele continue to suffer. The Fifth Brigade is still a dreaded force. Mugabe rationalizes his silence by stating, "If we dig up the country's history in this way, we wreck the nation and we tear our people apart into factions."[21] But in his efforts to establish and maintain himself as the supreme leader in Zimbabwe, it is Mugabe himself who creates chaos in his nation, and tears the lives of the Ndeble apart.

Organizations such as the Zimbabwean Catholic Commission for Peace and the Legal Resource Foundation, the Canadian Interfaith Coalition on Africa, and Amnesty International (to name a few), have all pressed Mugabe to open the dialogue regarding past events in Matabeleland. In 1997, then Secretary General of Amnesty, Pierre Sané, wrote an open letter to Mugabe. In this letter, Sané outlined the UN Security Council's criteria for "crimes against humanity". Sané stated, "Viewed in this light, the atrocities that have been documented in... [Matabeleland] are tantamount to crimes against humanity."[22] Despite condemnation for human rights abuses, there is no indication that Mugabe will ever admit to crimes against the Ndebele.

After Mugabe

Given Mugabe's advanced age, there will certainly be a successor but not necessarily a regime change in the near future. The transition between Mugabe and the government that follows him will be a crucial time for the Ndebele. Organizations such as the UN and the international community as a whole should have the opportunity to provide assistance in Zimbabwe to prevent government-instigated intimidation and to promote fair election practices, but they are heavily restricted. Only sympathetic observers are allowed as election monitors. Currently, the ZANU-PF leadership remains in power by continuing Mugabe's legacy of electoral fraud and perpetuating the violence and oppression against all opposition, despite losing a general election in 2008. The indifference, if not support, of the Mbeki-led ANC government in Pretoria proved crucial in perpetuating the Mugabe dictatorship, despite the complete economic ruin of the country. Movement for Democratic Change (MDC) opposition party leader Morgan Tsvangirai has promised a full and transparent investigation into past activities of the Gukurahundi if he is elected president.

The road map for reconciliation is already in place, should Tsvangirai or a repentant ZANU-PF president truly wish to heal the deep wounds of the Ndebele and move Zimbabwe forward as a united and democratic nation. *BSBTP*, along with other organizations and committees who have since examined this issue and are in agreement with its findings, has offered crucial recommendations. First, and most importantly, the atrocities against the Ndebele must be made public

– the people must be heard. Second, though the prosecution of the instigators and perpetrators has been blocked by Mugabe's amnesties, these criminals could certainly be removed from public office and positions of power from which they make decisions affecting the lives of Zimbabweans. Third, the Ndebele must receive material compensation to rebuild both their individual lives and their physical communities. Foreign expertise might be employed to provide extensive psychological support to the victims of the Gukurahundi. Last, changes to government laws would need to be considered with the intent of protecting the Ndebele (or any Zimbabwean) against violence and discrimination in the future. The past and the present hold horrific and heartbreaking experiences for the Ndebele, but with a new leadership committed to transparency, and a supportive global response, the slow path to reconciliation is possible.

NOTES

1 US Department of State: Bureau of African Affairs, "Background Notes: Zimbabwe." October 2008, p. 6. http://www.state.gov/r/pa/ci/bgn/5479.htm.
2 As quoted in Christopher Hope, *Brothers Under the Skin: Travels in Tyranny* (London: Macmillan, 2003), p. 99.
3 Chatham House: Royal Institute of International Affairs, "Zimbabwe's Gukurahundi: Lessons from the 1980–1988 Disturbances in Matabeleland and The Midlands", Meeting Summary – 4 September 2007. http://www.chathamhouse.org.uk/publications/papers/view/-/id/549/.
4 Jocelyn Alexander, "Dissident Perspectives on Zimbabwe's Post-Independence War", *Africa: Journal of the International African Institute* 68, no. 2 (1998), p. 167. http://www.jstor.org/.
5 As quoted in Hope, *Brothers Under the Skin*, p. 105.
6 Catholic Commission for Justice and Peace and Legal Resources Foundation, "Breaking the Silence, Building True Peace: A Report on the Disturbances in Matabeleland and the Midlands 1980–1988, Summary Report", (April 1999), p. 11. http://www.sokwanele.com/pdfs/BTS.pdf.
7 Ibid., p. 29.
8 Ibid., p. 27.
9 US Department of State, "Background Notes", p. 6.
10 Catholic Commission, "Breaking the Silence", pp. 22–23.
11 Ibid., p. 26.
12 Ibid., p. 14.
13 As quoted in Chatham House, "Zimbabwe's Gukurahuni".
14 As quoted in Geoff Hill, *The Battle for Zimbabwe* (Cape Town: Zebra Press, 2003), p. 83.
15 Ibid., p. 78.
16 Ibid., p. 78.
17 US Department of State, "Background Notes", p. 12.
18 Catholic Commission, "Breaking the Silence", p. 29.
19 UNHCR Refworld, "Assessment for Ndebele in Zimbabwe", Minorities at Risk Project, UN Refugee Agency, 31 December 2003, p. 2. http://www.unhcr.org/refworld/docid/469f3aeb14.html.
20 Hope, *Brothers Under the Skin*, p. 25.
21 As quoted in Iden Wetherell, "The Matabeleland Report: A Lot to Hide", *AfricaFiles* 12, no. 3 (1997), p. 1. http://www.africafiles.org/printableversion.asp?id=3843.
22 Pierre Sané, "Zimbabwe: Open Letter from Amnesty International to His Excellency the President Robert Mugabe", Amnesty International, http://asiapacific.amnesty.org/library/print/ENGAFR46031997.

2

Nightmare in Paradise: The 1964 Zanzibar Revolution and Genocide

Sandra Lockwood

✧

Throughout history, it has been the inaction of those who could have acted, the indifference of those who should have known better, the silence of the voice of justice when it mattered most, that has made it possible for evil to triumph.

Haile Selassie

In the early hours of January 12, 1964, a group of men armed with sticks and knives stormed the police armory of Zanzibar Town. Nine hours later, the political and racial landscape of Zanzibar had irrevocably changed – ethnic majority black Zanzibaris were now in control, and thousands of Arab and Indian Zanzibaris lay dead. Zanzibar's revolution stands out as an example of one ethnic group almost completely purging another. An estimated 5,000 to 12,000[1] Zanzibaris, primarily of Arab ethnicity, were killed or expelled within a week of the coup.

Zanzibar celebrates the anniversary of the Zanzibar Revolution each January with celebratory fireworks and gunshots. No mention is made of its accompanying genocide, which would seem a forgotten footnote to its history. It is worth taking a closer look at Arab and British colonial rule, the slave trade, the rise of African nationalism, and the actual coup that led to such bloody consequences. The Zanzibar Revolution may have taken the world by surprise, but it was over 200 years in the making. Black Zanzibaris endured political subjugation, economic inequality and racism, first under Arab, and then British colonial rule. Moreover, Zanzibar was the site of the largest slave market in East Africa.

Background

A view of Zanzibar's geography and early history helps put the revolution in perspective. Zanzibar consists of two islands just off the east coast of the African continent. The islands themselves are relatively small: Unguja, the main island, is 1,030 square kilometers in area, while Pemba to the north is only 611 square kilometers. What the islands lack in size they make up for in strategic location.

Zanzibar is located just 6° south of the equator, yet it has a mild tropical climate, along with abundant fresh water and fertile soil, making it an "island paradise". Its location, however, is both a blessing and a curse. Zanzibar lies directly in the path of the prevailing trade winds. From ancient times, these islands have been an important destination along the Indian Ocean trade route. By the 11th century, Shirazi Persians and Omani Arabs came to settle. Initially, the islands absorbed these small waves of settlement – the settlers mixed and intermarried with the indigenous people, creating a unique island culture and the "Shirazi" people.

In the 15th century, however, Portuguese exploration brought to an end the Arab dominance in the Indian Ocean. For two centuries Zanzibar was under Portuguese control, although the Portuguese did not colonize the islands, establishing only a fishing village at what would later become Zanzibar Town. By the 18th century the Omani Arabs had reasserted their influence in East Africa. A series of successful campaigns reestablished their dominance, and found Zanzibar an ideal base for their empire. It was small, easy to defend and close enough to the mainland to control a good 1,600 kilometers of coastline. By the 1780s, large scale colonization of Zanzibar began in earnest. In 1831, the Sultan Seyyid Said of Oman, head of the Busaidi dynasty, located the seat of his empire in Zanzibar.

Arab Colonization

The Sultanate, with its influx of Arabs, had major consequences for the islands. Violent land seizures pushed the indigenous black and Shirazi population from the fertile land of the west onto the unproductive land in the northeastern part of the island. The construction of Zanzibar "Stone" Town brought characteristic Islamic architecture, including the Sultan's palace and mosques. The location of Zanzibar Town is distinctive

– it is a natural harbour on a triangle of land jutting into the sea. Along the broad base of the triangle runs a large creek. East of this creek is N'Gambo, the black slum quarter, as blacks were unwelcome in Stone Town.

Until this time, Zanzibar Town had largely existed for entrepôt traffic – *dhows* from India and Arabia would come to offload and store such goods as cloth, iron, and salted fish. They would reload with ivory, coconuts and slaves from the mainland and wait for the regular change in the prevailing monsoon trade winds to blow them back home.

It is said that the Sultan himself brought the first clove sapling to the island.[2] So impressed was he with the prolific growth of the plant that he decided to devote the entire island to its production. Huge shipments of clove seedlings arrived along with new colonists with each prevailing monsoon wind. In just 20 years, Zanzibar produced 7 million pounds of cloves a year.[3] Thus, Zanzibar was transformed from just a trading post to a major producer, generating the world's largest clove crop.

The political consequences of Arab colonization were felt most keenly on Unguja. The Sultan and his inner circle of advisers carved up the land into plantations, whose landlords formed a political and administrative oligarchy answering directly to the Sultan. Prior to colonization, Zanzibar was not without political organization. The figure of the Mwinye Mkuu provided leadership for the black and Shirazi population. Agents of the Sultanate first tried to co-opt the Mwinye Mkuu. Through clearly disadvantageous treaties the indigenes were forced not only to "sell" their land, but to provide free labour or "corvée" for the new Arab landlords. Eventually the Sultanate crushed all indigenous political structures.

The indigenous Zanzibaris were coerced into labouring on the clove plantations, but their numbers were insufficient. Zanzibar imported a large slave population, and by the mid 1890s, over 40,000 slaves were labouring in the spice trade. However, Zanzibar's economy was not just built on cloves – its other "commodity" was the slaves themselves. The Arabs had engaged in slaving for over 2,000 years, but never on this scale. Zanzibar became the largest centre in East Africa for the misery that is the slave trade. Men, women and children were captured on the mainland and force-marched from their villages in the interior to the coast, where, already brutalized, weakened and malnourished, they were packed onto *dhows* and shipped to Unguja. Some died on the journey, and the rest were then unloaded at Stone Town to be sold at the notorious slave market. The English Captain Thomas Smee witnessed the market in 1811. He described the long "files" of slaves paraded before prospective buyers:

> I have frequently counted between 20 and 30 of these files in the market. Women with children newly born hanging at their breasts, and others so old they can scarcely walk are dragged about in this manner. Some groups appeared to be so ill-fed that their bones seemed ready to penetrate the skin. From such scenes one turns away from with pity and indignation.[4]

Between 1770 and 1896, 1,300,000 slaves reached Zanzibar, of whom 424,000 were exported, mainly to Arabia, Persia and India.[5]

In the mid 19th century, Britain became interested in Zanzibar because of its strategic location. Other European nations were engaged in colonial expansion – Germany was in Tanganyika and France in Madagascar. Britain viewed Zanzibar as crucial for its own ambitions in Kenya and Uganda, as well as for monitoring rival nations and for securing and maintaining its colonies in Asia. In 1856, the Sultan Seyyid Said died, leaving two sons vying for the throne. Britain saw an opportunity and, using gunboat diplomacy, it interfered in the succession, placing the brother sympathetic to British interests on the throne. The new Sultan Seyyid Bargash was now in its debt. Further, he needed Britain's cooperation to prevent German annexation of Zanzibar to Germany's new colony in Tanganyika. The Germans were not inclined to preserve the political institutions in lands they colonized.[6] Britain presented Bargash with a solution – a protectorate with a "dual mandate" – a power-sharing agreement whereby two governments, his and Britain's, would share sovereignty over Zanzibar.[7]

Naturally, the Protectorate came with conditions. Britain's second reason for acquiring Zanzibar was to abolish slavery. Pressure from missionary and humanitarian organizations, as well as the growing public opinion back home drove the abolition movement. The Sultan faced a dilemma – his Busaidi dynasty had been slaving for centuries, and his wealth was dependent on the revenue from trading and transporting slaves to Arab dominions. Furthermore, ending slavery had staggering economic consequences for the Arab plantation landowners. Bargash reluctantly signed the Protectorate agreement, reportedly lamenting,

"A spear is held at each of my eyes. With which shall I choose to be pierced?"[8]

British Rule in Zanzibar

In November 1890, Zanzibar became a British protectorate. British colonial rule had three phases: the abolition of slavery; the establishment of an administrative framework; and the transformation of the framework into a legislative body in preparation for eventual parliamentary democracy.[9] Historian Anthony Clayton notes that "on their arrival, the British saw themselves as reformers and reconcilers".[10] Certainly Britain was full of paternalistic good intentions. However, slavery did not end overnight. It was not until 1897 that Britain officially abolished this heinous practice. At that time, the slave population was estimated to be 150,000.

However, the morally-minded British had neglected to consider the consequences of these suddenly "free" men and women. Many blacks were terrified – they constituted a large group of people their former Arab masters now saw as undesirables on "their" land. The Arabs were not about to pay them, nor offer them food or shelter, and so the former slaves became valueless human beings. Those who were "hired" by their old masters found their wages insufficient for survival. The Arab landowners were understandably furious at the economic ramifications of this new "slaveless" order. To placate them, the British passed such arcane legislation as the taxing of "salaries" of these newly-freed men and the arrest for vagrancy for any found unemployed. Thus, many former slaves found themselves in a far worse situation than before. Some migrated to the margins of the island and mixed with the Shirazi to eke out a living fishing from the sea. Some became squatters on plantation lands, exchanging a subsistence living for labour. Many others flocked to the N'Gambo slum, worsening the already crowded and miserable living conditions there.

As for the Arab plantation owners, some went into bankruptcy or mortgaged their lands to Indian moneylenders in Stone Town. Others consolidated their plantations and looked to the mainland to import seasonal migrant labour. Understandably, there was a significant reduction in the production of cloves. Because Zanzibar was largely a one-crop economy, it had to import much of its foodstuffs. The decline in clove revenues, combined with the fact that Zanzibar did not have an agricultural food production infrastructure, made life difficult for Zanzibaris regardless of race.

After the abolition of slavery, second on Britain's agenda was the establishment of a strong administrative infrastructure. Britain had assured the Sultan that the Protectorate would operate with a power-sharing arrangement. However, as described by Michael Lofchie, the only political scientist to work in pre-revolutionary Zanzibar, "The establishment of a Protectorate was purely a matter of lending official solemnification to Britain's informal acquisition of paramount influence in Zanzibar politics."[11]

Before Britain's involvement, the Sultan had ruled Zanzibar single-handedly, aided by a close, nepotistic circle of officials and advisers, but now the Sultan had only symbolic power. Britain moved to establish an effective economic structure that would oversee all areas of political, financial, judicial and economic life in the colony. This great enterprise needed a correspondingly large bureaucracy, for which Arabs were readily recruited, educated and trained to run. Lofchie notes that even at the height of its influence in Zanzibar, Britain never had more than 200 of its own citizens on the ground. Britain's second great accomplishment in Zanzibar was the creation of a class of skilled Arab professionals.

Britain's third goal in Zanzibar was to take the cream of this new class and mould a legislative council, a precursor to a parliamentary government. In 1926, Britain formed the Legislative Council of Zanzibar, symbolically presided over by the Sultan. At first, this council was just an advisory body to the British Resident, the head official of the colony. The Legislative Council (later the Legislative Assembly) in no way reflected or represented the people of Zanzibar, being composed of an appointed Arab elite. It is vital to note that Britain always considered Zanzibar to be an Arab state. Britain rejected "direct rule" and did not wish to eliminate the Sultanate, as it envisioned that Zanzibar would eventually function as a constitutional monarchy, a political form obviously familiar to them.

It is worth mentioning that the British, upon arriving to set up shop in Zanzibar Stone Town, found it profoundly unsettling. They hated the "mixedness"[12] of Arab and Indian living side by side along with Sufis, Ismailis, Goans, and Sunni Muslim traders. Zanzibar was of course a major port for peoples from all over the world.

Zanzibar urban society by 1890 was marked by a high degree of heterogeneity, a population with a high awareness of a potentially infinite number of "elsewheres" and a consumerism, which in combination with the first two factors made for a distinct cosmopolitanism.[13] Blacks were not part of this cosmopolitanism – they lived exiled outside the town walls in the slum N'Gambo.

We can view British political reforms in Zanzibar as a way to "classify" the cosmopolitan chaos – to sort through the mix of peoples, and delegate jobs and positions according to race and class. Thus, Arabs were considered suitable for the bureaucratic and business positions, Indians were deemed good civil servants and tradesmen but blacks were relegated to the most menial positions.[14] Britain may have congratulated itself on its humanitarian position vis-à-vis the slave trade, but its race-based reclassification had the effect of perpetuating the blacks' position at the bottom of the social ladder. Moreover, it neglected to take into account decades of repressed hostility the black population felt towards the Arabs. This was a terrible mistake: "[t]he easy British belief ... that the past and its oppression had been forgotten was a dangerous complacency, as became clear in the later 1950s, and the pre-colonial legacy contributed to the pogrom character of the Revolution's bloodshed."[15]

The contemplation of a multicultural Zanzibar was beyond the capacity of the British, who kept to themselves. They ate, drank, and played billiards in their whites-only English Club and partied at their whites-only beachside resort. Obviously, such elitist establishments did nothing to alleviate racial tensions. Indeed, the British further stratified the racial pyramid by adding a white layer right at the top.

The Legislative Assembly is a key example of how elitism, especially in terms of race, became further entrenched in Zanzibar. Despite the entry of a "token" African member in 1946, the Arabs began to see the Assembly as a template for their government after independence. The Assembly remained an appointed body until 1956, when Britain opened six seats for election. This election occurred during a turbulent, highly charged political climate, when both Arab and African nationalisms were on the rise. The establishment of political parties, radical and militant in nature, contributed to an atmosphere of "pathologically communal suspicion".[16]

The Escalation of Conflict

The Arabs knew exactly where a popular, self-governing Zanzibar would put them. They constituted only one-sixth of the population, and the majority blacks would easily drown them out. It is worth noting that the Zanzibari Arabs were the second largest alien elite in Africa, the whites in South Africa being the first. The Arabs organized as the Zanzibar National Party (ZNP) to press Britain for immediate independence. By moving quickly they could take control before the blacks had even started to mobilize. They had a considerable advantage: they were educated, well off, and versed in the workings of the government. They marketed themselves as the "people's party" – patriotic, pro-Islamic, and anti-British, which appealed to many Shirazis. Strategically, they played down race, even appointing an African as party vice-president.

Black Zanzibaris, meanwhile, had many disadvantages. They were not an educated group. Despite Britain's efforts at school construction, the blacks could not afford to send their children. Shaaban Sudi Mponda, the sole African in the Assembly, begged the British to delay the election: "We Africans do not welcome this election with open hearts… We are a backward people due to lack of educational facilities."[17] As well, the black Zanzibaris could not put forth a united front. They were divided into three groups: the indigenous former Bantu tribes and Shirazi peoples, the descendants of slaves, and, significantly, a large group of migrants from the mainland.

Between 1957 and 1963, Zanzibar had three disastrous elections. Progressively with each, Britain tried to prepare the country for independence. Each time the Afro-Shirazi Party polled the most votes, but Arab-initiated vote-rigging schemes, gerrymandered ridings and general corruption marred the results and each time the ZNP formed the government. The blacks realized they were outmaneuvered. It became clear to them after the July 1963 election – held just five months before independence on December 10, 1963 – that under a British-style government Zanzibar would return to Arab rule. They would continue to be a subjugated people.

If political repression was not enough to create unrest, another wind blew across Zanzibar from the mainland – African nationalism. Many seasonal workers had come to Zanzibar and stayed on. African nationalism in Zanzibar had its roots in 1934 and the creation of the African Association for Immigrant Workers. Initially, it was just a football club. Post-revolution President and Afro-Shirazi Party leader Abeid Karume[18] was among its members. The African Association became influential in trade-union disputes, as in the 1948 strike at the Zanzibar docks, which immobilized the city for over 20 days. This strike was a unifying force for blacks and, although not seen so at the time, was a harbinger of the revolution: "[t]he colonial government understood the significance of the industrial discontent; but saw the demonstration and the mainlanders' role creating an African solidarity as only an unfortunate feature in an industrial fracas of no deep-rooted structural significance."[19]

Although this was considered a strike by the migrant population, these men now numbered over 50,000, a quarter of Zanzibar's total population of 200,000. By the late 1950s this migrant group was well versed in the "politics of protest" and aware of the rise of African nationalism on the mainland. Both Kenya and Uganda were moving towards independence, with black leadership at the helm.

Revolution

When revolution did come, it came as a spontaneous combustion. In its declassified files on the revolution, CIA operatives pointed to a number of men potentially responsible: the Communist Chinese sympathizer Mohammed Babu, leader of the Umma Party; the radical union leader Kassim Hanga; Afro-Shirazi Party leader Abeid Karume, who, on the eve of the revolution had given a rousing pro-black speech at the Seaman Union Club.[20] But it was none of these men who actually initiated the revolution, and they themselves were as surprised by it as everyone else. Zanzibar was a tinder keg waiting to explode, but it still needed a spark to ignite it. That spark came from John Okello.

Okello was Ugandan and a proponent of the African nationalism sweeping the mainland. He was also a Christian on a self-proclaimed mission from God. His autobiography, written two years after the revolution from the confines of a Kenyan prison, describes in detail his God-given dreams; how he was "chosen" to take back Africa for Africans.[21] Okello was no soldier, although he took the rank of "Field Marshal". He was self-educated and obviously had some natural talents – he was a charismatic speaker who easily drew crowds as he preached his brand of nationalism.

On the night of January 12, 1964, he assembled 800 men outside the Stone Town walls. He divided his "army" into 4 units of 200 each and assigned targets. Okello led the charge on the Ziwani Police Headquarters, the main armory. The Arab government could have easily prevented this first charge, but for the fact that it had fired all the British-hired policemen and security officers within days of assuming independence. Their loyalty to the new regime was suspect, as most were originally black mainlanders. These trained, knowledgeable men had been replaced by inexperienced Arabs, creating a large group of embittered, former policemen with no work, no salary, and no place to go. Okello easily co-opted them. There is a modern parallel to this – within days of the fall of Saddam Hussein, the Americans discharged the entire Iraqi army. These men could have been used to maintain order, prevent looting and give some semblance of security. Instead, the disaffected men drifted into many anti-American militias.

After distributing arms, Okello seized the radio station. Over the next two days, he broadcast a series of incendiary messages that incited the black population to violence. Today, these broadcasts seem like a kind of perverse Hollywood entertainment for their sheer outrageousness, but at the time, they must have been utterly terrifying. He announced:

> The Government is now run by us, the Army. We have the strength of 99 million, 99 thousand. I will take very strong measures, 88 times stronger than at present...[22] I am Field Marshal Okello! Wake up you Imperialists; this is the government of the Freedom Fighters. Wake up, you black men. Let everyone of you take a gun and start to fight...[23]

He then addressed the Sultan, "You are allowed 20 minutes to kill your children and wives and then kill yourself."[24] The Sultan escaped in his yacht. Okello made wild claims about his capacity to produce weapons: "500 guns a day, 100 grenades an hour,"[25] as well as boasts of his own immortality: "I am above the Government and cannot die."[26] Overnight he emerged as the de facto hero and leader of the revolution. He and a growing posse of thugs swept over the island raping, looting, and killing Arabs and Indians in their path. Okello did not claim the presidency. He assigned that role to Karume, who, along with other black leaders like Babu, stepped into the political vacuum to form the revolutionary government. Both Karume and Babu had probably never even met Okello. If so, it supports the hypothesis in CIA declassified documents – that Okello was an opportunist and a creature of spontaneity, and that the revolution was a spontaneous action.

We know that Okello was instrumental in instigating much of the carnage, but we know less about what happened on the ground. The few westerners in Zanzibar at the time were rounded up and expelled. However, two Italian filmmakers were able to charter a helicopter and shoot footage, flying low over Unguja on both the 13th and 14th of January. Gualtiero Jacopetti and Franco Prosperi had been in Africa for several years filming wildlife, but witnessed so many bloody episodes they began filming those instead, eventually releasing the controversial film *Africa Addio.*[27] Their Zanzibar footage records many horrors – mass graves, trucks piled high with bodies, long lines of men and women marching to an execution pit, countless bodies floating in the sea. While some may be disturbed by the sheer sensationalism, the film offers concrete proof of the genocide.

Accounts of the massacre suffer from both the paucity of verifiable information and the excess of gross misinformation. A group of American journalists expelled during the revolution reported that it was the work of Cuban radicals. Years later, the CIA traced this story back to the sighting of a single man, a Pakistani, wandering the island in Castro-style garb.[28] Cold War fears of communist plots drove this propaganda, aided by China and the Soviet Union being among the first to recognize Zanzibar's new status. Yet despite this lack of truthful reporting, how could the killings of so many have gone largely unnoticed? Surely a survivor somewhere must have made a record of the atrocities. So, why have first hand reports not surfaced? Many Arabs did escape and set up expatriate communities in Oman and other Arab states. But unless these survivors come forward to tell their story, the genocide will remain a misunderstood or ambiguous event.

Post-revolution

Perhaps Karume understood the political implications of the mass killings. One of his first actions as president was to expel Okello, who had become a liability. Babu, the foreign minister in the new government, declared that Okello had never been anything but a kind of disc-jockey at a broadcast station.[29] By the first anniversary of revolution, Okello's name had been purged from the official story.[30]

After his expulsion, Okello continued to earn a reputation as a troublemaker, and was declared persona non grata in both Tanzania and Kenya. He was apparently last seen in his native Uganda with Idi Amin in the early 1970s.[31] Okello's autobiography, an attempt to rehabilitate his reputation, recounts his heroic exploits in an obviously biased but nonetheless fascinating, first-hand account of the Zanzibar Revolution.

Responsibility and Acknowledgement

The interval of British tenure, from the establishment of the protectorate in 1890 through to independence in 1963, is marked with missed opportunities, inept decision-making, and a deplorable lack of foresight. The British considered Zanzibar only a "training ground" colony. They considered Zanzibar to be "intellectually lifeless",[32] and "a delightful anachronism".[33] It was a pretty place where junior colonial officials went to cut their teeth before moving on to India. Not surprising then, that when the revolution exploded, the British became bystanders. After evacuating any remaining British civilians, they offered no assistance and made no attempt to intervene or stop the bloodshed, oblivious to their own role. The British therefore abdicated any responsibility to protect the Arabs as they were being massacred.

If the British failed the Arabs during the massacre, they also failed the blacks during their rule in Zanzibar. Herein lies a glaring contradiction. Despite noble intentions, the British perpetuated the racism and class elitism that disenfranchised the black majority. While the British formally abolished slavery, they provided no alternatives for the blacks after centuries of Arab subjugation, nor did they provide educational opportunities. They pointed Zanzibar in a democratic direction, but did not establish truly representational government. We cannot help but hold the British partly accountable for exacerbating the oppressive conditions – created during Arab rule – that led to the massacre.

Perhaps the Zanzibar genocide became just one of many brutal stories emanating from the African continent at the same time, like the Mau-Mau uprising in Kenya and the Biafra War in Nigeria. The fact of the massacre is not in doubt – the *Africa Addio* footage is easy to find and view on the internet. Perhaps this atrocity has been swallowed up by the sheer scope of horrors that followed and continue to ravage Africa. Zanzibar's first president, Abeid Karume, is remembered as more of a dictator than a president. Although he "ordered" free education for all, Karume became displeased with many of his intellectuals and subsequently had them "liquidated".[34] Zanzibar's ten years under his tenure are "an era of grave human rights violations where people feared for their life on every minute of every day".[35] Revolutionary history is not easily challenged in these conditions.

The hardest lesson to be found in Zanzibar is that of history repeating itself. Wherever there is centuries of built-up animosity, racism, gross inequality, and dehumanization, tensions increase to the breaking point, and then the roles of the abusers and the abused are reversed. The Arabs, former colonizers and enslavers of the blacks, became the victims in a revolution of decolonization.

In February 2007, Rowan Williams, the Archbishop of Canterbury, visited Zanzibar. He went to the Anglican Cathedral, built on top of the slave pits; he toured the former cells of captives and held the fetters in his hands. He remarked:

> It is as if slavery is a kind of compulsion for human societies. You can go back again and again to treating others as objects, as possessions, and I don't think we can simply sit back and say it is a thing of the past and no more. All the modern forms of slavery; economic slavery, debt slavery, the slavery of sex trafficking – these things are still with us.[36]

The Zanzibar Revolution and genocide speak of the human compulsion for slavery – in its physical, as well as economic and psychological forms – and of the appetite of countries for colonization, with the often catastrophic results of decolonization. Given Zanzibar's history, it may be understandable, but still soul-wrenching, that the black majority, in freeing themselves, had to spill so much blood. January 12, 1964, brought a nightmare of incomprehensible brutality to the spice-scented tropical islands. For the following few days, Zanzibar was the bloodiest place on earth.

NOTES

1 The number of people killed varies widely from source to source. The real number will probably never be known, but could be as high as 20,000.

2 John Cohen (text), and Gualtiero Jacopetti and Franco Prosperi (film), *Africa Addio* (New York: Ballantine Books, 1966), p. 133.

3 Ibid., p. 133.

4 Ibid., p. 130.

5 Esmond Bradley Martin, *Zanzibar, Tradition and Revolution* (London: Hamish Hamilton, 1978), p. 32.
6 Michael F. Lofchie, *Zanzibar: Background to Revolution* (Princeton: Princeton University Press, 1965), p. 56
7 Ibid., p. 57.
8 John Cohen, *Africa Addio*, p. 136.
9 Michael F. Lofchie, *Zanzibar: Background to Revolution*, p. 59.
10 Anthony Clayton, *The Zanzibar Revolution and its Aftermath* (London: C. Hurst & Company, 1981), p. 4.
11 Michael F. Lofchie, *Zanzibar: Background to Revolution*, p. 56.
12 Anne Bang, "Cosmopolitanism Colonised? Three Cases From Zanzibar" in Edward Simpson and Kai Kress (eds.), *Struggling with History: Islam and Cosmopolitanism in the Western Indian Ocean* (London: C. Hurst & Company, 2007), p. 170.
13 Ibid., p. 174.
14 Michael F. Lofchie, *Zanzibar: Background to Revolution*, p. 61.
15 Anthony Clayton, *The Zanzibar Revolution and its Aftermath*, p. 4.
16 Ibid., p. 38.
17 John Cohen, *Africa Addio*, p. 144.
18 Abeid Karume, the leader of the Afro-Shirazi Party, became Zanzibar's first President. His government followed a Marxist ideology. One of his first acts was to confiscate private property and redistribute it to the poor in 3-acre parcels. He was assassinated in 1972.
19 Anthony Clayton, *The Zanzibar Revolution and its Aftermath*, p. 34.
20 Helen Hunter, "Zanzibar Revisited" in *CIA Historical Review Program*, released as sanitized 18 September 1995. https://www.cia.gov/library/center-for-the-study-of-intelligence/kent-csi/docs/v11i2a01p_0001.htm. Accessed 11/09/2008.
21 John Okello, *Revolution in Zanzibar* (Nairobi: East African Publishing House, 1967), p. 73.
22 Helen Hunter, "Zanzibar Revisited", p. 2.
23 Esmond Bradley Martin, *Zanzibar, Tradition and Revolution*, p. 57.
24 Ibid., p. 57.
25 Helen Hunter, "Zanzibar Revisited", p. 2.
26 Ibid., p. 2.
27 After its première in Rome, February 1966, the film *Africa Addio* was denounced by 20 African embassies in Italy as a racist piece of sedition. It won a 'Donatello David', an Italian film award; the Italian cabinet minister who was to present the award refused to attend the ceremony amid the controversy.
28 Helen Hunter, "Zanzibar Revisited", p. 5.
29 John Okello, *Revolution in Zanzibar*, p. 8.
30 Ibid., p. 8.
31 *Don Petterson, Revolution in Zanzibar: An American's Cold War Tale* (Colorado: Westview Press, 2002), p. 177. Petterson surmises Okello fell out of favour with Amin and was executed.
32 Esmond Bradley Martin, *Zanzibar, Tradition and Revolution*, p. 48.
33 Ibid., p. 49.
34 *Zanzibar Forum, History*, http://www.zanzinet.org/zanzibar/history/historia.html.
35 Ibid.
36 Rowan Williams, Archbishop of Canterbury, video accessible on YouTube at http://www.youtube.com/watch?v=NBTErUDIcz8.

3

Unpacking the "Mau Mau" Rebellion

Salima Charania

✧

Your history gets in the way of my memory
Agha Shahid Ali

History records a rebellion erupting in Kenya from 1952 to 1956 – the official (colonial) estimate sets the Kenyan death toll at 11,000. However, unofficial (indigenous) estimates are as high as 100,000. This chapter investigates the often subjective accounts that form the dominant historical perspective. It explores colonial motives, myth-making and shaping of "facts" that the British used to legitimize the violent suppression of the Kikuyu by military force in Kenya. These notions are juxtaposed with Kikuyu counter-narratives of this largely unacknowledged atrocity, in the hope of presenting a more balanced discourse. We shall see that the construction of myths to legitimize and perpetuate violent imperial oppression as "justified retaliation" by British forces in Kenya echo through the current justifications of the global war on terror.

Kenya became a British colony in 1884 as a result of negotiations in Berlin between the imperial powers of Britain and Germany, each vying for valuable economic resources in East Africa as they carved up the map. From there began the British Empire's colonial domination of Kenya. The characteristics of the occupation of Kenya followed the path of past conquests by the British Empire. The Kikuyu (an anglicization of *Gikuyu*), the largest cultural group in Kenya, lost much during the occupation. The British encouraged white settlers to come live in Kenya, with the promise of cheap land, readily available labour and opportunity to amass substantial wealth. Kenya's colonization had a significant impact on the Kikuyu, predominantly agriculturists who made their living by farming and raising livestock. Some ethnic groups, like the Luo, the third largest ethnic group in Kenya, did not participate in the anti-colonial movement as the Kikuyu did. The European land settlement initiative did not seize Luo lands, nor did the settlements create a crisis for their traditional culture. The lands used to lure the white settlers were areas of Kenya inhabited by the Kikuyu, considered to be the some of the most fertile farming land, such as the White Highlands. This rich land was confiscated from the indigenous Kikuyu and distributed amongst the newly arrived settlers. The Kikuyu and other ethnic groups, except for some Maasi who fought with the British against the Kikuyu in Kenya, resisted the occupation but were unsuccessful. The British increased their control of Kenya's natural resources with little opposition, within or outside Kenya, during the several decades before the uprising. The British further tightened their grip on Kenya politically and economically by implementing several strategies. Early on, the colonial government established African reserves, similar to homelands in South Africa, where each indigenous ethnic group was apportioned separate lands. David Anderson, in *Histories of the Hanged*, states "[a]mongst the many grievances of the Kikuyu, the loss of lands to Europeans was deepest felt. Since the arrival of the first European settlers in 1902, land in Kenya had been divided by race, just as it was in South Africa. In 1915 the Crown Land Ordinance had recognized 'native rights' in lands reserved for their use, and in 1926 the British consolidated this division by creating African Reserves for each of Kenya's 'tribes', leaving the 'White Highlands' solely for the Europeans."[1]

A British-appointed council of chiefs replaced the traditional Kikuyu council of elders, eliminating the indigenous system of organization. The newly-appointed chiefs acted as intermediaries, part of a system that became known as indirect rule. The British, therefore, created a powerful intermediary elite, endowed with privilege, wealth and special access to the colonial government. The land transfer was just the beginning – the settlers now needed Africans to work the very land they once owned. The indigenous peoples of Kenya were not keen to move from being independent agriculturists to becoming poorly paid wage labourers, enduring harsh working conditions for the newly arrived settlers. In order to further restrict the economic freedom of Kenyans, the colonial government imposed the hut and poll taxes: "[T]o solve the problem of getting Africans to work for settlers, the government introduced a hut and poll tax that forced Africans to work for wages to pay the taxes; at the same time, they prohibited them from growing cash crops, such as coffee, sisal, and maize."[2] However, labour shortages continued for the settlers – the indigenous Kenyans resisted being exploited. After various unsuccessful attempts at recruiting labour, the final and perhaps the most disturbing tool of subordination, the *Kipande* pass system, was enacted. The *Kipande*, or identity card, had various implications and consequences. Native Kenyan labourers, who were once free to farm their own land, were required to wear this identity card around their necks. Thus the *Kipande* became a symbol of slavery as it restricted native Kenyans' movement and facilitated their oppression. British settler employers recorded such information as registration number, the wearer's place of residence, the type of work performed, the rate of pay, whether or not taxes had been paid, and comments about the wearer's work characteristics. If the *Kipande* indicated the forced labour tax had not been paid, the wearer could be forcibly recruited as labour for settler farms.

It was against this backdrop of exploitation, overcrowded reserves, malnutrition, poverty and racism that unrest simmered over the decades, before the event now called the Mau Mau uprising. In the decades leading up to the crisis, the Kikuyu organized politically. Of their few organizations, the most prominent was the Kikuyu Central Association (KCU). There were attempts to strive for peaceful resolutions to grievances against the long-standing oppressive regime. Conditions in the reserves worsened – they were overpopulated, the land was becoming exhausted from over farming and hunger was widespread. The "squatters", as they were later referred to by the white settlers, worked on settler farms on land originally confiscated from the Kikuyu, and they endured poor treatment and deplorable living conditions. However, as years passed and the Kikuyu political organizations failed to achieve their resolutions, the resistance took a violent turn. In 1948, the "Mau Mau" secret society formation began. It was said to be formed by Kikuyu labourers who worked on white settler farms. By that time approximately 250,000, a quarter of the Kikuyu peoples, had become forced labourers on white settler farms. By 1952 violent protests began taking place on settler farms, Nairobi slums and on Kikuyu reserves. During this time, Kikuyu fled by the thousands from the reserves to the Kenyan forests, which became the base for Mau Mau fighters. While sporadic protests against whites and Africans loyal to the British did occur, the act that led the colonial government to declare a state of emergency was the October 7, 1952 assassination of Senior Chief Waruhiu, a Kikuyu who had greatly benefited from his collaboration with the British. Senior Chief Waruhiu and other British-appointed Kikuyu chiefs were disliked by Kikuyu labourers who saw them as sellouts – reaping the benefits of colonial patronage while turning against their own people. It was only after the assassination of Chief Waruhiu that the British took the resistance as a serious threat to colonial rule. The colonial government cracked down on the movement, outlawing its members. Following the imposition of martial law, political leaders, most notably Jomo Kenyatta, thought to be the mastermind behind the movement, were arrested and detained. Despite Kenyatta's repeated denunciation of the Mau Mau, he was jailed for seven years. Many years later it was revealed that there was no evidence directly linking Kenyatta to the movement. Kenyatta later became the first president of post-colonial Kenya.

The state of emergency and the British imposition of military strength did little to stop the intensity of the Mau Mau movement. The Mau Mau lacked the sophisticated strategy, as well as sufficient weaponry, to effectively fight the British. Knowing that their arms were no match for the might of the British, the Mau Mau based themselves in the thick forests of Mount Kenya, launching irregular night-time raids on neighbouring settlers' farms, post offices and police stations, as well as on Kikuyu suspected as loyal to the colonial regime.

The British retaliation against the movement was an aggressive two-pronged strategy. The first was launched in the remote mountain forests of Kenya, pitting twenty thousand British troops, with Royal Air Force support, against approximately twenty thousand Mau Mau "insurgents" with home-made weapons and no outside support. This campaign would last over two years before the British brought the area under control. The second, and lengthier, campaign was geared towards the civilian population of approximately 1.5 million Kikuyu, considered to be a serious threat to colonial powers, as the British believed they had taken the "Mau Mau oath". Those captured – an estimated eighty thousand "insurgents" – were held in detention camps established by the British.[3]

There are numerous accounts of atrocities taking place in the detention camps. One such record tells us that "[p]risoners were routinely tortured and suspects killed with impunity. Settlers advocated killing all

Kikuyu and even using an atomic bomb."[4] The British military response was swift and coordinated. The movement's base camps in Mount Kenya's forests and the surrounding areas were heavily bombed. The retaliation was not only limited to the "insurgency" – the British strategy to crush the uprising, in fact, included innocent civilians. Lands and livestock were confiscated, crops and homes burned down. Those suspected of harbouring Mau Mau were interrogated and tortured, a shoot-on-sight policy was adopted, and thousands of Kikuyu were herded into so-called protected villages which were in actuality a way to control the population rather than to protect them.[5]

The British colonialists were able to rationalize the violent actions taken to suppress the freedom movement by offering various justifications. Two factors that contributed to this atrocity being constructed as a just war were the widely held ethnocentric beliefs of colonialism and the creation of the Mau Mau myth. From the start, the British did not take the rebellion as a serious call for freedom from the British regime. For them it was unfathomable that these people, whom they were benevolently looking after, would want to have freedom or would be capable of self-governance. As Rosberg aptly notes in *Myth of "Mau Mau": Nationalism in Kenya*,

> [e]thnocentrism has been an important element behind the general acceptance of this myth. At a more immediate level of explanation, we may observe a concrete set of interrelated beliefs held by Europeans in Kenya. The most important of these were (1) an implicit conviction that the colonial system was perfectly capable of responding to the legitimate social and political grievances of the African; (2) the belief that 'Mau Mau' was but another manifestation of earlier African religious movements; (3) and the belief that in employing secret oaths, the African was rejecting modernity and reverting back to primitive behaviour patterns.[6]

Policies employed during the uprising reflect such thought. For example, the establishment of detention camps was based on the ethnocentric belief that colonialism was partly a mission to civilize Africans, an inferior race of people who were essentially savages. Upon the advice of British psychiatrists in Kenya, the British set upon a campaign to "re-educate" suspected Mau Mau and their sympathizers in these detention camps. This "re-education" reportedly included a range of practices, from Christian schooling to torture – which included electric shock, castration, rape and other violent and degrading treatment – geared towards crushing the eighty thousand Kikuyu who passed through the camps and, along with them, the rebellion.[7] Building a narrative of Mau Mau as needing to be helped, civilized and "rehabilitated" provided a seemingly rational foundation for establishing detention camps. This weaving of the myth of cultural imperialism both set the stage for and perpetuated these atrocities.

The Kikuyu tradition of oathing was a cultural practice that was appropriated and moulded into a colonial myth that supported the suppression of the uprising. Rosberg explains, that "Europeans' stereotyped views of the Kikuyu character also help explain their assumption that the oath was central to the 'Mau Mau' movement."[8] Further he says, "[a] third factor which served to reinforce the colonial community's conviction that the 'Mau Mau' was essentially an irrational rejection of modernity was the widespread use of oaths and oathing ceremonies. For Kenya's Europeans, no other single feature of 'Mau Mau' so clearly unequivocally symbolized the atavistic and primitive character of Kikuyu politics. The very word 'Mau Mau' probably contributed to this impression."[9]

The role of oathing was multi-dimensional and complex. Because of the secrecy that surrounded the Mau Mau oath, it has engendered much speculation. Oathing is common across many societies – it can be a symbolic act designed to create solidarity around shared values or goals. It is interesting that the British, for whom oaths of allegiance to the monarchy are foundational in their history, would find the acts of oathing among the Kikuyu so foreign. Oathing was a part not only of Kikuyu culture, but also of other ethnic groups in Kenya. During the time prior to the rebellion, Mau Mau fighters reportedly took oaths promising to kill whites and anyone else who stood in the way, and to take their weapons for the movement.[10] There were taboos surrounding the breaking of the oath. It was said that if the oath was broken it would spell death for the one who broke it. Further, those who refused to take the oath could be considered British sympathizers, and also targeted. When the British found out about the oath, they reacted with fear. The colonial secretary of state, Oliver Lyttleton wrote:

> The Mau Mau oath is the most bestial, filthy, nauseating incantation which perverted minds can ever have brewed. I am not unduly

> squeamish, but when I first read it I was so revolted that it got between me and my appetite… I can recall no instance when I have felt the forces of evil to be so near and so strong.[11]

It is difficult to ascertain how much about the Mau Mau oath is real and how much was British propaganda. The British deemed that the oath played a significant role in the rebellion, made it a capital offence to take the oath and required captured Mau Mau to take a counter-oath to cleanse them of evil.[12] The British understanding of the role of the oath shaped the response to the rebellion. It was unfathomable to the British government and settlers that their benevolence towards their trusted servants would be reciprocated with such a violent revolt. They glossed over their own racism and their expropriation of Kikuyu land, which effectively ghettoized and enslaved the Kikuyu. The British chose to believe that the revolt was based on the mysterious Mau Mau oath that turned their loyal servants into savages. Believing that if they could "re-educate" these "savages" and remove the effects of the oath, they would once again return to the way things had been.[13]

Dane Kennedy in his article "Constructing the Colonial Myth of the Mau Mau" aptly notes that "[p]olitically mobilized groups invariably invent myths to justify their aims and undermine those of their rivals, but only those groups that possess or acquire power sanctioned by the state are able to enshrine their myths in textbooks and other organs of orthodoxy…"[14] The use of myths to propagate imperialism started early in colonial history. Colonization in Africa was justified by the British, as they truly believed they were on a "civilizing mission". Official rhetoric propagated the myth of benevolent imperialism whose aim was to fulfill the moral obligation of a superior British empire to transform "backward" heathens into progressive citizens by imposing their economic knowledge and Christian values.[15]

This constructed ethos was further built upon during the period of the rebellion. The Mau Mau was defined in several ways, at different times. From the start the conflict was portrayed, both externally and internally, as a war against Mau Mau terrorists. Back home in Britain and among the settlers, tales of the savage Mau Mau spread quickly. The Mau Mau were "portrayed as a barbaric, anti-European, and anti-Christian sect that had reverted to tactics of primitive terror to interrupt the British civilizing mission in Kenya".[16] Mainstream news magazines such as *Life* presented their readers with pictorial evidence of Mau Mau savagery upon the innocent British settlers. A war against "terrorists", "insurgents" or "rebels" is easily digestible, as we know today. It is important to note, before further exploring these events, that the term "Mau Mau" is highly contested. The members of the movement referred to themselves as "the movement", the "African government" and most commonly as "Land and Freedom Army", a name that lived on after the rebellion. Various etymological explanations have been offered but not by the Kikuyu themselves. Perhaps the use of this term, so un-English and foreign-sounding, helped in moulding the perceived meaning of the term to fit the desired narrative. It has been suggested that:

> [t]he British probably maintained the term Mau Mau because it conjured up images of a secret society and hid the fact that it was a rational political organization fighting for land and freedom. The British government and the police did everything they could to make sure Mau Mau was depicted to the world media as a group of criminals leading an irrational attack against the forces of law and order.[17]

Another tragic event that took place during the rebellion has also shaped the way the Mau Mau movement is remembered. Some ethnic Kenyans, suspected to be British loyalists and collaborators with the colonial regime, were targeted by the movement as well. The Lari Massacre, in which the Mau Mau reportedly carried out a bloody attack on Kenyan British loyalists, ended with hundreds of civilians hacked and burned to death. Although the Mau Mau were blamed for the massacre, the details of what actually happened are not clear. Mau Mau activists have adamantly insisted that they were specifically targeting Chief Luka, his family and other loyalists at Lari, while the massacre included hundreds of civilians, including women and children, whose bodies lay among the dead. The Lari Massacre was used as a tool of state propaganda in two ways according to Anderson in *Histories of the Hanged*. It was used by the British to effectively eliminate any sympathy for the Mau Mau that may have existed and make it easier for the British to push forward their rationale that this was not a nationalist fight for independence. Anderson goes on to say, "[t]here were two principal targets for British Propaganda over Lari. First, the attack was used to convince public opinion back in Britain of Mau Mau barbarity… The second target for propaganda was Kenya's African population. Luka and his followers were presented as typical of loyal Kikuyu who were now potential targets of Mau Mau savagery." Anderson adds that "the state's counter-terror in the aftermath of the attack was only vaguely hinted at, and then most often in terms that glorified the idea of righteous vengeance against the culprits".[18] The outcome of the massacre was difficult to untangle. Casualties were borne by both sides; however, even a pro-Home Guard publication later noted that the number of "terrorist" casualties far outnumbered those suffered by the British loyalists and security forces combined.[19]

Kenya gained independence from Britain on December 12, 1963, when the British finally accepted that continuing colonial rule in Kenya was unsustainable both politically and economically. Official history records the number of white civilians killed during the uprising as 32, while the number of African civilians killed by Mau Mau is put at 1,819. Of the "insurgents", it is believed that 11,000 were killed, 80,000 detained and more than 1,000 were hanged as criminals.[20] Unofficial counter-narratives suggest the number of Kikuyu killed is much higher. One might ask what the legacy of the Mau Mau rebellion was back in Britain. In Elkins' words:

> Back in Britain there would be no soul-searching or public accounting for the crimes perpetuated against the hundreds of thousands of men and women in Kenya. When Ian Macleod took over the Colonial Office in the months after Hola, he wrote to Kenya's new governor, Patrick Renson, assuring him that he had "decided to draw a veil upon the past". The final lasting image of Britain's moral war in the empire was not going to be revealed by a thorough investigation into the torture, murder, and starvation of Kikuyu men, women, and children. Instead, there was a great deal of sympathy, if not admiration, for the professional soldiers, British colonial officers, and ordinary settlers who fought the terror of the Mau Mau, even if terror pushed them to casual brutality and violence.[21]

The question remains as to how this was allowed to happen – and why atrocities still occur today. In a coincidence of history, power brokers effectively convince the world that suppression was, and still is, justified. The same rhetoric of "othering" that was used against the Mau Mau is being fed to our media today with respect to the "War on

Terror". The term "Islamofascism" has been coined to justify invading sovereign countries in the Middle East, for crushing the fanatical Taliban and furthering "our" mission to liberate and educate Afghan women. It is the positioning of an opposing or less powerful view outside the realm of rationality that allows the powerful dominant voices to shape the interpretation and recording of events. Feeding on racist, ethnocentric sentiments and public anxiety about the "other" can strengthen support of aggression in the name of security. Anderson's account of measures used against the Mau Mau resonates today with the Western nations' justifications for the "War on Terror": "[i]n the midst of the war, draconian anti-terrorist laws were introduced suspending the human rights of suspects, imposing collective punishments, facilitating detention without trial, permitting the seizure of property of convicts..."[22]

Marshall S. Clough, in *Mau Mau Memoirs*, quotes Josiah Mwangi Kariuku, a Kenyan socialist politician who had himself worked on settler farms until 1946, and later provided a counter-narrative from the point of view of the oppressed:

> The future historian of these times may find it difficult to get our side of the story....But in my narrative of the camps and our strange life together inside them he may perhaps sees some glimpses of truth and justice of the movements of unity, and he may begin to understand why we do not regard the soldiers of the forest as "hardcore", "terrorists", or murderers, but as the noblest of our fighters for freedom.[23]

While colonial narratives and myth-making allowed for wide acceptance of this atrocity in Britain, other internal factors and conflicting counter-narratives to this day contribute to the way the Mau Mau rebellion is remembered in Kenya. The failure of the Mau Mau movement to achieve its military and political goals has complicated how the legacy of the movement is recorded. Former participants are divided among themselves on how the movement is to be remembered. Also, without representation among the political elite of post-colonial Kenya, the former members of the movement lack access to record their story.[24]

Not all Kikuyu were part of the Mau Mau movement, adding further nuance to the way the events are remembered within Kenya. The Kikuyu political leaders in Kenya after independence either disassociated themselves from the Mau Mau movement, or they later identified themselves with the movement in order to establish political power. Thus there are divisions in the collective memory of the events. Even Jomo Kenyatta, a Kikuyu jailed by the British as a suspected Mau Mau leader, dissociated himself from the movement and relegated the Mau Mau to obscurity when he became the first president of independent Kenya. It was not until Kenyatta's political party, KANU, was voted out after forty years in government in 2002 that the new government brought with it a change in how the Mau Mau is viewed by the nation. The new government rescinded the 1952 British-imposed ban which had designated the Mau Mau as an illegal organization.[25] Although the Kikuyu became the political elite in the years after independence, many who had not been linked to the Mau Mau used the memory of the movement to justify and maintain their dominance in post-colonial Kenya. This entitlement based on exclusive Kikuyu participation in the fight for freedom has left a lasting legacy in Kenyan politics to this date. Moloba notes, "[t]hey saw themselves as members of an ethnic group that played a decisive role in the struggle for independence and therefore deserved 'a bigger share of the national cake'."[26] Subsequent Kikuyu presidents in Kenya have used the memory of the revolt to justify why they should lead the country.

The 2007–08 Kenyan election crises erupted in Kenya after incumbent President Mwai Kibaki was re-elected. Supporters of Raila Odinga, Kibaki's opponent, alleged there had been electoral tampering. Ethnic fighting erupted between the Kikuyu, the community to which Kibaki belonged, and supporters of Odinga, who were primarily Luo. The political and ethnic violence that ensued left hundreds dead and thousands more homeless. As a suggested resolution, Kofi Annan called on Kenya to establish a Truth and Reconciliation Commission to address the humanitarian situation, the political crisis and land and historical injustices. The political situation in Kenya to this day remains volatile.

History may be shaped by the "official" story, but it need not remain static as counter-narratives become circulated. The remnants of the official British story, together with the Kenyan government's selective amnesia about the events surrounding independence, have, for now, combined to appropriate the Mau Mau legacy. This shaping of the narrative has so far allowed the Mau Mau episode to remain an unacknowledged atrocity. But, as Anderson reveals, "[e]lsewhere in central Kenya the steady haul of human bones keeps surfacing. There are unmarked graves from the Mau Mau war all over Kikuyuland. Some of them hold the remains of rebels and suspects, killed by the security forces. Other graves hold the remains of people executed by Mau Mau... The land itself is inscribed with memories of Mau Mau."[27] As Kenyans continue to reap this grim harvest, the Mau Mau Rebellion still casts a shadow across the Kenyan psyche. It is the very darkness of the shadow, however, that may prompt Kenyans – and their former colonizers – to move toward greater understanding and acknowledgement of this episode in their history.

NOTES

1 David Anderson, *Histories of the Hanged* (London: Weidenfeld & Nicholson, 2005), p. 21.
2 Richard H. Robbins, *Global Problems and the Culture of Capitalism—4th Edition* (Boston, MA: Pearson Education, Inc., 2008), p. 317.
3 Caroline Elkins, *Britain's Gulag* (New York: Henry Holt and Company, LLC, 2005), preface.
4 Richard H. Robbins, *Global Problems and the Culture of Capitalism—4th Edition* (Boston, MA: Pearson Education, Inc., 2008), p. 325.
5 http://www.bluegecko.org/kenya/tribes/kikuyu/maumau.htm
6 Carl G. Rosberg Jr and John Nottingham, *The Myth of "Mau Mau": Nationalism in Kenya* (New York: Fredrick A. Praeger, 1966), p. 321.
7 Richard H. Robbins, *Global Problems and the Culture of Capitalism—4th Edition* (Boston, MA: Pearson Education, Inc., 2008), p. 326.
8 Carl G. Rosberg Jr and John Nottingham, *The Myth of "Mau Mau": Nationalism in Kenya* (New York: Fredrick A. Praeger, 1966), p. 333.
9 Carl G. Rosberg Jr and John Nottingham, *The Myth of "Mau Mau": Nationalism in Kenya* (New York: Fredrick A. Praeger, 1966), p. 331.
10 Richard H. Robbins, *Global Problems and the Culture of Capitalism—4th Edition* (Boston, MA: Pearson Education, Inc., 2008), p. 321.
11 Richard H. Robbins, *Global Problems and the Culture of Capitalism—4th Edition* (Boston, MA: Pearson Education, Inc., 2008), p. 321.
12 http://www.psywar.org/maumau.php
13 Richard H. Robbins, *Global Problems and the Culture of Capitalism—4th Edition* (Boston, MA: Pearson Education, Inc., 2008), p. 325.
14 Dane Kennedy, "Constructing the Colonial Myth of the Mau Mau", *The International Journal of African Historical Studies*, Vol. 25, No. 2, pp. 241–60, 1992, p. 242.
15 Caroline Elkins, *Britain's Gulag* (New York: Henry Holt and Company, LLC, 2005), 5.
16 Caroline Elkins, *Britain's Gulag* (New York: Henry Holt and Company, LLC, 2005), preface.
17 Richard H. Robbins, *Global Problems and the Culture of Capitalism—4th Edition* (Boston, MA: Pearson Education, Inc., 2008), p. 322.

18 David Anderson, *Histories of the Hanged* (London: Weidenfeld & Nicholson, 2005), pp. 178–79.
19 Wunyabari O. Maloba, *Mau Mau and Kenya: An Analysis of a Peasant Revolt* (Bloomington: Indiana University Press, 1998), p. 101.
20 http://www.psywar.org/maumau.php
21 Caroline Elkins, *Britain's Gulag* (New York: Henry Holt and Company, LLC, 2005), p. 363.
22 David Anderson, *Histories of the Hanged* (London: Weidenfeld & Nicholson, 2005), p. 5.
23 Marshall S. Clough, *Mau Mau Memoirs* (Boulder, Colorado: Lynne Rienner Publishers, Inc.), p. 1.
24 Wunyabari O. Maloba, *Mau Mau and Kenya: An Analysis of a Peasant Revolt* (Bloomington: Indiana University Press, 1998), p. 169.
25 David Anderson, *Histories of the Hanged* (London: Weidenfeld & Nicholson, 2005), p. 343.
26 Wunyabari O. Maloba, *Mau Mau and Kenya: An Analysis of a Peasant Revolt* (Bloomington: Indiana University Press, 1998), p. 172.
27 David Anderson, *Histories of the Hanged* (London: Weidenfeld & Nicholson, 2005), p. 343.

4

THE BIAFRAN WAR FOR INDEPENDENCE: NIGERIA IN THE 1960S

Patricia Kelly

✧

If unity is the ideal framework for the development of the African man, it must not become his grave...
Republic of Biafra Ministry of Information, 1968

When we are poised the wounds of battle to heal,
We shall remember those who died in mass.
Biafran National Anthem

Most people old enough to remember the 1960s can recall the photographs of starving, sad-eyed Biafran children with their bloated bodies and frail stick-like limbs. These were the poster children for African food aid, iconic images of the Nigerian Civil War that would be repeated over the decades across Africa in areas of decolonization, ethnic "cleansing" and violence. But what is largely unknown is the repression and atrocity that preceded and followed those images. The repression of the Igbo people of Nigeria actually began before the commencement of war, and it has continued to the present. The persistence of a political culture in Nigeria that denies human rights to minorities like the Igbo inhibits acknowledgement of past atrocities. The meaning of Biafra stretches backwards and forwards in time. It is important to examine events that led to the moment when those iconic photographs were taken, and subsequent events that have contributed to the collective memory held by the Igbos to this day. In Nigeria and in other places in Africa, events continue to play out with appalling similarity. The question that remains is how reconciliation can be reached before a country unwinds into chaos and death.

Pre-Civil War Period

The country of Nigeria was created in 1914 as a colony and protectorate of Britain. The borders of 1914 enclosed peoples of 250 linguistically diverse ethnicities and of at least two predominant religions – Islam and Christianity. The majority of Nigeria's population belonged to one of the three major ethnic groups: the predominantly Muslim Hausa-Fulani of the north, the mostly Christian Yoruba of the west, and the predominantly Catholic Christian Igbos of the east. However, a significant minority of Nigerians – 40 percent – belonged to one of the remaining ethnic groups. The northern peoples were settled in what was by far the largest area which, although land-locked, had access to the sea by the River Niger and the River Benin; both the western peoples and the eastern peoples had access to the Atlantic coast.

From a western perspective, Nigerian history – from 1914 to the end of its civil war in 1970, and through to the present – seems a tragic political experiment involving many foreign interests. During this period, millions of Nigerians became the victims of unprovoked massacres. The civil war itself resulted in the deaths of at least 3 million. It could be argued that the young country of Nigeria, despite inheriting a system of parliamentary democracy and having successfully educated a workforce of nationals, lacked at least one factor or precondition required for the success of liberal-style multiculturalism as described by Will Kymlicka: the existence of reliable human rights protections.[1] The absence of reliable human rights provisions during a time of ethnic crisis and chaos helped to ensure that atrocities committed against the ethnic Igbos in 1966 would remain relatively unacknowledged until the twenty-first century.

The civil war that followed the secession of the eastern region of Nigeria and its declaration of autonomy as the Republic of Biafra received extensive global attention, bringing humanitarian aid to the region. It is well known that millions of ethnic Igbos starved or were bombed during their civil war with the Federal Republic of Nigeria from 1967 to 1970. However, the slaughter of thousands of ethnic Igbos in

1966, the year preceding the civil war, went unrecognized internationally and was minimized at the time by Nigerian military leaders of northern descent. These earlier atrocities, unacknowledged through the constitutional and administrative changes in Nigeria during the 1960s, were, however, a catalyst for the declaration of independence by the Eastern Region from Federal Nigeria in May, 1967 and the ensuing thirty-month civil war.

Igbos maintain that prior to the amalgamation of north and south Nigeria by the British in the early 1900s, there was little ethnic conflict between groups, as traditionally most tribes chose to remain independent of each other. Decolonization by the British initially created three administrative regions that not only resulted in the eventual political domination of independent Nigeria by one ethnic group – the Hausa-Fulani of the north – but also created domination by one ethnic group within each of the administrative regions. (A fourth region, the midwest, would be created in 1963.) It remained to be seen how the institutions of a democracy – a constitution and free elections – would affect the socio-economic standing of the peoples of so many different ethnic groups.

Desiring successful independence for the colony of Nigeria, Britain introduced in the 1950s a parliamentary system and the first of three constitutions of that decade before granting full independence in 1960. Nigeria, the most populous country in Africa, was to be a model of transition to democracy for all other former colonies in Africa. Britain ruled its colony indirectly until 1960, educating and establishing a political and bureaucratic elite loyal to the democratic traditions of Britain in each of the three regions. The Christian Igbos and a smaller minority group, the Ibibios of the eastern region, emerged as dominant socio-economic groups, in both the eastern region and in the north and west. As minorities, they had to rely on coalition governments with northern representatives for political power in the 1960s.

Democracy did not flourish in Nigeria following independence in 1960. The census of 1962–63 showing a majority of Nigerian citizens to be Hausa-Fulani was quite controversial, as it gave the north a federal parliamentary majority. Economic decisions at the national level would almost certainly be influenced by the wishes of the dominant ethnic group. Violence accompanied the general election of 1964. Elections for the Western Region in 1965 were suspected to have been rigged. Ethnic diversity was by now a "built-in minority problem".[2]

Tumbling Into Chaos

By 1966, Nigeria was an unstable federation with a constitution that promoted development of the four regions at the expense of a strong, centralized federal government. The regions, viewing themselves as unequal in power, considered the federation's central authority impotent. The first military coup, in January 1966, established a Supreme Military Council and Federal Government with an Igbo, Major-General Ironsi, as leader. His attempt to unify the government and country by decree failed, and in May, a group of mostly northern military officers staged a counter-coup. Ironsi was assassinated, and a northerner, Lt.-Col. Gowon, assumed the position of military head of state. An ad hoc constitutional conference in September, with delegates from each region, considered political options for Nigeria: to become a federation with strong central authority, to become a federation with weak central authority, to become a confederation, or to try an entirely new political configuration.[3] Minorities within the four regions, now renamed provinces, preferred to be part of a coalition within a federation; easterners and northerners remained wary of any configuration that would give political and administrative power to the others or to westerners.

The first open attack on Igbos began in late May of 1966, directly after Ironsi's attempt to unify the country by decree – a rule that initially, at least, had popular support. Ethnic Igbos in the Northern Region were attacked and killed by northern civilians. It is notable that Ironsi, an Igbo himself, did not send troops to support the Igbo population. A second attack occurred against civilians in late July, two months after Ironsi's assassination. The third attack against civilian Igbos and easterners happened on September 29th, 1966, known as "Black Thursday". Soldiers and civilians massacred anywhere between 5,000 and 50,000 Igbos in northern and western Nigeria. It is estimated that between 700,000 and 2 million Igbos returned to the Eastern Region as refugees. The frequency of these attacks and the targeting of civilians from their ethnic group convinced Igbos that they were not safe within Federal Nigeria. It remains unknown whether the attacks were indeed planned and instigated at the highest levels of Nigerian military authority, or whether they were spontaneous. Either way, the attacks were supported by the people of the Northern Region. The Military Governor for the Eastern Region, Lt.-Col. Ojukwu, with a mandate from the regional representatives, began to prepare for eventual secession from Nigeria.

The political chaos of 1966, and into 1967, stemmed from the fact that there were three leaders – Ironsi, Ojukwu, and Gowon – each with a regional mandate, each trying to determine the ideal configuration of power in a country where his own ethnic group was a minority. Both Ironsi and Gowon believed that military rule was essential to restoring order and preventing dissolution of the country. Gowon was a reluctant national leader, but he was urged by both the British High Commissioner, Sir Francis Cumming-Bruce, and the American ambassador, Elbert Mathews, to try to keep the country unified. Nigeria in the 1960s was a major African exporter of rubber, palm, cocoa, and a minor exporter of petroleum, and they informed Gowon that "not another dime in foreign assistance would come to Nigeria" if the country dissolved into its constituent regions.[4] Gowon's response was to divide Nigeria into twelve states, reducing the Igbo territory and thereby Igbo influence. Areas that had formerly been part of the Igbo-dominated Eastern Region came under the power of the smaller minorities of the Efiks, Ibibios, Annangs, and Ijaws. The Eastern Region lost Port Harcourt and the surrounding area, thus becoming landlocked. As a result, the Eastern Region seceded in May, 1967, declaring itself the Republic of Biafra.

The Nigerian–Biafran Civil War

Britain chose not to intervene at this time, nor did any government in Europe or North America. The major powers adopted a "wait and see" attitude.[5] Prior to secession, during the atrocities against the Igbos and easterners in 1966 and 1967, the international powers had been uninvolved, perhaps because they were ignorant of the events. The international community did become involved during the civil war but then only with humanitarian support to the eastern Nigerian peoples. In terms of political involvement it largely remained a bystander.

The Eastern Region of Nigeria could have existed as the viable state of Biafra. It had a well-educated population, proximity to the Atlantic Ocean, oilfields within its territory and the major petroleum seaport of Port Harcourt. However, very few countries recognized Biafra as a sovereign state. Only Gabon, the Ivory Coast, Tanzania, Zambia and Haiti recognized Biafra. Among western nations only France decided to follow the direction of other French-speaking countries, and Portugal provided Biafra with communication and air landing space on

São Tomé, its island possession off the coast. Meanwhile, Britain supported the "unifying government" of Gowon and his Nigerian forces and supplied them with small arms, as did the Soviets. The United States, preoccupied with its war in Vietnam, did not become involved. Overall, foreign powers, fearing the Igbo drive for self-determination would provoke similar sentiments in other African countries, passively supported Nigerian unity. Neither the Biafran nor the Nigerian government was satisfied with the response from the international community. Essentially, Nigerians were left to their own devices.

The consequences of the ensuing thirty months of civil war took a disproportionate toll on the people of Biafra. They were subjected to bombing raids that violated conventions of war. Humanitarian relief was intermittently blocked to the shrinking enclave of Biafra. The Biafran forces wanted to accept relief by air, fearing that relief brought through a land corridor would be tailed by Nigerian forces, but the Nigerian government would not authorize relief flights into its airspace. The estimated Biafran death toll in early 1968 ranges from 200 per day (British sources) to 6,000 per day (World Council of Churches). In his book, *Surviving in Biafra*, Alfred Uzokwe describes families in the area relying on subsistence plots of cassava and yam and the international supplies of cornmeal, stockfish, rice and milk to prevent the protein-deficiency condition of kwashiorkor.[6] At the end of the war, three million Nigerians, mostly Biafrans (former Eastern Nigerians) had perished from starvation or indiscriminate warfare.

Perception of Atrocities

The atrocities of the 30-month civil war received extensive coverage in the press, in periodicals, and in subsequent literature. On the other hand, the "pogroms" against the easterners of May and July, 1966 and "Black Thursday" of September, 1966 went unnoticed at the time by the international community and ignored by the Nigerian military governments of the late 1960s. Why was coverage and attention so different during these two periods?

Perhaps the presence of international aid and relief providers in Biafra during the civil war channelled "facts on the ground" to the rest of the world. The international effort in the civil war was described as the "largest privately-run international relief operation in history".[7] Aid came to Biafra primarily through organizations such as CARITAS, the World Council of Churches, and the International Red Cross. It was humanitarian in nature and not tied to any political position or ideology. Fortunately for Biafrans, Christian missionaries chose to stay in the region following its secession, providing a direct link to foreign countries during the conflict. The Vatican was also involved in trying to secure a cease-fire and negotiations for a peace settlement in 1968. Biafra absolutely had to depend on alternative recognition of its crisis as nearly the entire international community refused to intervene on its behalf politically or militarily.

It may be that the Igbos of the newly formed Republic of Biafra were more successful at drawing attention to their plight than they had been as simply another ethnic minority within Nigeria prior to secession. The Biafran Ministry of Information made a case, using journalists' accounts, to the international community of crimes against humanity perpetrated by the Nigerians prior to and during the war. In addition to ensuring that its case for secession be recognized internationally, the Biafran government worked strenuously to unite its civilians patriotically against Nigerian forces with exaggerated accounts of the successes of its forces. Most Biafrans chose to believe the propaganda until soldiers began to return home with grave injuries. But while the Biafrans may have lost faith that they were winning the war, they had no doubt that they were victims of ethnic cleansing and had been so for some time.

In the 21st Century

The Human Rights Violation Investigation Commission of Nigeria (HRVIC) studied the atrocities of the 1960s and the continuation of human rights abuses in Nigeria to the present day, leading to the Oputa Panel Report of 2002. The seven-volume report, which contains records of public hearings (Volume Four), a section on Reparation, Restitution, and Compensation (Volume Six), and summary conclusions and recommendations (Volume Seven) was released unofficially by the Civil Society Forum and the US-based Nigerian Democracy Movement in January 2005. In the Chairman's introduction, Justice Oputa states that the Commission "firmly reject[s] that view that we should simply forget the past".[8] He notes that the key word from Nigerian President

Obasanjo's address was "reconciliation" and the report recommends reconciliation for the people of Nigeria instead of trials.[9] The Report was released only unofficially nearly three years after its completion in May, 2002. Its release was delayed first by a High Court ruling and later by an Appeal Court ruling that determined certain former military officers could not be compelled to testify before the Commission, and that, "the law does not back the Human Rights Violations Investigation Commission."[10] In February 2003, the Oputa Panel's work was further thwarted when the Supreme Court ruled that the panel had "no powers to summon witnesses outside the Federal Capital Territory," and further "that the 1999 Constitution made no provision for tribunals of inquiry".[11] It has proved challenging to get Nigeria's government and justice system to seriously and honestly examine the events before and during the Civil War – to say the least.

Atrocities continue to this day in Nigeria, as well as in many other states in the region. Global dissemination of news and politics via the Internet has helped expose human rights abuses and atrocities to a world-wide audience but, as with Biafra, this only makes the atrocity public – but not necessarily acknowledged. A government and its judiciary functionaries can deny any involvement or, as in the case of the Nigerian Oputa Panel, a country's highest courts can block the process of public hearings that could reveal war crimes and their perpetrators.

Contemporary Nigerian politics have a dismaying resemblance to those in the post-independence 1960s. It is true that civilian rule by democratic elections, lost in 1966, returned in 1999 with the election of Olusegun Obasanjo. However, atrocities against civilians have been just as egregious under the governance of Obasanjo as during the preceding military dictatorships of Generals Muhammadu Buhari, Ibrahim Babangida, and Sani Abacha in the 1980s and 1990s: in a frightening parallel to the 1960s, more than 11,000 Nigerians died in ethnic, political, or religious clashes between 1999 and 2006.[12] As in 1966, millions of Nigerians were internally displaced as a result of the violence. Human Rights Watch reports that many of those deaths occurred in "highly organized massacres along ethnic and religious lines [and that] no one has been held to account for their role in organizing or inciting those massacres".[13] It is the culture of impunity in Nigeria that allows atrocities to continue. The pattern was set in the fledgling democracy of the 1960s, and continued through subsequent military and civilian governments.

As in the 1960s, military officers and government officials at the highest levels disregard or condone atrocities: they refuse to use their powers to enforce law and order, to hold perpetrators of atrocities accountable to the public, or to institute meaningful reform. In worse cases, authorities actively participate in atrocities by using political "godfathers", cult gangs, and groups of thugs to intimidate the population during elections, or to eliminate opposition. Yet Nigerians, scarred by the war, insist upon remembering and revealing. Interviews, surveys, and focus-group discussions of the war experience and its consequences conducted by the International Red Cross and Greenberg Research in 1999[14] reveal that Nigerians continue to have strong feelings about the war experience, even if they were young or had not been born at the time of the war – only 2 percent of respondents did not have an opinion or could not answer a question.[15] Nigerians remember well the role of the International Red Cross in providing assistance during the war, and clear majorities of respondents indicate that in such situations the international community should take responsibility for administering punishment through an international criminal court, and that it should provide assistance to civilians during wartime. A majority of Nigerians of south-eastern origin support both punishment and assistance – 66 and 81 percent respectively – while a majority of Nigerians from the other regions support only international assistance to civilians during war – 84 percent. Respondents included former army officers, combatants and civilians – many of whom had lost at least one family member during the conflict.

While many social and political factors can contribute to a climate conducive to human rights abuses, a Scandinavian study by A.H.M. Kirk-Greene lists three factors, all present in Nigeria in the 1960s, that make armed conflict – and its concomitant atrocities – more likely: the translation of traditional stresses into modern politics, the domination of any sense of post-colonial national identity by pre-colonial loyalties, and the blatant exploitation of ethnic identity. These factors, entrenched in Nigerian history since 1960, may be difficult to reverse. But one path to reconciliation for Nigerians may be to keep alive the memory of their friends and relatives who suffered through the many changes of government in the 1960s. Nigerians should also continue to educate the international community about their dead. It is partly because the death toll in the Civil War overshadowed the number of Igbos massacred in 1966 that the previous Igbo massacres have remained generally unknown outside Nigeria. An overwhelming number of Nigerians, including those of the south-east, believe in the possibility of a lasting peace.[16] Perhaps so many remain optimistic, despite historical and structural obstacles, because forty years later they remember each single atrocity – their dead and aggrieved relatives are not simply numbers but individual souls. An effective campaign to prevent further atrocities may be inspired by the memory of one.

The real challenge is to transform these stories of the "ones" into a collectivity, a public memorialization that may prompt leaders to reach for reconciliation rather than weapons. The creation of borders in Africa by colonization and decolonization has unleashed tensions that are still present. In recent years in Nigeria, Igbos have been talking anew of an independent Biafra. Its future remains uncertain.

NOTES

1 Will Kymlicka, *Multicultural Odysseys: Navigating the New International Politics of Diversity* (Oxford: Oxford University Press, 2007), p. 182.
2 A.H.M. Kirk-Greene, *The Genesis of the Nigerian Civil War and the Theory of Fear* (Uppsala, Sweden: The Scandinavian Institute of African Studies, 1975), Research Report No. 27.
3 John J. Stremlau, *The International Politics of the Nigerian Civil War, 1967–1970* (Princeton, New Jersey: Princeton University Press, 1977), p. 37.
4 Ibid., p. 35.
5 Ibid., p. 30.
6 Alfred Uzokwe, *Surviving in Biafra: The Story of the Nigerian Civil War* (Lincoln, NE: Writers Advantage, 2003), p. 63.
7 John J. Stremlau, *The International Politics of the Nigerian Civil War, 1967–1970*, p. 242.
8 Human Rights Violation Investigation Commission, *Oputa Panel Report*, http://kwenu.com/record/2005/ndm_oputa.htm, 2005, p. 6.
9 Ibid., p. 8.
10 Human Rights Violation Investigation Commission, *Oputa Panel Report*, http://kwenu.com/record/2005/ndm_oputa.htm, 2006.
11 Ibid.
12 Human Rights Watch, *Criminal Politics: Violence, "Godfathers" and Corruption in Nigeria*, http://www.hrw.org/en/reports/2007/10/08/criminal-politics-0, p. 18.
13 Ibid., p. 42.
14 International Committee of the Red Cross, *People on War; Country Report, Nigeria* (Greenberg Research, Inc., 1999).
15 Ibid., p. 12.
16 Ibid., p. 10.

5

The Algerian Harkis: Témoignages d'une Histoire Cachée

Dylan van der Schyff

The history of the Algerian supplétifs [the Harki subalterns] is one of a great hope that turned into an atrocious drama... Confident in our promises, in our strength, in our justice and our loyalty, they found themselves abandoned to the mercy of their implacable adversaries.

French General R. Parlange

The story of the Algerian Harkis is one of betrayal and lost hope. Hidden from the world, its presence is felt in the French conscience as a vague sense of shame and disgust. And if it seems remarkable to consider that no one speaks of the horrible event that took place in October 1961,[1] when French police massacred up to 200 peacefully protesting Algerians in the streets of Paris – the bodies thrown in the Seine – then the silence that surrounds the plight of the Harkis is even more striking. At the end of the Algerian war, the indigenous Muslim force that fought on the side of France was abandoned by the French and massacred by the FLN – between 50,000 and 150,000 were killed. The survivors were made to live in camps in southern France, often for up to fifteen years – or, as Dalila Kerchouche puts it, "the length of a childhood". Many families were split up; and once released from the camps, the refugees faced the seemingly impossible task of integration into a culture that was completely foreign to them.

Until recently this drama was recalled as a distant nightmare that both the Algerian and French governments would have preferred to let disperse into the fog of time. However, the *témoignages* (testimonies) that recall the events of this tragic history carry such weight that they cannot be easily pushed aside. Although the French and Algerian governments have done their best to cover up the atrocities they committed during colonization and the war, there are those among the children of the victims, now grown and integrated into French society, who want answers. But because the story of the Harkis has been repressed – out of fear and shame – in the memories of those who lived through it, and because much of the official documentation of this history is trapped within the bureaucracy of the French government, it is only recently that the events and their effects have begun to be pieced together into a cohesive history. Thanks to the emerging *témoignages* of those who fought and suffered during the war and in the camps, and of their children, who struggle to make sense of their past, the world may become aware of this sad but important part of 20th-century history.

This chapter will look at two *témoignages* that are representative of the Harki struggle. Bachaga Boualam's *Les Harkis au Service de la France* tells, through his own experience and that of his comrades in arms, of the formation of the Harkis and the role they played during the war. Dalila Kerchouche's book *Mon Pére, Ce Harki*, recounts her experience as a child of Harki parents in France. Mixing autobiography and journalism, Kerchouche explores her roots and searches for identity at the beginning of the 21st century. Both of these accounts make it clear that the Harkis are neither the traitors, nor the deserving recipients of reprisal and scorn, that they have often been made out to be. Rather they are portrayed as a misunderstood and maltreated people who were tragically caught up in larger geo-political forces and almost forgotten.

In France the word Harkis[2] properly refers to the force of supplementary Muslim soldiers engaged by the French during the Algerian war (1957–1962). In Algeria, the term has become synonymous with the words "traitor" and "collaborator". In both countries the word signifies a social pariah. Perhaps a better way to begin to understand the origins of the Harkis is to consider that the Arabic word *harka* is used to describe, among other things, a defensive position taken up against an external enemy.

In May of 1954, France lost control of Indochina. And when fighting broke out in Algeria on the 1st of November that same year, it seemed to many that yet another step was being taken in the new struggle for geo-political power. In the environment of the early Cold

War a new kind of warfare was emerging that would be fought from decentralized positions and over new ideologies. Where the previous conception of warfare was largely concerned with conquering or regaining lost terrain, this new warfare of subversion demanded control over the population – hearts and minds became just as important as the acquisition of territory. And inasmuch as Algeria was seen as having a strategic geographical position in Africa and the Mediterranean, it also represented an outpost of the Western imperial ideology that was increasingly understood as being threatened in the global arena by the expanding force of Stalinist communism and the religious influence of Islam. Tunisia and Morocco had already gained their independence and it was feared that they would provide support to the east and west for forces planning subversive action in Algeria.

Insurgency in Algeria was initially carried out by bands of roving rebels whose mission was to instil terror and confusion in the hearts and minds of the Algerian people. Bachaga Boualam writes:

> [The Harkis] are the children of these burned villages, of these destroyed schools, the farmers of this razed land, the husbands of these raped women, the fathers, the brothers of these children with slit throats, organising themselves in self-defensive *harkas* under the authority of their caïd[3] and of the French officers so that the time of the assassins may end and peace may return to the villages.[4]

According to Boualam, the Harkis initially played a defensive role. Armed by the French, they organized themselves into defensive *harkas* in order to protect their own people from the growing violence. And while some of these men had fought for France in the past,[5] many were simple shepherds whose sole concern was for the safety of their families and villages. It seems very unlikely that larger geo-political concerns or modern nationalistic conceptions could have had a conscious presence in the minds of these people, who simply wished for a secure existence. It was, however, in the best interests of France to take advantage of this resistance to the rebels, and the Harki force grew rapidly – from 500 in 1954 to over 60,000 by the time the war ended in 1962.

Boualam describes the feeling of hope that encouraged the Harkis to join the French forces – a hope, he claims, that extended to the greater population of Algeria. He singles out May 13th, 1958, as the day that this hope was declared:

> It was said that the Europeans hated the Muslims, that the Muslims feared the Europeans. Well, hundreds of thousands of men, women, children, French, Spanish, Jews, Europeans, Muslims, from the towns, from the villages, descended from their mountains, fraternised everywhere and sealed their union. It was said that the army was separated from the nation but all of a sudden we had to take notice that, of all the national collectives, it was the army that was the closest to the people… we the Harkis knew all of that. It was why we took up arms.[6]

No could have imagined that soon many of those who had expressed so much hope, so much goodwill and *fraternité* in the face of the escalating conflict, would be forced to leave their houses and families, and flee from their country in order to save their very lives.

While France was all too ready to extend the role of the Harkis from the localized defensive *harkas* to that of a counter insurgency force in its own right, it had not learned from its tragic mistakes in Indochina. The French thought that by utilizing a native force that was habituated to the land and its customs they could attain better intelligence on the ground. In this the French were not completely mistaken – the Harkis fought bravely. And by protecting the agricultural workers and the schools from the rebels, they helped to lift the weight of terror so that life in the villages could continue. But as in Indochina, where the French severely underestimated the power of psychological warfare – as introduced by Mao Zedong and applied by Ho Chi Minh – the superior training and armaments of the French Army could not effectively counter an enemy that used terror as its principal weapon of engagement. The assistance of the *supplétifs* was not enough to stem the growing fear; and the well-trained French force of 400,000 was unable to quash an insurgency that began as a handful of poorly trained and badly armed rebel bands.

Under the centralizing power of the Algerian Front de Libération Nationale these rebel bands grew in force. The FLN had not only mastered the new form of subversive warfare on the ground but also managed to extend its political influence to an international level. Their attacks became more and more effective and they eventually succeeded in forcing the hand of the French government, which could no longer bear the cost of this protracted and increasingly bloody conflict. Following the referendum that led to Algerian independence in 1962, the *supplétifs* were disarmed and demobilized. The Évian accords that followed independence made the provision that:

> No one will be able to be the object of police measures, justice, disciplinary sanctions or discrimination of any kind by reason of: opinions stated at the time of the events which occurred in Algeria before the day of the poll of self determination; acts committed at the time of the same events before the day of the proclamation of the cease fire. And no Algerian can be forced to leave the Algerian territory, nor be prevented from leaving it.[7]

However, no specific provisions were made regarding the future of French loyalists or their families, whether they were Pied-noirs, Jews or Harkis, and the slogan became "the suitcase or the coffin".

The FLN ideology created a level of opposition between the French and the native inhabitants of Algeria that had not been present since the very first colonialists arrived in 1830. Although there had certainly been animosity and skirmishes between the French settlers and the native Algerian population in the past, the situation was more complicated than a clear conflict between the oppressor and the oppressed. Other groups were involved, and the greater population seemed to have mixed feelings towards the French colonists. Nevertheless, the story of Algerian resistance was presented as a continuous, unified and ideologically consistent struggle that was led heroically by the FLN. The complexities of Algerian history were collapsed into a simple binary of good and evil – a quasi-mythology in which the FLN and the Algerian people were one, both politically and historically, and where collaborators with the French were understood to be traitors, sub-human national and religious enemies.[8] In times of violence and chaos, ideology avoids the complexity of reality and is often hard to resist. The Harkis became a symbol of the "evil" that threatened an independent Algeria – "… terrified, the Harkis watched this explosion of joy that took place in front of the bodies of the *supplétifs* that hung from electrical poles."[9]

In March of 1962 the massacres began. In the chaotic climate of political instability and internal conflict that followed independence, the massacres – sometimes perpetrated on entire families at a time – were often accompanied by torture and rape. Both the French and the FLN had committed atrocious acts during the war and this was a final and brutal reprisal. The *Comité National de Liaison des Harkis* has claimed that 150,000 were killed and 16,000 were rescued by French officers who, disobeying orders, evacuated their Harki comrades to France. More conservative estimates put the number of dead at 50,000.

The French government was fully aware of the massacres – as evidenced by reports made by French officials still in Algeria at the time – but was slow to act. French officers were threatened with military sanctions for bringing their Harki allies to France outside of the "general plan of evacuation" – any Algerian found in France unofficially would be sent back immediately. In reality there wasn't even a contingency plan for the evacuation of the Harkis and the killing continued for months. Thanks to the initiative of several French officers, the *supplétifs* and their families finally began to arrive in France late in 1962. But rather than allow the Harkis to immigrate properly, the French government decided to place them in camps in order to "aid with integration". Between 1962 and 1969 some 42,500 people came through these makeshift camps that were set up using tents or old military barracks. Most were hidden in the forests of southern France and their existence was officially suppressed.

After the long journey from Algeria – made with other Harki families in the hold of a ship – Dalila Kerchouche's family was accommodated in a floorless tent. For their first few months in France they huddled together and endured the coldest winter of the decade without proper clothing or enough food:

> The Harkis saw the worst winter of the decade – the elders of the region still remember it. ...without heating, fire or light my parents and their five children held each other, the one against the other on the beds, in order to warm themselves. The icy wind blew through the vents in the fabric. Dressed in a light robe, my mother was freezing. The little ones, shivering in their summer clothing, clung to her skirt, not accustomed to this cold that froze them to the bone.[10]

Soon they found themselves shuffled from camp to camp. According to Kerchouche, the conditions in the camps were extremely unsanitary. The toilets were so filthy that no one could use them – people were forced to relieve themselves where they could. And without proper showers and sinks to wash in, the children became covered in scabs. The French government did everything it could to keep the Harki camps hidden from the public – surrounded by barbed wire, the camps were closed to journalists.

France had also repatriated a large number of Pied-noirs from Algeria, but these descendants of European settlers were quickly accommodated in apartments and houses. The experience of the Pied-noirs, although surely not without its own hardships, testifies to a rather clear double standard held by the French government of the day. Not treated as proper immigrants but unable to return home, the Harkis were at the mercy of those who controlled the camps. The money that the men made at work in the camps was often siphoned away from them. And although the Harkis had technically been granted certain rights – even citizenship in many cases – many were not aware of them or were too afraid to claim them.

Eventually, revolts against camp conditions began to arise and many Harkis were sent to disciplinary camps like the one at Bias. This camp was an old prison and was surrounded by barbed wire and a high wall – it was here that Kerchouche was born in 1973. At Bias, children as young as nine were taken from their parents without explanation. Most of them were taught a trade and put to work. Men that showed any sign of a rebellious nature were taken to a nearby psychiatric hospital, and those who returned were often broken shells of their former selves.

Slowly, however, the Harkis began to emerge from the camps into a society where they found themselves misunderstood and often despised. Afraid, they tried desperately to fit in:

> My family spent almost twelve years behind barbed wire. Twelve years is a long time, the length of a childhood... [My parents] did everything to be accepted – too much even. All their lives they lived with guilt, with the fear of accusation and of being sent back to Algeria.[11]

Although the Kerchouche family received a great deal of kindness from some of the native French citizens they encountered outside the camps, they were also subjected to ongoing discrimination, hate, and misunderstanding. One of Kerchouche's brothers found it necessary to change his name – to something less Arab-sounding – in order to succeed in his profession; while another, unable to deal with the psychological trauma of the camps and integration, committed suicide. However, despite all the hardships and against incredible odds, Kerchouche's parents managed to raise highly functioning members of French society. Kerchouche herself is a respected journalist.

Although the Algerian War was one of the most drawn-out and bloodiest conflicts in the decolonization of Africa, it was almost immediately overshadowed by several other major events once independence was achieved. The world's attention rapidly shifted towards the Vietnam War, the Soviet invasion of Czechoslovakia, and the events of May 1968 in France. This made it relatively easy for the French and the Algerians to suppress and rewrite the history of the war with their own interests in mind. While the French concealed their embarrassment and shame, the FLN distorted events in order to amplify its own heroic image.

In the wake of the major political and social upheavals of the 20th century, the history of the Harkis is one of many that testify to the destructive and tragic consequences of modern geo-politics. Borders have been redrawn and histories have been rewritten instrumentally in order to further the economic and political interests of the major powers. And as a result, innocent people have been separated from their families and culture, used as scapegoats to further political propaganda, betrayed by the powers they once served, massacred, or simply forgotten. The Harkis have been subjected to all of these violations. These people became the pawns and ultimately the victims of global political forces that were beyond their control, and they have suffered both physically and psychologically.

Desperately clinging to remnants of their old life, those who survived the massacres and the camps were dispersed into a culture they did not understand. Their children continue to pay the price as they battle with themselves and their society to piece together their own identity. Caught between assimilation into France and the disturbing circumstances that brought them there, they struggle to make sense of conflicting feelings of shame, anger and fear. They are further alienated by the overwhelming ignorance and misunderstanding that surround them. Kerchouche writes:

> Who is [my father] in the end? A soldier who swore fidelity to France, ready to spill his blood for her? A traitor to the Algerian nation who collaborated with the enemy? That doesn't seem like him. But what exactly did he do during the war? Was he for a French Algeria? Did he support the colonies, torture the *fellagas*, rape the women and pillage the *mechtas*… These are the running clichés of the Harkis. … This is what history taught me: to hate my father… [As a child] I joined the camp of the vanquished, the humiliated. My future appeared so much more sombre. Mute, I swallowed my anger. Like my father, I was incapable of defending myself.[12]

Of all the questions that Kerchouche asks, the one she keeps returning to is "Why?" Why were these people who fought so bravely to protect themselves – who were so loyal to their French comrades, and who trusted France with their lives – treated this way? For Kerchouche the sad response is that the Harkis were treated as subhuman for the simple reason that they were Arabs. She goes on to claim that the system the French administration has in place is still quasi-colonial and discriminatory; and that the treatment of the Harkis is the greatest political and social scandal to occur in France in the last forty-five years.

Recently the French government has shown tentative signs of recognizing the role that the Harkis played during the Algerian conflict. On December 5th, 2007, the president of the French Republic, Nicolas Sarkozy, received Harki representatives and announced measures to ameliorate the integration of the Harkis in France – without officially recognizing the responsibility of France in the abandonment and subsequent massacre in 1962, and without substantial acknowledgement of the suffering the Harkis underwent in the camps. Understandably, many see this as too little, too late.

The official sentiment in Algeria is still hostile towards the Harkis – they have recently been compared to those French who collaborated with the Nazis between 1940 and 1944. And although official statements have been made declaring that the descendants of Harkis that live in Algeria should not be held responsible for the acts of their predecessors, laws have been passed that make it almost impossible for those with Harki paternity to hold positions of responsibility. However, one should be careful not to confuse a people with their government. As Kerchouche points out, during her visit to Algeria she was generally greeted warmly by the people she encountered, who seemed to be, above all else, curious about the history she was researching. And in France too, there are many citizens of European descent who are demanding to know the truth about their government.

Could a truth commission similar to the one held in South Africa in 1995 be applied in this situation? It seems very unlikely that revealing the truth about the Harkis would result in major civic upheavals or continued reprisals. Rather, it could benefit French society by allowing a permanent and important part of the population to feel understood, perhaps having the effect of reducing the animosity between French citizens of Arab and European descent. Unfortunately, it does not seem likely that a Harki truth commission will come to pass in France. Those who lived through the war are nearing the end of their lives and there is no real pressure on the French government to take part in such an inquiry. A full acknowledgement of the treatment of the Harkis would expose cracks in France's strict assimilationist immigration and cultural policies, thereby opening the door for other minority groups to make claims; and it would draw attention to clear hypocrisy with regard to the cherished French doctrine of *liberté, fratenité,* and *égalité* – a situation the French government most certainly would not allow.

While the hope that bound the original *harkas* together is most certainly lost, it is beginning to seem possible that a history of the Harkis may still be heard. Several cohesive organizations have emerged in the last two decades that are dedicated to collecting and disseminating information – the *témoignages* continue to emerge and exert an influence. And although it seems unlikely that the Harkis might eventually hold real political power, their story draws its strength from a more fundamental source: a shared sense of humanity that recognizes the violation of basic human rights in the feverish game of global power politics.

NOTES

1 In 2001, some forty years after the event, the massacre was officially acknowledged by the city of Paris with the unveiling of a memorial plaque near the Pont Saint-Michel. Centrist and right-wing French politics, as well as the police union, have objected to the plaque, citing increased threat of civil unrest, alleged tolerance of terrorism, and encouragement of disrespect for the police.

2 The term "Harki" has also been extended to include all Muslim Algerians who supported the attachment of Algeria to France during the Algerian war, whether they were soldiers or not.

3 A caïd is an Arab military chief or judge.

4 Bachaga Boualam, *Les Harkis au Service de la France* (Paris: France Empire, 1962), p. 18.

5 Muslim troops fought with distinction in Crimea, Mexico, Madagascar, and against the Nazis in World War II. Martin Evans and John Phillips, *Algeria: Anger and the Dispossessed* (London: Yale University Press, 2007), p. 37.

6 Boualam, *Les Harkis au Service de la France*, p. 27.

7 *Accords d'Évian*, Chapitre II, partie A, article 2.

8 Martin Evans and John Phillips, *Algeria: Anger and the Dispossessed*, p. 5.

9 Dalila Kerchouche, *Mon Pére, Ce Harki* (Paris: Seuil, 2003), p. 40.

10 Ibid., p. 61.

11 Ibid., p. 26.

12 Ibid., pp. 24, 25.

6

Unmarked Graves and Old Wounds: The Spanish Civil War

Michael Donovan

✧

I have shut my windows.
I do not want to hear the weeping.
But from behind the grey walls.
Nothing is heard but the weeping.

Federico García Lorca

Between 1936 and 1939 the blood of half a million was spilled onto the soil of Spain. Many fell in combat, many perished in outright executions and others simply "disappeared". At war's end, the victorious Franco acknowledged his fallen supporters with honour. On the losing side of the conflict, however, there would be no tributes for the dead, and for the survivors only more repression. Today Spanish civil society is restlessly awakening from its national amnesia of the horrors of those years. The question is how the Spanish state can, despite the consternation any official process may cause, acknowledge and reconcile the "forgotten" atrocities in its continuing struggle to prove its democratic credentials.

The three young fellows piled into the sedan, their spirits high, a slight scent of Spanish brandy on their breath. The engine fired up assertively with the low growl of a late model Studebaker Presidente. The driver placed it in gear and navigated the bulky machine carefully along the streets of Madrid. It was a warm June day, and the three señoritos opened the windows and lit up their cigarettes. Tobacco has a soothing effect on the nerves. Even fascists get uneasy before a killing.

Spain in the spring of 1936 was churning with fear and hope, with anxiety and faith, providing an undercurrent for many tales of tragedy.

Never in the history of the nation-state had the force of the past conflicted so fiercely with ideas for the future. Those who held dear the notion of traditional Spain imagined themselves locked in a struggle to preserve the old order of empire: the monarchy, the church, the landlords and the military. They reviled liberalism as a French toxin, and detested the socialist "Reds".

In opposition stood a diversity of political ideas that would boggle the mind today. A variety of political parties, aiming for social reform through the Republic, appealed to intellectuals, minor officials and small business owners. Different factions of socialism and communism received support from the middle class or trade unions. And at the far left of the spectrum were the anarcho-syndicalists, whose philosophy allowed no quarter whatsoever for centralized authority – be it federal rule, capital ownership or the church.

Traffic was lighter than normal on that June day, as most of the city's builders were on strike. The car rumbled along the Paseo del Prado, site of the May Day parade a month earlier. Then the avenue had pulsated with the energy of thousands of socialists and communists. Mandolin musicians struck the notes of the Internationale, *and a multitude of banners were unfurled: "Unite Proletarian Brothers!", "No Peasants Hungry!", "Long Live Socialism!". Cheers of support erupted for the "Working and peasant women: An anti-fascist militia!" and for the "[w]idows, mothers and orphans of the Asturias miners",*[1] *who were remembering the nearly two thousand miners massacred by the army in 1934*[2] *– a massacre spearheaded by one General Franco.*

Peeking through closed shutters, the conservative rank had been shocked and repulsed by the swagger of the poor, the women, the working class. The Reds, buoyed by their February election victory, seemed set to hurl Spain into a crazed socialist revolution bringing land reform, separation of church and state, legalized divorce and greater administrative autonomy for the regions. The mighty Catholic Castilian Empire would disappear forever. The fascist Falange Youth had responded by taking on the Young Socialists, fighting them in the streets, and garnering such support that their membership swelled to 30,000 by early summer. Three Falangists, the aforementioned señoritos, sat peering out the window of their parked Studebaker. The strikers' picket line a hundred yards away was breaking up as the builders headed home for the evening. Two strikers were now approaching the car on the opposite side of the street. The time had come for the Falange to defend the glory of Spain! The driver pulled out from the curb as the one in the back flicked his cigarette out the window and gripped his submachine gun. The third reached into his pocket for his revolver. They slowly passed the workers. The two might have belonged to the Socialist UGT union or the anarchist CNT, but to these assassins they were Reds and nothing more. One of the builders was talking rapidly to the other, his calloused hands flitting through the air in gesture. The other seemed not to be listening but casually watched the sedan go by.

With a squeal of tyres, the motorcar swung sharply around and braked fiercely as it drew up on the men. In just two seconds, twenty-five bullets spewed from the sedan. The body of the chatty one hadn't yet hit the ground by the time the other was dashing down the road at top flight. A figure sprang from the vehicle and blasted six rounds at his fleeing quarry. Some time later, a stray dog would find a bit of his right ear, but this fortunate survivor of the shooting wouldn't perish until the Battle of Jarama eight months later.

The military coup began on July 17th, 1936, with General Franco's radio broadcast from Spanish Morocco, "Spaniards! All those of you who feel a holy love of Spain; all those in the ranks of the Army and Navy, who have made an act of profession in the service of the Motherland; those who have sworn to defend her against her enemies, until death, the Nation calls you in her defence."[3]

By this time, social strife throughout the country was so great that the generals hoped for a quick assumption of power. In cities across the peninsula, the army marched out of their barracks to take command of government buildings and radio stations, but in cities to the east and north they met with fierce opposition. The most stubborn resistance came from the anarchists. With a membership of a million and a half, and a history of defending themselves, workers, farmers, miners and fishermen roused to dash Franco's hopes for a quick *coup d'etat.* When the dust settled, Spain was divided down the middle into a Republican zone and Franco's Nationalist zone.

Amid the confusion of those first few days, the dithering Republican government was pushed aside as the revolutionary parties vaulted into action, forming militias and taking control of the commercial, industrial and agricultural enterprises. George Orwell observed in Catalonia: "It was the first time that I had ever been in a town where the working class was in the saddle. Practically every building of any size had been seized by the workers ... almost every church had been gutted and its images burnt. Churches here and there were being systematically demolished by gangs of workmen."[4]

Complete destruction of churches and convents in areas of the Republican zone was the reaction to hundreds of years of Church oppression extending back to the Inquisition. The anarchists in particular loathed its existence, viewing it as the state's psychological whip for flogging the people. The resultant backlash left perhaps 4,200 clergy members dead;[5] some perished in their burning churches while others fell to mob violence.

According to historian Antony Beevor, approximately 38,000 perished in the "Red terror", with about half those deaths occurring in Madrid and Catalonia in the summer of 1936.[6] Other victims included supporters of Franco's coup, and "known exploiters" like workplace managers, lawyers and shopkeepers. Most of the violence in those early days was a product of spontaneous rage, not organized persecution. The anarchist intellectual Frederica Montseny attempted to bring order and remarked on "a lust for blood inconceivable in honest men before". Indeed, many individuals of conscience defended their local churches and priests, as well as those who had held positions of authority before the war but had not abused those positions.

Meanwhile in the ever-expanding Nationalist zone, the atrocities of the "white terror" numbered perhaps as high as 200,000 during the three years of fighting and its aftermath.[7] General Yagüe's attitude towards the enemy around Badajoz, near the Portuguese border, was generally representative of the senior officers: "Of course we shot them. What do you expect? Was I supposed to take 4,000 Reds with me as my column advanced, racing against time? Was I expected to turn them loose in my rear and let them make Badajoz red again?"[8] Typically the murderers were not Spanish at all, but Moors. Most of Franco's best troops were Moroccan and, being historically on the wrong end of Spanish colonial domination, had less compunction before letting loose with machine guns.

The Falange grew to several hundred thousand, and in territory newly conquered by the army, would move in for a second round of terror or "purification". Those suspected of voting the wrong way were executed – their numbers included intellectuals, teachers, doctors, union leaders and government officials. Reliable figures for executions exist for some areas: Seville 9,000; Grenada 8,000; Majorca over 3,000; Navarre over 7,000. The British consul in Málaga reported 20,000 executions from 1937 to 1944, with the Republicans killing a thousand in 1936.[9] Dissent was totally impossible. Even the Catholic clergy in the conquered Basque region could neither stop the slaughter nor protect itself from it.

Franco's forces mobilized for a *cruzada*, or crusade, when General Mola declared, "Those who are not with us are against us."[10] Franco's Spain also practised the limitless militarism that typically accompanies extreme nationalism. In the spring of 1937, Nationalist bomber aircraft, actually German squadrons sent by Hitler in coordination with Franco, carpet bombed Guernica, the historic capital of the Basque people. The largest bombs flattened buildings, and anti-personnel munitions tore into the disoriented residents, while fighter airplanes strafed those trying to flee. Lastly, as if the horror could get no worse, a chemical weapon, white phosphorus, was dropped from the sky to choke and to burn flesh indiscriminately. This act of destruction may have been the first example in history of indiscriminate air attack on civilians. Picasso memorialized the hundreds[11] who perished in his famous painting *Guernica*. Historic Guernica was not the only example of the "collateral damage" of the day – bombardments of civilians by artillery and aircraft – but perhaps the best-known. During the long siege of Madrid, Hemingway wrote about the simple cruelty of one barrage: "They killed an old woman returning home from market, dropping her in a huddled black heap of clothing, with one leg, suddenly detached, whirling against the wall of an adjoining house."[12]

The term "fifth column" was coined at this time. As General Mola's four columns marched on Madrid in 1936, he broadcast a radio message for the support of a so-called fifth column inside the city. He did, indeed, have many supporters in Madrid, but with the exception of some spies collaborating with him, they provided minimal assistance. However, the spectre of a fifth column obsessed the anti-espionage agents who set on the hunt for fascist spies. This notion also excited the foreign press. A few years later a similar fervour would prompt the commitment of over 130,000 Japanese Americans and Canadians to internment camps.

International interest in the fight against fascism was also sparked among intellectuals, leftists, and workers, even in countries that were not yet threatened by fascism. The historical record describes the warmest reception for the tens of thousands of foreigners from dozens of countries who fought on the side of the Spanish Republic. Interestingly, many were from educated Jewish families and were well aware of the treatment meted out to their people by Franco's ally Hitler

Madrid fell on March 28, 1939, with Franco declaring the war officially over on April 1. He enacted a Law of Political Responsibilities, which, in effect, made every Republican supporter guilty of a capital crime. Hundreds of thousands of Republicans were interned in concentration camps or forced into slavery; the executions continued in large numbers for the next four years. Refugees in France were encouraged to return to Spain, where they were then imprisoned. Political parties and trade unions were banned, and women's rights severely curtailed. The Church had its dominant position in the state restored; divorce, civil marriage and abortion were outlawed.

Since Franco's claim to legitimacy as head of state derived from the war, he needed to keep alive the national myth of the righteousness of the cause, but in a general way, with no meaningful public dialogue. The vanquished had to suffer in silence. Even after Franco died in 1975 and democratic elections were restored, the left and right agreed on *el pacto de olvido* or the "pact of forgetting". The prevailing notion was that the war should be forgotten, that it was best not to revisit past grievances and thereby open wounds. And yet people did not forget. One socialist, Juan Moliner, discussed in the 1980s his father's death: "[O]ne has to live with those people knowing that they have killed him, live with those people without saying a word."[13] Inhabitants of small towns remember the loyalties of their neighbours' families; they may know the locations of unmarked graves. In other instances, they can only speculate on where the remains of their ancestors lie. Even today, Spaniards are reticent to speak of the Civil War – a recent survey showed that 50 percent of Spaniards never discussed the war at home.[14]

The question whether Spain *should* officially address the memories is easy to answer, since a large grassroots movement is forcing the issue onto the Spanish government. The subject is becoming harder to ignore. There are now dozens of organizations, like the Association for the Recovery of Historical Memory (ARHM), pressing for compensation for victims, exhumation of mass graves followed by respectful reburials, and official memorialization of the atrocities.

The more difficult question is *how* Spain will deal with the collective memory of its civil war. The state has reacted with the Law of Historical

Memory.[15] This law provides compensation for several categories of victims, mandates that local governments must help locate and exhume mass graves, declares Franco's kangaroo courts illegitimate and orders the removal of Francoist symbols from public buildings. The law is controversial, partly because the church and some political conservatives criticize it, but also because some think its scope is not broad enough. In June 2006, almost 65 percent of Spaniards thought *everything* in relation to the war should be investigated, while only 28 percent believed it best to investigate nothing regarding the war, and further, to refrain from discussing it.[16]

Spain's civil society is clearly ahead of its political parties on the issue of the Civil War. As early as three decades ago, Catalans quietly began removing Francoist symbols from the public domain and replacing street signs with their own handwritten ones. Today, many more people are demanding action from local and regional governments, forming organizations, launching memorial websites and tending mass graves. Joaquim Sempere, a professor of sociology in Barcelona, makes the case that "here and now, a law to recognize victims has more value for the state than for the victims. It is the state that is asserting its own claim to be representative of the people..."[17] In other words, the state needs to assert its democratic character by demonstrating that institutional collaboration with Francoism no longer exists.

It is fair at this point to question the motivations for the "pact of forgetting". Could it have been a means to smooth the transition to democracy, or was it simply a concession that the left felt compelled to make to garner its share of political power? Since 43 percent of Spaniards say that they have Civil War victims in their family,[18] clearly the state needs to catch up to civil society on this matter. But how could the state take the initiative? It could be said that such official inquiry might be of limited usefulness. First, Francoism in its worst manifestation disappeared years before the man himself did, and the instigators and perpetrators of the atrocities are long gone. Further, the regime's apologists today do not recognize the illegality of Franco's rule. And finally, the perspective that Spain swiftly flipped from dictatorship to democracy is not universal; some see, rather, an evolution of the political landscape over many decades as Francoism softened, leading into a monarchy and finally a parliamentary democracy.

In principle, the state supports the grassroots movements on reconciling with the past, but its own laws are in conflict with the possibility.

One prominent judge, Baltasar Garzón, has ordered numerous mass graves to be opened as part of an investigation into the disappearance of 114,226 people. Unfortunately, most of Spain's highest level magistrates oppose this move, viewing it as a violation of the "pact of forgetting" as enacted in the Amnesty Law of 1977. And so we see that the state has enacted a Law of Historical Memory that is insufficient and laden with judicial complications. Spain is in the difficult position of needing to heal the wounds of the past for the sake of nation-building, while at the same time, placating its separatists. All that is certain is that history will continue to play a part in the present.

Contemporary Echoes

But it isn't just Spaniards who could benefit from revisiting history. Spain is not alone in having a dark chapter in its history that bears acknowledgement, even though this chapter may contain a cruel lesson. The horrors of extreme nationalism and violent ideological conflict continue to unfold in other countries. Other western powers, as well, have never been good at acknowledging their own ignominious actions. The Spanish Civil War may have been a training ground for Mussolini's soldiers and Hitler's pilots, but Britain, France and the United States were also partially responsible. Their embargo on arms sales to the Republic, while Franco freely purchased oil from the Texas Oil Company and sold ore to British capitalists, all but doomed the democratic republic.

Today, the dangers of extreme nationalism and unitary leadership still scowl at us from the shadows of Washington. The reactionary Bush regime in Washington from 2001 to 2008, although more constrained by domestic law, might as well have been using the Spanish Nationalists' playbook from 1936. They exploited the shock and confusion of the 9/11 attacks on the World Trade Center in much the same way Franco's regime used the social unrest in Spain sixty-five years earlier. Bush invoked God, and famously launched his crusade with, "You are either with us or against us," reminiscent of Franco's *cruzada* and General Mola's marshalling declaration: "Those who are not with us are against us."[19] In both cases, power became concentrated in one man. A mainly pliant press in the United States turned out propaganda chillingly similar to Spain's in the 1930s: unquestioning patriotism, combined with praise for conservative family values and for the brave military. Then followed limitations on individual freedoms, demonization of liberals and dissenters, establishment of secret prisons, reduced human rights, spying, and a disdain for democracy. Almost comically, the "patriotic" American rejection of "French fries" in favour of "freedom fries" is reminiscent of the earlier Spanish disapproval of "Russian salad".

Far more serious than culinary re-naming is the unchecked militarism that often accompanies extreme nationalism. One example – there are many – is the November 2004 American attack on Fallujah, Iraq, another historic city like Guernica. The artillery attack and aerial bombardment damaged eighty percent of its homes, destroying at least a quarter of them.[20] Snipers shot anyone attempting to flee. One refugee explained to reporter Dahr Jamail that the US military "used these weird bombs that put up smoke like a mushroom cloud. Then small pieces fell from the air with long tails of smoke behind them."[21] These fragments burned people's skin and could not be extinguished with water. Initially the Pentagon denied using chemical weapons, but eventually had to admit that "shake and bake",[22] or white phosphorus, was used. The victorious army prohibited aid organizations and the media from entering the ruined city afterwards, but one Red Cross official spoke of at least 800[23] civilian dead.

The consequences of the Iraq invasion, too, have been devastating for its population. One survey of Iraqi refugees in Syria conducted by the United Nations describes that one in five are "victims of torture and/or violence", seventy-seven percent were affected by bombardments or shelling, and eighty percent witnessed a shooting. All had experienced at least one traumatic event.[24] Approximately 4.2 million Iraqis are refugees in neighbouring countries or internally displaced and may be similarly traumatized. Spain's past is Iraq's present.

For the purpose of public relations, those directly killed by the US military are automatically defined as "insurgents" or "foreign fighters". The relationship between the Iraqi population and the fighters from Algeria, Syria, Yemen, Saudi Arabia, and many other countries is not one of great interest to the western powers. Here it is interesting to recall those earlier foreign fighters who came to fight on the Republican side in Spain, stirred by ideas of solidarity. Similar sentiments may, indeed, have brought foreign fighters to Iraq, stirred to action partly by the humiliation and torture shown in the Abu Ghraib photographs, to stand in solidarity with their Iraqi counterparts, Muslim defenders against the West's crusade.

Can Spain Learn from South Africa?

Spain is, at least in civil society, dealing with the indignity of its not so distant past. The shame was cloaked for decades by the Francoist narrative of a glorious defeat of Communists at the hands of true patriots. But now an awareness of "forgotten" atrocities is beginning to bloom in the national psyche from the grassroots, and a sense of reconciliation with the past and healing are beginning to take hold.

However, the state has a daunting task ahead, as many Spaniards in influential positions – in the Church, the right wing parties, the judiciary and the senior civil service – refuse to swallow this dose of national shame in the name of nation-building. It is not clear at present if reopening this discussion will strengthen national unity, but avoiding the matter will certainly do nothing to settle a restless Spanish society.

Spain's political leaders believed, at the time, that the "pact of forgetting" would give them the surest guarantee of a peaceful transition to democracy. This approach contrasts with that of post-apartheid South Africa, where its leaders feared the fragile country would degenerate into civil conflict if it didn't deal with its past. A Truth and Reconciliation Commission (TRC) was launched in South Africa, which has become the gold standard for many other TRCs and is generally understood to have been healthy for South Africa. Perhaps Spain may look to the South African experience for ways to deal with its turbulent past.

Comparing the national experiences of the two countries is not as superficial as it may initially seem. South Africa was racially divided – between black and white. Spain's division was political, between "Red" and "white" in ideological terms. But in both cases, the division was class-based. South Africa's whites owned the capital and land, and ran the mines and plants. The economically underprivileged blacks organized into politicized trade unions and supported the African National Congress (ANC) with its socialist roots. In Spain the Reds typically got their support from the landless farmers and the workers. Although there were middle-class supporters of the Republic, it was the millions of unionists that formed the core of the Reds. Generally, the economically and politically powerful in Spain aligned with "white" or status quo nationalism, as did prosperous whites in South Africa.

In South Africa, the question of economic restructuring of the nation had to be dropped from the discussion before the powerful would relinquish their monopoly on political power. In a sense this compromise is not so much a "pact of forgetting" the abuses during apartheid, but a setting aside of the radical socialist roots of the ANC in order to move forward with reconciliation. Consequently, the ANC now provides minimal social programs, rather than the radical economic redistribution it set out to deliver, while the nation's wealth continues to concentrate upwards, albeit now into a multiracial bourgeoisie. Similarly, in Spain the economic question is of no relevance today. Little differentiates the economic policies of the left from those of the right. Provided Spain addresses the past without threatening the economic interests of the business class, it is doubtful that any serious civil strife could occur. The revolutionaries who had fire in their bellies for a complete eradication of the capitalist system are no more.

A Formal TRC for Spain?

Might Spain launch a South African-style TRC? It could be said that the "pact of forgetting" is what allowed Spain to move forward with political reform. Interestingly, just six years after Franco's death, an attempted military coup turned into a virtual non-event as no one rose up in support, and the King remained loyal to democratic reform. That Spain's appetite for a stable parliamentary democracy showed that much strength in 1981 indicates plausibly that the past might have been addressed even at that time. Spain has made much progress post-Franco, and in 1986 joined the European community as one of its democracies.

The possibility of Spain reconciling with its past is bolstered by other factors as well. The King has made it clear that as a member of the European Union, Spain's military is under civilian control and its regions have a good deal of autonomy. Those with royalist, imperialist, or separatist views are a minority and no longer particularly active. With only minor grumbling from the Church and the remaining Franco appointees, there are but few smouldering embers left to flare up violently. The Basque separatists remain the most visible flashpoint. However, their demands remain so intransigent that they recognize no policies from Madrid – either in support of or against reconciliation with the past. On the whole, therefore, while some of the older generation continue to fear confrontation and question the robustness of their democracy, and the effectiveness of the law to protect them, it appears that their perception does not reflect the reality.

Further, with the organic recognition presently spreading from the grassroots, it is debatable whether an official TRC would produce positive results at this time. Spain's present condition stands in contrast with the abrupt fall of apartheid in South Africa, with a TRC swiftly following. And so a Truth and Reconciliation Commission in Spain could well have only one side's participation, and even then, incomplete participation – many victims in the Basque country, Catalonia, Galicia, Andalusia and other regions would rather have more autonomy, or even outright independence, than reconciliation with Madrid.

No matter how Spain chooses to come to terms with the events during its civil war, its ghosts still whisper, and not just to Spaniards. Unrecognized atrocities, wherever and whenever they are committed, linger in collective memory. When nations can formally recognize their own past atrocities, they come to terms with their own past but at the same time call attention to current crimes against humanity. Spanish philosopher George Santayana's oft-paraphrased maxim comes to mind: Those who cannot remember the past are condemned to repeat it.

NOTES

1 An account of the May Day parade is given in John Langdon-Davies' *Behind the Spanish Barricades: The Classic Eye-Witness Account of Spains Civil War* (McBride, 1937), pp. 4–6.
2 Neal Ascherson, *Spanish Civil War* (Granada Television, 1983).
3 Richard Kish, *Franco* (Wayland Publishers Ltd., 1976), p. 11.
4 George Orwell, *Homage to Catalonia*, p. 1.
5 BBC News, May 3, 2003.
6 Anthony Beevor, *The Battle for Spain: The Spainish Civil War 1936–1939* (Weidenfeld and Nicholson, 2006), p. 87.
7 Ibid., p. 94.
8 John T. Whitaker, *We Cannot Escape History* (The MacMillan Company, 1943), p. 113.
9 Anthony Beevor, *The Spanish Civil War*, p. 74.
10 Ibid., p. 260.
11 A death toll of 1654 has appeared in print throughout the decades. Recent research suggests the number may have been as low as 200–300.
12 Ernest Hemingway, *NANA Dispatch: Shelling of Madrid*, 11 April, 1937.
13 Neal Acherson, *Spanish Civil War.*
14 Instituto Opina, July 18, 2006.
15 Actually: the Bill to recognize and extend rights and to establish measures in favour of those who suffered persecution or violence during the Civil War and the Dictatorship.

16 Instituto Opina, July 18, 2006.
17 Joachim Sempere, *El Pais*, February 2, 2007.
18 Instituto Opina, July 18, 2006.
19 See cit. 10.
20 *Washington Post*, April 19, 2005.
21 Dahr Jamail, January 19, 2005, "What is the US Trying to Hide in Fallujah?".
22 James T. Cobb, *Field Artillery*, March–April 2005.
23 Dahr Jamail, November 16, "Iraq: 800 Civilians Feared Dead in Fallujah".
24 William Spindler, January 22, UNHCR.

7

Blind Spot: The Allied Bombing of Dresden

Scott-Ryan Abt

✧

> *The aim is the destruction of German cities; the killing of German workers; and the disruption of civilized life throughout Germany. It should be emphasized that the destruction of houses, public utilities, transport, and lives; the creation of a refugee problem on an unprecedented scale; and the breakdown of morale both at home and at the battle fronts by fear of extended and intensified bombing, are accepted and intended aims of our bombing policy. They are not by-products of attempts to hit factories.*
>
> **Arthur 'Bomber' Harris, Air Chief Marshall, Royal Air Force**[1]

States and their militaries – which hold a monopoly on the truth among their populations during conflicts – have long used the fog of war to obfuscate and obscure atrocities perpetrated against an enemy. Yet the dark but hidden truth is that immoral, illegal and murderous acts do occur in war, and further, that they are committed by both sides of a conflict. This holds true even for World War II, the "last good war". We need to re-examine long-held certainties about the moral righteousness of actions undertaken during this war, and in coming years we will also need to look back at current conflicts with a critical eye.

In fact, the period of time that elapses between the acceptance of the "official" rationale for and morality of war that is disseminated amongst its citizenry by a government and a more rigorous analysis of some of the deeper, underlying realities for a particular conflict has become shorter. Perhaps in part because of the way that the American government lost control of the version of the "truth" that it wanted its people to see during the Vietnam War, there has been a decline in public acceptance in western countries of government claims to the necessity of initiating war and to the moral high ground during its prosecution. During the Vietnam conflict, the evening news nightly presented to ordinary Americans disturbing images that caused many of them to wonder if their government had been telling them the whole story. It was this lack of control of the "truth" by the American government (and therefore any claim to the moral high ground) that played a role in bringing that war to an end and changed the way militaries around the world use the media to provide their versions of events, both while they are happening and after the fact.

Until recently, the public assumed that government knew best and would lead a country to war only as a last resort, once all other options were exhausted. And in wartime the public was willing to accept their government's assertion that all members of an enemy state were necessarily evil and that all measures to demoralize and destroy the adversary were legitimate and justified. This sentiment no longer holds true, even in the pursuit of a "just" war. One need only look to the shift from western society's acceptance of the righteousness of the Allied cause during the First and Second World Wars to today's more questioning and critical attitude to the Iraq or Afghanistan conflicts. Partly because of emerging knowledge that in previous wars all sides were responsible for atrocities, and also because of the realization that atrocities are certainly being committed by all belligerents in current conflicts, observers, casual or otherwise, now question claims to "the truth" by either side. Today, saturation bombing campaigns and civilian deaths are not made public. To do so would be to risk the wrath of public opinion. But at the end of World War II, as indicated by Harris' statement above, the truth did not have to be hidden. It was the clear aim of Bomber Command to kill as many Germans as possible with every raid.

State-sponsored propaganda did not allow most people on the Allied side of World War II to feel much sympathy for German victims of that conflict. Amongst the Germans conversely, any examination of the suffering they themselves endured has been unpopular, chiefly as a result of collective guilt over the Holocaust and Hitler's expansionist aggression, until quite recently. In any war, the enemy civilians are presumed to be willing participants in the war even though they have little, if anything, to do with decision-making, they are painted as one and the same as their government, which is portrayed as the aggressor. Amongst the allied nations in World War II, the only good German was a dead one, regardless of whether he was a fully paid up member of the Nazi Party, a conscripted soldier fighting in Italy, or someone just trying to eke out a quiet existence on a farm in Bavaria as the world crashed down around him. It is still difficult today, in light of the horrors that Germany under the Nazi regime unleashed on Europe from 1933 to 1945, for anyone to understand the scope and depth of suffering felt by ordinary Germans, let alone to have any sympathy for them. Yet suffer they did.

Over sixty years have elapsed since countries of the West went to war with one another. It would be difficult to imagine that these countries, now liberal democracies, would do so again. On the face of it, they are no longer divided by ideology – they have too much in common with one another, and there is simply too much at stake for this to reoccur. The benefit of over sixty years of absence of conflict among these nations has allowed some of the wounds of the 1930s and 40s to have healed and for this reason, a re-evaluation of the history of the period can and should take place. And yet the quest for the truth "can be problematic",[2] because much of what happened during the dying days of the war has been swept under the rug.

In February 1945, with World War II drawing to a close in Europe, the defeat of the Nazis was certain. The noose had been tightening around Germany's neck for some time. On the Eastern Front, the Soviet Red Army, after Stalingrad and Kursk, had been able to push the decimated German Wehrmacht back and out of the Ukraine, across Poland, and was on the verge of crossing the Oder River and entering Germany itself. In Western Europe, the Allied landings in Normandy in June 1944 and subsequent liberations of the Low Countries continued a successful push to the western bank of the Rhein River. Much of the German forces in the west had been moved to the Eastern front for a final Goetterdaemmerung-type clash with the Soviets. However, in a last ditch attempt to stem the advancing Allied tide in the west, the Germans threw everything that remained at their disposal at the Allies, in what became known as the Battle of the Bulge in the Ardennes region of northeastern France. Though initially successful in breaking through the Allied salient and thereby surrounding the US 8th Army, by January of 1945 it was all over, due mostly to overwhelming Allied resources and troops. The inability of the Germans to replenish their supplies was caused mainly by successful Allied air bombing of factories, fuel plants and oil depots. However, despite heavy losses, it was apparent that Germany still had some capacity and some will, at least officially, to continue fighting for some time, which contributed to the decision for American and British forces to bomb the German cities of Dresden, Leipzig, Chemnitz and Magdeburg.

Indeed, British and American aerial bombing of many German cities had been going on for some time. Industrial and military targets such as Hamburg, Luebeck and Kiel in the north, Essen, Dortmund, and Gelsenkirchen in the northwestern Ruhr Valley and Duesseldorf, Leverkusen and Cologne just further south, and Friedrichshafen, Stuttgart, Ulm and Freiburg in the south were heavily bombed and this caused irreparable damage to the German war effort, and as such were considered "fair game" for bombing.

However, the debate today centres on whether or not Dresden had any importance as a military target, or if there are other reasons why it was destroyed and much of its population annihilated. What is not open to question is that Dresden was, at that time, the temporary home of hundreds of thousands of refugees fleeing from the east, just ahead of the advancing Soviet Red Army. Initial estimates put the civilian death toll on that day at 25,000 people. Today the number is believed to be closer to 35–50,000[3] who died on the night of February 13th alone.

Richard Rapier Stokes, British MP and First World War hero, stated in the British House of Commons, March 6, 1945: "Tens of thousands who lived in Dresden are now buried under its ruins. Even an attempt at identification of the victims is hopeless. What happened on that evening of February 13? There were 1,000,000 people in Dresden, including 600,000 bombed out evacuees from the east. The raging fires which spread irresistibly in the narrow streets killed a great many from sheer lack of oxygen." Stokes further demanded to know, "Is terror bombing now a part of our policy? Why is it the British people are the only ones who may not know what is being done in their name?"[4] The truth is that this kind of bombing – saturation, as opposed to strategic – had been going on well before Dresden and in fact for the Allies, Dresden was but one of about seventy urban centres in Germany that were completely obliterated between 1943 and 1945. By February 1945 it was simply another city that needed to be razed as a part of the effort to bring Nazi Germany to its knees. While bomber commands, both British and American, claimed at the time that bombing was done as precisely as possible, the fact that most industrial, military and transportation targets were in crowded urban areas (the construction of most of which dated back to the Medieval era) made a high number of civilian deaths a certainty. After the indiscriminate bombings of London, Coventry and other British cities by the German Luftwaffe in September 1940, there was then, and has been since, little in the way of international sympathy for the civilian German victims of this event. In fact, Stokes' voice would have been one of only a handful at the time. However, in 2008, we can question, with some historical perspective, the necessity of the bombing of Dresden to determine whether or not it is an unacknowledged atrocity. Several questions need to be answered: What happened? What were the immediate impacts and what did subsequent suffering look like? What justification for this action was presented by the perpetrators at the time? What were possible motivations for the perpetrators? Why has this event been unacknowledged? Should it be acknowledged? If so, why and how?

Impact and Aftermath

The evenings of February 13th and 14th were the end of Dresden. Despite differences of opinion among bomber commands, the saturation bombing of German cities was still taking place in early 1945, ostensibly to once and for all crush the remaining morale of the German people and therefore bring an end to the German government's ability to prosecute the war. Strategic bombing had been used successfully by the Allies to disrupt aircraft manufacture, especially the production of vital ball bearings, and also to strike at the fuel supply that remaining aircraft would need to meet incoming Allied bombers. Dresden would not be spared what befell other major German cities in the two previous years.

Over 700 bomb-laden Lancasters arrived over Dresden around 10 p.m. on February 13th. Thousands of tons of explosives caused immediate destruction and chaos, tearing roofs from houses and shattering windows. The centre of the city, constructed in medieval times, was a tightly packed maze of wooden buildings, ideal tinder for the thousands of four-pound incendiary bombs that fell in the next twenty minutes. As a result, although many people died instantly, the majority of victims in Dresden were incinerated or suffocated in the ensuing firestorm and massive building collapse caused by the firebombing. While firefighters attempted to contain the blaze, by midnight the entire city was engulfed. Civilians and refugees cowering in basements and cellars were trapped and certain to die, mostly from a shortage of oxygen caused by the voracious fire. Because the streets were so narrow, fire leapt from building to building, creating a ceiling of flames and a hellish inferno. When the fires had nowhere else to go, they converged into a column, searching for more oxygen and stretching far into the sky. The whirlwinds stirred up by the firestorm reached 95 miles per hour and sucked people into the flames, where they were melted and burned alive.[5]

The next night, as the city continued to smoulder and burn, the bombers returned, and let loose a repeat of the previous night. According to Randall Hansen, though the intended target was the city centre, in fact what was hit was the area south of the city around the train station and its marshalling yards, which were to have been the main target the previous night. Naturally, there were people gathered there who had fled the inner city after escaping death – as it turned out, only to face it again the next day. Richard Taylor remarks that "it was as if the enemy had anticipated Dresdeners' every move, and then killed them like cattle cunningly driven into holding pens."[6] The city was decimated, with anywhere between 35,000 and 50,000 people killed instantly. Further, hundreds of thousands either became or continued to be homeless refugees when at least 95,000 homes were destroyed.[7]

Subsequent nights saw further raids on the nearby cities of Leipzig and Chemnitz, with similar results. But what is only now beginning to be discussed is the misery and hardship for those who managed to survive the bombing in Dresden and these other cities. Many of them, some 600,000, were refugees arriving from Breslau (Wroclaw, today in Poland) just sixty miles to the east, which had fallen some weeks earlier to the Soviet Red Army. It is fair to say that the terror and the chaos of Dresden was not something most endured just once. Indeed most of those who arrived from Breslau had little choice but to keep moving in search of food and shelter, but their options were more limited by the day. Would continuing to move toward Allied lines in the west really have been a welcome choice for them, based on what they had just witnessed in the destruction of Dresden by the Allies? Finally, it must also be said that while staying out of the clutches of the Soviets was a matter of life and death for refugees and Germans in Dresden alike, it would be untrue to say that Volksdeutsche (ethnic German) refugees from the east, many of whom were in Germany proper for the first time in their lives, received a warm welcome from Dresdeners or Germans in other similar cities. They represented, to many people in Dresden, a drain on scarce resources, and as such were forced to keep moving, some for months and years after the war had finally ended. The suffering of these refugees, and all other German non-combatant victims remains unacknowledged to this day, not only in Germany, but in the rest of the world.

Allied Justifications

Why did American and British bomber command make the decision to decimate Dresden and purposely cause such a high number of civilian casualties at a point in the war when the defeat of Nazi Germany was almost assured? It would be unfair to accuse those in command – RAF Marshall Arthur Harris, US Air Force Chief of Staff Carl Spaatz and RAF Chief of Air Staff Charles Portal – of deviousness, of thinking that their orders could go unnoticed in the fog of war, Dresden being only one of many targets at that point. Rather, for them, Dresden was just another city that had to be completely wiped out for the war to be brought to a conclusion, refugees or no refugees. Understandably, the life of an Allied soldier on the ground was more important to them than that of a German civilian. The justification that the destruction of German cities would save Allied lives at the expense of German ones was again dusted off some months later and reused in the same way ahead of the death and destruction caused in Japan by the atomic bombing of Hiroshima and Nagasaki.

Whether Dresden was a justified military target revolves around the question of how much manufacturing and industry was in place in the area at the time. The fact that the city was so weakly defended would indicate that the answer was, "not much". While Dresden may have been a key manufacturing centre earlier, by this point in the war it was not.

It has also been suggested that another purpose of the bombing of Dresden and other cities was to impact the morale of the German people. While this may have been a motivator, the result may have been the opposite. According to Ferguson, "If anything, the indiscriminate character of the air attacks aroused more defiance than defeatism,"[8] amongst Germans in a way similar to the attitude of Londoners during the Blitz of 1940. Rather than undermining enemy morale (as a plaque in the Canadian War Museum asserts), collective punishment may have served to reinforce a false patriotism and resolve amongst Germans at the time.

Another important justification for bombing Dresden was its position as a hub in terms of transportation and communication, specifically rail traffic. "Dresden had by this time become the main centre of communications for the defence of Germany on the southern half of the Eastern front and it was considered that a heavy air attack would disorganize these communications and also make Dresden useless as a controlling centre for the defence."[9] Dresden was a key connection point for troops moving from the Eastern Front to the Western Front and vice versa. This alone was enough justification for the Allies to bomb the city.

Yet another significant line of reasoning presented by the Allies at the time was that Dresden was one of only a few major urban centres in Germany yet to be bombed – most others had not only been bombed but utterly destroyed. It was thought that the destruction of cities west of the Oder River was a necessity for two political reasons. First, it was believed that the Nazis would not surrender until such time as the entire country had been destroyed. Ordinary Germans and the Nazi rank and file may have had enough, but it was the top leadership including Hitler, Himmler, Goering and Goebbels that would not allow for capitulation. In fact, it was Hitler himself who promised that because they did not deserve victory, the German race would go down with him in the end, saying, "We may be destroyed, but if we are, we shall drag a world with us."[10] Second, the Allies did not want to provide any opportunity or location for the German government to continue to function once Berlin had been destroyed. At the time, Dresden represented the most viable location for that to be attempted, and this fact justified, for the Allies, its destruction.

Other Motivations

There are other possible reasons why the Allies may have engaged in the saturation, or terror, bombing of Dresden that may be revealed by the context of other events of the time. The Germans, when they were engaged in their own bombing of British cities in 1940, showed little regard for precision bombing of targets. Why then, the argument ran, should Allied forces show restraint, especially when lack of restraint would seem to be able to bring the war to a quicker conclusion – being gentlemanly would only prolong the war. In short, they had the means and they were prepared to unleash terror because they knew the Germans had little reserve to withstand it and that public opinion at home would not raise its voice against it.

More important to note is that few in positions of high command in the Allied Forces, especially Churchill, had any doubt about who the next enemy would be once the Nazis were inevitably defeated – the Soviets. There was tension among the "Big Three" Allies – Roosevelt and Churchill had an informal and uneasy alliance with Stalin. The capitalists had joined forces with the communists against the fascists, but it was clear that Stalin had long viewed his forces as having borne most of the sacrifice and expected that this would be taken into account once the threat from their common enemy, Germany, was extinguished. The Yalta Conference, during which the Big Three (Churchill, Roosevelt and Stalin) agreed upon the division of postwar Germany, had concluded just two days before the bombing of Dresden. Still, it was still not a *fait accompli* as to which parts of Germany would be "liberated" – occupied – and by whom. For this reason, the Allies may have felt the need to strike viciously at the remaining German cities, not only to mollify the Soviets, but also to demonstrate that they could be just as violent, exacting and vengeful as their Eastern partners. The bombing of German cities like Dresden and to greater effect a few months later of Hiroshima, would dissuade the Soviets from warring with their erstwhile allies once the Nazis were out of the way. Harris, in fact, says that "The intentions of the attack are to hit the enemy where he will feel it most, behind an already partially collapsed front… and incidentally to show the Russians when they arrive what Bomber Command can do."[11] In the end, the destroyed city was included in the Soviet Zone of occupation which eventually became communist East Germany.

Reasons for Forgetting

If the destruction of Dresden and the resultant deaths is indeed an atrocity, why have we at best counted it as only one in a series of other violent and horrifying events, or at worst turned a blind eye to it with the rest of the long lamentable catalogue of human cruelty, to borrow a phrase from Winston Churchill? Why are some events worthy of being remembered and others not?

Among the Allies, re-examination of atrocities they committed in World War II has been taboo until very recently. Several factors may have impeded that discussion. It could be a case of the victors writing history, which would seem a simple answer. The assumed righteousness of that conflict may have also prevented questioning. Less convincingly, it could be argued that such discussion has been stilled out of respect to surviving veterans, who are viewed as having sacrificed for their country and for the notion of humanity itself. What was done in the name of the survival of the free world seemed reasonable and justified at the time and in many quarters still does seem so. The thinking, particularly in North America, has been that if some of the enemy, innocent or otherwise, had to die to ensure the defeat of fascism, so be it.

What is possibly of more interest is why this event was also forgotten in Germany for many years. May 12, 1945 was, for Germans, *Stunde null*, or Hour Zero. It represents the merciful end of the war, the end of the Nazi Party and the Third Reich, and the utter destruction of their country. It is from there that life began again and, as a result of the reconstruction of the country, Germany can claim to be a postwar success story. But *Stunde null* also represents the start of a national amnesia. At the time, there may have been no other way forward but to instantly forget the past. Germany could not wallow in self pity, not even briefly. As the aggressor, it was never allowed to, especially once the reality of the concentration camps became clear both inside and outside Germany. Consequently, any thoughts of the suffering and/or responsibility of ordinary Germans were turned aside in a national "forgetting" of the war. Some may have kept silent about their past roles for fear of being implicated and possibly put on trial. Others may have wanted to make the past disappear. But for most ordinary Germans the enormity of actions taken in their collective name was too painful and too incomprehensible. They could never have any right to victimhood. They would be considered perpetrators, collaborators, bystanders, perhaps a handful, rescuers, but victims? Never.

However, the current generation of young adults *"die wissen wollen was der Opa im Krieg getan hat"* (want to know what Grampa did in the war). Germany now, as a whole "is terribly, terribly anxious to come to terms with what happened" not just to the Jews in their midst, but also what happened to *them,* to attempt to understand the impact this has had on the national psyche.[12] Their increased interest in a dark chapter of their country's history has caused a closer examination of the participation of ordinary Germans in World War II as well as a re-evaluation of the shame that settled on every German following the war.

A renewed discussion needs to be conducted with discernment so as not to fall into the right-wing argument that somehow compares the suffering of Germans with that of Jews. Such an argument "represents moral parity between the allies and the Axis",[13] and is untenable. The world has become well-informed about the Holocaust and its sheer magnitude. It is impossible to equate the experience of German wartime victims with that of the Jews in Europe: the Holocaust was a far greater atrocity. But the fact that we cannot *equate* the experience of civilians in Dresden with that of European Jews should not prevent us from seeing them as victims. Acknowledging an atrocity like the bombing of Dresden brings the realization that all non-combatants in war are victims, regardless of nationality, faith or heritage. Their governments act in their names, but rarely with their consent. Ordinary Germans had little say in the march to war in the 1930s, indeed little more than the average American or Iraqi had in the lead-up to the American invasion of Iraq in 2003. Nevertheless, they suffered the consequences of that war.

Reasons for Remembering

Should this event merely be a footnote to history? Should we simply accept the explanation given at the time – that it was an unfortunate but necessary price to pay to bring the war to an end – and move on? Should we avoid shining light on the tragedy of Dresden because it would be too painful? Or should we, rather, uncover this and other past atrocities in order to explore the deeper meanings these events may reveal? History needs to examine not only the "official" story, as described by governments and militaries, of events that took place in the "fog of war", but also the stories not revealed by official sources – the personal stories of the victims. Older documentation of historical events, along with long-held assumptions, must be re-examined in light of such evidence.

As well in our re-examination of Dresden, we need to be cognizant that "history is written by the victors" and that victors describe atrocities in a certain light – strictly from their own viewpoint. Dresdens have occurred around the world before and since February 13, 1945. Today we hear excessive civilian deaths described as "collateral damage", an expression that turns away from any notion of individual human suffering. Destruction and deaths are still occurring, and sadly seem unlikely to stop. While the media may occasionally update us on the latest "collateral damage", we mostly get biased reports. We hear the story from the side that holds the "moral high ground", but it is in actuality the story of the suffering of thousands (or millions) of ordinary people (today in Iraq, Afghanistan, the Congo or Gaza, to name but a few). No one sees their individual suffering and it is often forgotten until generations later.

The purpose of revisiting events like the bombing of Dresden is not to revise history to further any particular agenda, but rather to realize that no side in any conflict has a monopoly on either the truth or on suffering. We look back upon the tragedy of Dresden not simply to determine if it was an atrocity, but to recognize that governments and militaries have long used the chaos of war to obscure atrocities. Post-conflict, the victors record a history that claims the moral high ground in order to justify its own crimes and to direct the public gaze away from them. Examining past events and historical accounts more closely can reveal patterns of rhetoric that are disseminated by governments and militaries as they engage in war and its seemingly concomitant atrocities. These examinations may re-open for us lost opportunities to learn from history, rather than to stand by as it tragically repeats itself around the globe.

NOTES

1 Harris, in Randall Hansen, *Fire and Fury: The Allied Bombings of Germany 1942–45* (Toronto: Doubleday, 2008), p. 155.
2 Mary Gooderham, "I Never Thought I Would Go Back", *Globe and Mail,* Saturday Nov 8, p. F5.
3 Hansen, p. 259.
4 'Parliamentary Debates (Commons)', vol. 408, March 6, 1945 (in Hansen, pp. 259–60).
5 Hansen, p. 245.
6 Taylor, in Hansen, p. 246.
7 Niall Ferguson, *The War of the World* (New York: Penguin, 2006), p. 564.
8 Ibid., p. 565.
9 Harris, in www.spartacus.schoolnet.co.uk/2WWdresden.htm.
10 Hitler, in Martin Kitchen, foreword, *A World in Flames* (London: Longman, 1990).
11 Harris, in Ferguson, p. 567.
12 Mary Gooderham, "I Never Thought I Would Go Back", *Globe and Mail,* Saturday Nov 8, p. F5.
13 http://www.germannotes.com/hist_ww2_dresden.shtml

8

Broken Promises and Blind Eyes: The Expulsion of Ethnic Germans from Czechoslovakia and Poland after World War II

Lianna Laberge

✧

O Germany –
Hearing the speeches that ring from your house, one laughs.
But whoever sees you, reaches for his knife.
Bertolt Brecht

The European Theatre of World War II ended in May 1945. The Armistice, however, did not stop the conflict, violence and killings. From 1945 to 1948, 15 million people were expelled from their homes in eastern provinces of Germany and Eastern Europe.[1] Their crime was simply being ethnic Germans. Viewed, often incorrectly, as having being sympathetic to Hitler's Nazi party, and tarred with the collective guilt of fascist actions, they were the target of built-up feelings of hatred and revenge by the Czech and Polish peoples as well as by the Soviet army. Caught on the wrong side of the newly drawn European borders, the ethnic Germans were forced to leave lands that had been their homes for generations, abandon all their possessions and march west to Germany. Called "population transfers" and "resettlements", these forced moves were instigated by Czech and Polish governments and acquiesced to by Great Britain, the United States and the Soviet Union. Behind the euphemistic terms lay a grim and horrific reality. Suffering from actions perpetrated by vengeful soldiers and citizens, two million ethnic Germans

– ordinary men, women and children – lost their lives. In episodes of great horror, they suffered from rape, murder, torture and disease.[2] Anger and revulsion at the atrocities of the Nazi occupation of Poland and Czechoslovakia, gratitude for the Soviets' contribution to the victory over Hitler, and general war weariness induced the Western world to turn a blind eye to the sufferings of the ethnic Germans in Eastern Europe.

> In the Robert Koch Hospital here, which I visited this morning, there are more than sixty German women and children, many of whom were summarily evicted from a hospital and an orphanage in Danzig last month, and, without food and water or even straw to lie on, were dispatched in cattle trucks to Germany. When the trains arrived in Berlin they said that of the eighty-three persons crammed into two of the trucks, twenty were dead. A woman recovering from typhoid had, she stated, seen her husband beaten to death by Poles and she had then been driven from her farm near Danzig to work the fields. Now she has survived the journey to Berlin with two young sons, and, without money, clothes or relations, cannot see what the future holds.[3]

The seeds of this horror were planted after World War I, when the peace treaties of Versailles, St Germain and Trianon imposed new European borders. In a short period of time, five million ethnic Germans, who had lived peacefully for seven hundred years on the frontiers of the Oder-Neisse Rivers in Poland and the Sudeten Germans from the Sudetenland became instant citizens of five newly-drawn European countries, among them Czechoslovakia and Poland.[4] Deeply attached to their *Heimat* or homeland, these new citizens were reassured by the Czech and Polish governments that they would be granted a level of cultural autonomy. These pledges, however, were soon broken and in the following inter-war years, Sudeten Germans in Czechoslovakia and ethnic Germans in Poland suffered from job and education discrimination, land confiscations and high unemployment. In 1938, Viscount Walter Runciman reported on the discrimination faced by ethnic Germans living in Czechoslovakia:

> Czech officials and Czech police, speaking little or no German, were appointed in large numbers to purely German districts; Czech agricultural colonists were encouraged to settle on land confiscated under Land Reform in the middle of the German populations... there is a very general belief that Czech firms were favored against

> German firms... and that the state provided work and relief for Czechs more readily than for Germans.[5]

Between 1919 and 1938, the Sudeten Germans in Czechoslovakia, desperate for relief from the ongoing discrimination and ignored by the government of President Eduard Benes, appealed to the international community for help in attaining self-determination. Hitler, already forming his expansionist policies, used the situation to his advantage. He threatened to use force to help the Sudeten Germans. Fearing another war and hoping to appease Hitler, the United Kingdom, France and Italy met, and without the presence or consent of the Czech President, signed the Munich Agreement in September 1938. As a result of the Munich Agreement, the Sudetenland was transferred back to Germany. Not content with the Sudetenland, Hitler invaded Czechoslovakia in March 1939.[6]

Hitler was also able to use the continuing discrimination of ethnic Germans in Poland to further his expansionist policies. Citing examples of outrages and murders perpetrated against ethnic Germans in Poland, Hitler, ignoring England and France's support for Poland, turned to the Soviet Union. On September 1, 1939, the two countries signed the Molotov-Ribbentrop Pact. The treaty planned for the division of Poland between the two signatories. It set the stage for Hitler's invasion of Poland and provided the spark that unleashed the firestorm of World War II.[7]

Czech President Eduard Benes, having fled Czechoslovakia, and now in exile in Britain, worked tirelessly during the war years on a plan to undo the Munich Agreement and regain the Sudetenland without the nuisance of its ethnic German population. As early as 1941, and looking forward to a victory against the Third Reich, both the Czech and Polish governments-in-exile began plotting for the eventual expulsion of the ethnic Germans from their respective countries. Despite having promised that there would be no dismemberment of German lands in the Atlantic Charter of 1941, both the United States and the United Kingdom eventually supported the population transfers for political and strategic reasons. Consequently, Czechoslovakia would reclaim the Sudetenland. Further, during the war when it had become apparent that Stalin was going to keep part of Poland, the Allies realized that Poland would require compensation for lost territory. It was planned, therefore, that after the war ended, the German province of East Prussia would be given to Poland and its 2.5 million Germans transferred west to Germany. In this way, Stalin would keep his lands in the east of Poland and the ethnic Germans in Poland would be expelled from their homelands in order to make way for new Polish citizens. Once again, without their knowledge or consent, the fate of the ethnic Germans in Eastern Europe was decided by others.

While the rest of the world looked to peace and recuperation after the German capitulation in May 1945, this was not to be the situation for the Germans in Eastern Europe. Although the Allies had planned for the orderly transfer of the German population from Czechoslovakia and Poland, the reality was much more grim and deadly. While the Allies were meeting at the Potsdam Conference to plan for the orderly transfer of the Germans, the "wild expulsions" began. In Czechoslovakia, as the German army retreated, the Czech militia as well as Czech citizens, incited by the inflammatory statements of Eduard Benes and other leaders, began attacking the "traitorous" and "disloyal" ethnic German citizens. Using inflammatory speech, the leaders of Czechoslovakia encouraged Czech citizens to "get rid of all those Germans who plunged a dagger in the back of the Czechoslovak State" and to "clean out the republic as a whole and completely of Germans... Every one of us must help in the cleansing of the homeland."[8] Even religious leaders such as Monsignor Bohumil Stasek encouraged the expulsion by preaching that "once in a thousand years the time has come to settle accounts with the Germans, who are evil and to whom the commandment love thy neighbour does not apply."[9] Germans living in Czechoslovakia, forced to wear white armbands with the letter N (for *Nemec*, Czech for German), were easy targets for angry mobs. Germans were driven from their homes, beaten, raped and killed. In his book *Fires of Hatred*, Norman Naimark reports, "Czechs beat up Germans, shot at them, forced them to do humiliating and life-threatening tasks and showed them no mercy. People were randomly killed and villages were burned to the ground. Germans were hung by their heels from trees, doused in petrol and set on fire. In outright pogroms, Czech militia rampaged through towns and villages, shooting Germans at will."[10]

A report from the *London Daily Mail* describes what happened to those who survived the initial horror.

> Shortly before 9 PM young revolutionaries of the Czech National Guard marched through the streets calling on all German citizens to be standing outside their front doors at nine o'clock with one piece of hand luggage each, ready to leave the town for ever... Then they were marched out of town at gun-point to the Austrian border.
>
> It was pitch dark when they reached the border. The children were wailing, the women stumbling. The Czech border guards pushed them over the frontier towards the Austrian border guards. Then more troubled started. The Austrians refused to accept them; the Czechs refused to readmit them. They were pushed into a field for the night, and in the morning a few Romanians were sent to guard them. They are still in that field, which has since been turned into a concentration camp. They have only the food, which the guards give them from time to time. They have received no rations... A typhus epidemic now rages among them, and they are said to be dying at a rate of 100 a day.[11]

In Poland the situation was equally horrific. As in Czechoslovakia, the ethnic Germans living in Poland were beaten, tortured, and murdered. Their homes and lands were confiscated. German women and girls were raped and abused. Fearful of Polish retribution, thousands of Germans committed suicide.[12] Germans were also sent to labour and internment camps both in Poland and the Soviet Union. Large numbers died en route of starvation and illness. Often former Nazi camps were turned into camps for Germans designated for expulsion. The conditions were horrific. A report to the Foreign Office describes conditions in the Polish interment camps:

> The concentration camps were not dismantled, but rather taken over by the new owners. Mostly they are run by the Polish militia. In Swientochlowice (Upper Silesia), prisoners who are not starved or whipped to death are made to stand, night after night, in cold water up to their necks until they perish. In Breslau there are cellars from which, day and night, the screams of victims can be heard.[13]

A survivor of the camp related her experience. "Every time of the day we women were raped and our shirts torn from our bodies... I cannot speak about the kinds of animalistic perversities that the German women had to endure."[14]

As the wild expulsions were taking place in Poland and Czechoslovakia, the Western Allies were meeting in Potsdam. Warned by General Eisenhower that there were up to 10 million Germans being chaotically evicted from their homes in Czechoslovakia and Poland, and hoping to maintain a level of control, the Western Allies passed article XIII of the Potsdam Protocol. The first paragraph of Article XIII reads: "The Three Governments having considered the question in all aspects, recognize that the transfer to Germany of German populations, or elements thereof, remaining in Poland, Czechoslovakia and Hungary will have to be undertaken. They agree that any transfers that take place should be effected in an orderly and humane manner."[15] There was another reason the Allies wished to slow and control the transfer of ethnic Germans. The Allies were worried about the effect on their domestic budgets of the cost of feeding, clothing and housing the millions of new citizens in Occupied Germany. In the summer of 1945, the Red Cross was warning of a humanitarian crisis in Occupied Germany, stating that "the hurried transplanting of fourteen million human beings would raise a number of problems from the humanitarian standpoint, especially in a Europe strewn with ruins and where starvation was ripe."[16]

The first of the so-called "orderly" transfers began in January 1946.[17] As these transfers continued, the brutality towards the ethnic Germans decreased, but the train trips to Germany were dangerous and the passengers continued to suffer from illness, starvation and death. The promise of "humane and orderly" transfers proved almost impossible to keep. Bertrand Russell was one of the few writers who recorded what was happening in Eastern Europe. In 1945 he reported that:

> In Eastern Europe now mass deportations are being carried out by our allies on an unprecedented scale, and an apparently deliberate attempt is being made to exterminate many millions of Germans, not by gas, but by depriving them of their homes and of food, leaving them to die by slow and agonizing starvation. This is not done as an act of war, but as a part of a deliberate policy of "peace"... It was decreed by the Potsdam agreement that expulsions of Germans should be carried out "in a humane and orderly manner". And it is well known... that this proviso has not been observed."[18]

The story of a survivor confirms Russell's observations. Describing the atrocities perpetrated upon train passengers during the "orderly transfers", she related that "[a]t every railway stop it took place. When the train stopped moving between twelve and fifteen Poles jumped on and pillaged... In this manner we and the passengers in the other wagons were pillaged again and again... some of the passengers were left with only their underwear on."[19]

Arriving in Germany after harrowing journeys, the expellees found a country in ruins. As the Red Cross had predicted, the expulsion produced a humanitarian crisis. In the years after the war, the refugees, eastern Germans viewed as strangers in Occupied Germany, lacked the basic fundamentals of life – food, shelter and work. A memorandum by British military commander Robertson describes the situation of the expellees.

> The influx from the East has created in Western Germany a propertyless class whose numbers, embittered by dispossession and by the misery of months spent in transit camps and emergency accommodation, are obliged to exist in standards which they cannot willingly accept and which are noticeable lower than those of the native Western Germans.[20]

Many would continue to be moved. The German government relocated some from the crowded Eastern provinces to the less populated Western provinces. Other expellees, seeing no hope for themselves in Europe, accepted invitations to immigrate to North America and Australia. For many, living conditions in Germany would not improve until the 1950s and it wasn't until the "economic miracle" of the 1960s in Germany that the majority of expellees were integrated into Western society.[21]

Alfred de Zayas has described the expulsion of the Germans as "the largest mass transfer of population in history, a veritable demographic revolution in central Europe and a form of genocide in the course of which two million human beings perished".[22]

This tragedy received little notice at the time it took place and today it is little known in the western world. There are a number of reasons why the world has turned a blind eye to the atrocities perpetrated against the ethnic Germans. The enormous anger and revulsion the world felt towards the Nazi Germans overrode any qualms the West had about the retribution exacted on the ethnic Germans. All Germans were deemed collectively responsible for the Nazi atrocities and all were to be collectively punished. Believing the delusion that homogeneous countries would be easier to manage, the Allies were able to calm their misgivings about the expulsions by explaining that the population transfers would actually promote world peace and harmony by producing homogeneous nation states. Speaking before parliament in December 1944, Churchill stated, "Expulsion is the method which, so far as we have been able to see, will be the most satisfactory and lasting. There will be no mixture of populations to cause endless trouble… A clean sweep will be made."[23] Using the euphemisms "population transfer" and "displacements" also assuaged the collective conscience. Pushed to the fringes of German society, the expellees' requests for acknowledgement and compensation were unacknowledged by their own country. The German Federal Republic regarded their requests as revisionist demands that ran counter to Germany's forward-looking, post-nationalist policies.[24] As late as 2000, Antje Vollmer, Vice President of the Bundestag declared: "The topic of the [German] expulsion belongs in the Museum of German History."[25]

The expulsions of the ethnic Germans from Eastern Europe did not produce the desired European stability. Germany now contained twelve million expellees who harboured an understandably strong animosity towards their Czech and Polish neighbours. This animosity did not make for cordial relationships. The Sudeten Germans who continued to agitate for the return of their homeland further strained relations with Czechoslovakia. It would take until 1973 and the signing of the Prague Treaty for Germany and Czechoslovakia to recognize each other diplomatically. In this treaty, the countries abandoned territorial claims against each other and acknowledged the inviolability of their borders. A further step was taken in 1997, when through the efforts of Vaclav Havel, the Czech and German governments apologized to each other for the brutalities each inflicted on the other during and after World War II.[26] In the German-Czech Declaration, both sides declared their desire to continue to develop relations in a "spirit of good neighbourliness and partnership". Both sides have shifted their focus from conflict and blame to discussions based on reconciliation and consensus building.

In Poland the wounds also took a long time to heal. Willy Brandt visited Poland in 1971 and in a gesture of reconciliation visited the site of the Warsaw Ghetto. The image of the Chancellor kneeling in front of the memorial to victims of German aggression deeply impacted mutual perceptions, yet it would take two more decades before the Polish people were willing to apologize for their treatment of the ethnic Germans during the post-war expulsions.[27]

Although positive steps have been taken, issues still remain. Many Polish and Czech peoples continue to deny the brutality of the expulsions, and in Germany, many former Sudeten Germans continue to agitate for restitution for the properties they lost when expelled from Czechoslovakia after the Second World War.

The ethnic Germans living in Eastern Europe during the inter-war years were the victims of broken promises. Forced to become citizens of countries that ignored their minority rights, they spent the inter-war years suffering abuse and discrimination. Despite the assurances contained in the Atlantic Charter, most ethnic Germans in Eastern Europe were forced to leave their home countries after the Second World War and settle in a country that had neither the desire nor ability to welcome them. Promised an orderly and humane transfer in the Potsdam Agreement, they instead suffered from neglect, if not torture, abuse and murder. Deeming ethnic Germans collectively responsible for the atrocities of the Nazis, the world was willing to turn a blind eye to the abuses visited upon them, lured by the vision of a stable and peaceful Europe. Incited by the Czech and Polish governments, and supported by the United States, Great Britain and the Soviet Union, the human rights abuses suffered by ethnic Germans during the post-war expulsions need to be acknowledged and remembered. The ethnic Germans were victims of a policy meant to create stability but one which brought chaos. More critically, they were victims of a state-sponsored inhumanity that caused immeasurable suffering and the loss of millions of lives.

NOTES

1 The numbers for the expelled and killed ethnic Germans in this paper are taken from Alfred-Maurice de Zayas in his book *The German Expellees: Victims of War and Peace*. Estimates of the number of ethnic Germans expelled from Eastern Europe range from ten million quoted in Emil Nagengast's paper "The German Expellees" in the volume *Ethnic Cleansing in Twentieth Century Europe,* eds. Steven Béla Várdy and T. Hunt Tooly, to the fifteen million quoted from de Zayas' book.
2 Alfred-Maurice de Zayas, *The German Expellees: Victims of War and Peace* (New York: St. Martin's Press, 1986).
3 Ibid., p. 109.
4 Ibid., p. 14.
5 Ibid., p. 18.
6 It should be noted that not all Sudeten Germans looked to Hitler for help. The large Sudeten Social Democrat Party wanted nothing to do with Hitler. They had desired autonomy for the Sudeten Germans but not through a union with Hitler. See Alfred Maurice de Zayas, *The German Expellees: Victims of War and Peace* (New York: St. Martin's Press, 1986), p. 19.
7 Ibid., p. 21.
8 The quote is to be found in an article by Alfred-Maurice de Zayas, "Anglo-American Responsibility for the Expulsion of the Germans 1944-48" in *Ethnic Cleansing in Twentieth Century Europe*, eds. Steven Béla Várdy and T. Hunt Tooly (Duquesne: Duquesne University, 2000), pp. 147–156. See also Norman Naimark, *Fires of Hatred: Ethnic Cleansing in Twentieth-Century Europe* (London: Harvard University Press, 2001), p. 115.
9 Ibid., p. 115.
10 Ibid., p. 115
11 Alfred-Maurice de Zayas, *The German Expellees: Victims in War and Peace* (New York: St. Martin's Press, 1986), p. 86.
12 Norman Naimark, *Fires of Hatred: Ethnic Cleansing in Twentieth-Century Europe* (London: Harvard University Press, 2001), p. 126.
13 Alfred-Maurice de Zayas, *The German Expellees: Victims in War and Peace* (New York: St. Martin's Press, 1986), p. 93.
14 Norman Naimark, *Fires of Hatred: Ethnic Cleansing in Twentieth-Century Europe* (London: Harvard University Press, 2001), p. 119.
15 Alfred-Maurice de Zayas, *The German Expellees: Victims in War and Peace* (New York: St. Martin's Press, 1986), p. 83.
16 Alfred-Maurice de Zayas, "Anglo-American Responsibility for the Expulsion of the Germans 1944–48", *Ethnic Cleansing in Twentieth Century Europe*, eds. Steven Béla Várdy and T. Hunt Tooly (Duquesne: Duquesne University, 2000), p. 157.
17 Alfred-Maurice de Zayas, *The German Expellees: Victims in War and Peace* (New York: St. Martin's Press, 1986), p. 111.
18 Bertrand Russell is quoted in Alfred-Maurice de Zayas, *The German Expellees: Victims in War and Peace* (New York: St. Martin's Press, 1986), p. 108.
19 Philipp Ther, "A Century of Forced Migration: The Origins and Consequences of 'Ethnic Cleansing'", *Redrawing Nations: Ethnic Cleansing in Europe, 1944–1948,*

eds. Philipp Ther and Ana Siljak (Lanham: Rowman and Littlefield Publishers, Inc., 1997), p. 55.

20 Robertson quoted in Philipp Ther, "A Century of Forced Migration: The Origins and Consequences of 'Ethnic Cleansing'", *Redrawing Nations: Ethnic Cleansing In Europe, 1944–1948*, eds. Philipp Ther and Ana Siljak (Lanham: Rowman and Littlefield Publishers, Inc., 1997), p. 60.

21 Ibid., p. 61.

22 Alfred-Maurice de Zayas, "Anglo-American Responsibility for the Expulsion of the Germans 1944–48", *Ethnic Cleansing in Twentieth Century Europe*, eds. Steven Béla Várdy and T. Hunt Tooly (Duquesne: Duquesne University, 2000), p. 157.

23 Alfred-Maurice de Zayas, *The German Expellees: Victims in War and Peace* (New York: St. Martin's Press, 1986), p. 80.

24 Emil Nagengast, "The German Expellees and European Values", *Ethnic Cleansing in Twentieth-Century Europe*, eds. Steven Béla Várdy and T. Hunt Tooly (Duquesne: Duquesne University, 2000), p. 290.

25 Ibid., p. 290.

26 Norman Naimark, *Fires of Hatred: Ethnic Cleansing in Twentieth-Century Europe* (London: Harvard University Press, 2001), p. 138.

27 Ibid., p. 138.

9

No One Else to Ask: Investigating the Ukrainian Holodomor

Jean Kosar

✧

In the steppes
The yellowed grass does not speak
It is silent and bends as though it were alive
It does not want to disclose the truth,
But there is no one else to ask.

Taras Shevchenko

Starvation is a slow, agonizing process. The body consumes itself, exhausting the fat reserves first and then attacking muscle. The body's organs begin to shut down, causing swelling and accelerated breathing and heartbeat. Any exertion can result in heart failure. Dysentery, scurvy, jaundice and typhus may attack the weakened body. In the end, the victim reaches a state of semi-consciousness and lapses into death. In the early 1930s in Ukraine, millions of people – entire families of children, elders, mothers and fathers – suffered and died in what has come to be called the Holodomor, the murder by starvation of Ukrainian peasants by the Stalinist regime in Moscow. Vasily Grossman, in his novel, *Forever Flowing*, describes the suffering of the starving families:

> Every starving person dies in his own particular way. In one hut there would be something like a war. Everyone would keep close watch over everyone else. People would take crumbs from each other. The wife turned against her husband and the husband against his wife. The mother hated the children. And in some other hut love would be inviolable to the very last. I knew one woman with four children.

> She would tell them fairy stories and legends so that they would forget their hunger. Her own tongue could hardly move, but she would take them into her arms even though she had hardly the strength to lift her arms when they were empty. Love lived on within her. And people noticed that where there was hate people died off more swiftly. Yet love, for that matter, saved no one. The whole village perished, one and all.[1]

It seems inconceivable that a famine could be a tactic used to teach a whole people a lesson, but this is what happened when Stalin decided that Ukrainian nationalism had to be crushed. This use of starvation was not new. When famine struck Russia in 1891, there was an international effort to relieve the suffering, but at the time, Lenin observed that, by destroying the old regime and the peasants' faith in God and the Tsar, famine could be used to usher in a modern socialist world.

Under the Tsar, Ukrainian peasants had laboured as serfs to provide the Russian nation with food. When the communists took the reigns of government, new hope arose in Ukrainian revolutionaries that they would be masters in their own nation. However, Lenin and the Bolshevik leadership had little time for coddling national aspirations in Ukraine. Instead, they embarked on a policy of "war communism" which required the expropriation of agricultural produce from the breadbasket of the steppes. This policy was an early attempt on the part of the Bolsheviks to allocate goods to industrialized workers and was seen as a step toward full socialism, but the lack of real planning and the devastation of the Civil War precipitated a disastrous decline in productivity which ultimately resulted in the famine of 1921 and 1922. At this point, Lenin decided to take a step back and the Soviet government implemented his New Economic Policy. "War communism" was replaced by a progressive tax system and a policy of encouraging free consent to the collectivization of agriculture. At the same time, Moscow embarked on a policy of Ukrainization – a promotion of the Ukrainian language, art and culture designed to placate the advocates of an independent Ukraine.

However, this encouragement of Ukrainian nationalism eventually flew in the face of Marxist ideology, which viewed patriotism as counter-revolutionary. One's loyalty to one's class trumped adherence to capitalist constructs like "king and country". After Lenin's death in 1924, Stalin's government became increasingly uncomfortable with liberalism in Ukraine. Taxing the more successful peasants, labelled "kulaks", was not a way to fulfil Marxist doctrine. In order to increase productivity, utilize new technologies, like tractors, and follow the Marxist creed, the peasant farms would need to be collectivized. The dream was to create huge agricultural factories which would provide all peasants with equal opportunity and prosperity. The work and the produce would be shared throughout the Soviet Union and ultimately the socialist revolution could be exported to the world. Every collective farm (*kolkhoz*) would have access to modern farm machinery (which most individual Ukrainian peasants could not afford). The bourgeois nationalism of Ukraine and the pernicious desire for private land in the peasantry would be swept aside and replaced by a global socialist society that would embrace modern industrial techniques. The Bolsheviks realized that Russia had fallen far behind the West in the push toward modern industrial economies. Their plan was to catch up by launching huge initiatives in transportation and factory-building. If they failed, they feared that the revolution itself would be lost. Stalin's Five Year Plan, his replacement for Lenin's NEP, called for a 150 percent increase in agricultural production to feed workers on the great projects designed to force the backward economy of the Soviet Union into the modern world. It was believed that only through collectivization could the targets for increased agricultural production be reached.

The peasants of Ukraine appeared to be the most resistant in the Union to the concept of collectivization. The Soviet government realized that in Ukraine, collectivization would have to be imposed. In depicting the peasants' choice to join the *kolkhoz*, Soviet propaganda staged photographs of meetings in fields between sunburned farmers and eager Komsomol (Communist youth) missionaries, framed by banners extolling socialism and the prosperity of the *kolkhoz*. In actuality, the Party cadres sent from the city to push collectivization in the villages were greeted with stony silence when they asked who was in favour of socialized agriculture. When asked who was against it, "The peasants all raised their hands ... 'and who is against the Soviet regime?' Then no one answered."[2] Already Ukrainians had begun to fear the wrath of the centralized government in Moscow and its fervent disciples in the field. They were reluctant to be singled out as dissenters in a country with a history of violent suppression of nonconformity. Already the Marxist paranoia about counter-revolutionary influences and capitalist sabotage had taught them to hold their tongues. For many peasants, however, the collectivization of their farms was not a step forward to a brave new world, but rather a return to the past of serfdom, albeit with a new master – this time the Russian government.

On December 27, 1929, Stalin announced the "eradication of all kulak tendencies and the elimination of kulaks as a class".[3] At first, the moniker of "kulak" was applied to landowners who used hired labour. Kulaks were the exploiters of the peasant workers in the industry of agriculture, according to Marxist pronouncements. In Ukraine, there were very few true kulaks, perhaps as few as one percent of the population; however, in the increasing doublespeak of Soviet communism, the application of the word "kulak" was broadened. It came to mean anyone who owned livestock, anyone who had prospered under Lenin's economic liberalism, and ultimately anyone who resisted collectivization. A vast number of families were arbitrarily designated as kulaks and expelled from their homes and farms, with all their worldly goods confiscated by the Party officials. Victor Kravchenko describes what was expected of the party activists assigned to the task:

> Comrade Stalin ordered us to complete collectivization by spring ... The local village authorities need an injection of Bolshevik iron ... You must assume your duties with a feeling of the strictest Party responsibility, without whimpering, without any rotten liberalism. Throw your bourgeois humanitarianism out the window ... Beat down the kulak agent wherever he raises his head. It's war – it's them or us![4]

Although Stalin credited the peasants with expelling the kulaks, the reality was that there was considerable resistance to the policy in Ukraine – many village officials, at risk of being charged with having bourgeois sympathies, reported that their villages had no kulaks. Some opportunists used "dekulakization" to get even for past wrongs or to feather their own nests with the confiscated goods from kulak homes, but in most cases, suspected kulaks were only shunned through fear. However, the Party had set quotas for kulak accusations and demanded that these capitalists be flushed out of every community. If the village officials were unable to identify them, perhaps loyal Marxists from urban areas would have to do the job. Eventually, entire kulak families were loaded into cattle cars and shipped off to Siberia to provide labour for the burgeoning Soviet industrial complex. Vasily Grossman, himself a Jew, compares the treatment of the kulaks to the treatment of Jews by the Nazis during the Second World War:

> The so-called kulaks were pariahs, untouchables, vermin ... the kulak child was loathsome; the young kulak girl was lower than a louse. They looked on the so-called "kulaks" as cattle, swine, loathsome, repulsive; they had no souls, they stank ... they were enemies of the people and exploited the labour of others ... the kulaks are parasites; they are burning grain; they are killing children ... the rage and wrath of the masses must be inflamed against them, they must be destroyed as a class because they are accursed!
>
> Just as the Germans proclaimed that Jews are not human beings! Thus did Lenin and Stalin: kulaks are not human beings.[5]

Kulak children could find themselves abandoned when both parents were deported to Siberia. The children would wander the villages, begging for food and for shelter but villagers were afraid to extend help for fear of being branded as kulak sympathizers. Lenin's widow, Krupskaya, urged Marxists to wage the class war against adults only, but no one appeared to be listening.

As Nicholas Werth tells us in *The Black Book of Communism*, deportation operations were brutal, chaotic and completely uncoordinated from start to finish. Cattle cars were jammed with men, women and children, with no provision for food, water or sanitation. Many died on the way to the Siberian labour camps and once survivors arrived, they found nothing with which to start their new lives – no shelters or means of building them, no food, and not even any chance to work. The resulting deaths of millions of men, women and children went unrecorded. Because one of the reasons given for this transfer was for kulaks to supply labour for the work camps, the results were a dismal failure. In fact, the program resulted in a financial loss to the state. The average value of goods confiscated from kulak families was 564 rubles per farm (equivalent to fifteen months' wages for an average labourer), but the cost of deportation per farm was closer to 1,000 rubles.[6]

As Ukrainian farms were being cleansed of the scourge of the kulaks, the Soviet state rededicated itself to the grain requisitioning program and a policy of crash collectivization. After the mass deportations of kulaks, the remaining peasants saw the procurement program as a threat to their very survival. Resistance took many forms, including hoarding of money and food, the slaughter of livestock (in order to prevent it from being subsumed into the *kolkhoz* – between 1928 and 1932, Ukraine lost 50 percent of its livestock) and 14,000 riots and peasant revolts. Many of those who resisted were deported or killed.

In March of 1930, Stalin published his famous response to the stalwart resistance of the Ukrainian peasantry: *Dizzy with Success.* Although he claimed "the fundamental turn toward socialism in the village may be considered already secured", he denounced "coercive measures against the middle peasants" (those not rich enough to have been dekulakized). He wrote "some of our comrades have become dizzy with success and for the moment have lost clearness of mind and sobriety of vision" and concluded that "it is impossible to establish collective farms by force. To do so would be stupid and reactionary."[7] This article precipitated a temporary respite in the crash collectivization of the Ukrainian peasantry. Within three months, fifty percent of Ukrainian peasants had abandoned the *kolkhoz* and returned to their private farms. However, they were not allowed to repossess their livestock or farming implements, nor was it possible for them to return to their original plots of land. Taxes on independent farmers were doubled and tripled while farmers on the *kolkhoz* were exempt from taxation. Fear remained that resistance to collectivization would result in a charge of "kulak". Eventually, most of the resistance crumbled, and by 1932, seventy percent of farmers worked on the collective farms.

Although the Russian government was successful in forcing the Ukrainian peasantry onto the *kolkhoz,* it was considerably less successful in managing the huge industrial farms it had created. Promised deliveries of tractors never materialized and farm managers had little agricultural expertise. Even the livestock suffered neglect under collectivization. Petro Grigorenko relates his own uncle's dilemma on the *kolkhoz*:

> He spoke of his state farm as a shining example of the total economic mismanagement of the Soviet system. He showed me how the pigs were being maintained and said, "the miracle is that they are not dead yet. But they will be soon. And the director, the one responsible for this state of affairs, will not be penalized. 'Kulak supporters' like me will be called enemies and there will be no way we can prove our innocence."

> I advised him to leave the farm. To this he replied, "then they will surely arrest me, saying that I wanted to hide from punishment. At least while I am here I can save my pigs and fight with the director."[8]

In the end Grigorenko's uncle was arrested and killed under charges of counter-revolutionary activities.

It is unclear whether the harvests in 1932 and 1933 were poor, average or slightly better than average, but it is indisputable that the government functionaries assigned to expropriate grain were told to take greater and greater proportions of whatever was there, leaving peasants facing the winter without food. In three years, the government's procurement quotas had doubled but in the face of the chaos in the countryside, these targets could not be met. Ukrainian communist leaders advised Moscow that the procurement targets were impossible, only to be accused of counter-revolutionary leanings and threatened with removal from office. While peasants ate earthworms, acorns and even horse manure, local granaries held stocks of "state reserves" of food for "emergencies" and exports of grain continued. In fact, some of the stockpiled food began to rot while families starved all over Ukraine. Until districts were able to meet their procurement targets, they were blockaded – no shipments of commercial goods were allowed in. Even seed shipments were ruled out, though it was understood that without seed there would be no harvest in the following year.

The "ear law", passed in August 1932, made the theft of socialist property punishable by death. One could face execution by gleaning a few grains of wheat or taking a few potatoes grown on the *kolkhoz*. An internal passport system was instituted to ensure that people remained in their villages. Lenin had accepted international aid during the 1921 famine, but in 1932, the situation in Ukraine was kept a secret. Members of the international community, including Walter Duranty, an American pro-Marxist reporter, were taken through manufactured communities in Ukraine and shown happy collectivized families eating hearty meals and extolling the glories of socialized agriculture. The reality was quite different. While these happy scenes were being enacted, Victor Kravchenko was observing the following:

> The most terrifying sights were the little children with skeleton limbs dangling from balloon-like abdomens. Starvation had wiped

> every trace of youth from their faces, turning them into tortured gargoyles; only in their eyes still lingered the reminder of childhood ... Everywhere we found men and women lying prone, their faces and bellies bloated, their eyes utterly expressionless ... on a battlefield men die quickly, they fight back, they are sustained by fellowship and a sense of duty. Here I saw people dying in solitude by slow degrees, dying hideously, without the excuse of a cause. They had been trapped and left to starve each in his own home ... We were oppressed by the unnatural silence. Soon we came to an open space which, no doubt, was once the marketplace. ... Sprawled on the ground were dead men, women and children, thinly covered with dingy straw. I counted seventeen. As we watched, a wagon drove up and two men loaded the corpses on the wagon like cordwood.[9]

Perhaps the most tragic victims were the children. Robert Conquest, in *The Harvest of Sorrow*, estimates that two and a half million infants perished between 1932 and 1934. Of those children who did survive, many were left orphans, unable to cope with the deaths of their parents and extended family groups. Some migrated to cities to beg or commit petty crimes. These *bezprizornie* formed gangs and when the problems associated with them became too pressing, they were summarily shot by the GPU, the predecessor to the KGB. Soviet authorities suggested that the presence of homeless children in cities like Kiev was a counter-revolutionary plot perpetrated by kulaks in order to shame the state. Ironically, some of the children who survived these brutal times later found employment as GPU/KGB officers. They had been so brutalized themselves that they were able to enact horrific acts necessary to support the regime that had orphaned them.

In January 1933, Stalin announced that collectivization had finally fulfilled the glorious dreams of Marxism. According to Stalin, there was no more poverty in rural villages. The days of serfdom, when the labour of peasants enriched capitalist aristocrats, were gone and the peasants were enjoying the fruits of their collective labour. To support this positive spin, the central government instituted a three- to five-year prison sentence to anyone guilty of uttering the word "famine". While Stalin extolled the success of collectivization, Party members and officials witnessed trains loaded with corpses and starving people begging and dying in village market squares and at train stations. They wondered whether they should "blow the whistle". Did the Politbureau know? Writers like Mikhail Sholokov and public officials from Ukraine and

Russia attempted to broach the subject but Stalin characterized attempts to describe the horrors of the famine as fables, stories and counter-revolutionary propaganda.

By the end of 1933, at least 7,000,000 Ukrainians had starved to death and the spirit of Ukrainian nationalism was utterly broken. Finally, food aid was provided for the starving survivors of the famine. As was often the case, Soviet functionaries looked on the bright side:

> A ruthless struggle is going on between the peasantry and our regime. It's a struggle to the death. This year was a test of our strength and their endurance. It took a famine to show them who is master here. It has cost millions of lives, but the collective farm system is here to stay. We have won the war![10]

Russian authorities continue to deny that this famine was man-made and used as a terror tactic, but the evidence for the purposeful decision to crush Ukrainian resistance is overwhelming. The Russian Communists had convinced themselves that people had to suffer in order for the world to reach a new stage. They extolled toughness and turned their backs on pity, which they saw as a weakness that would betray the doctrine of Marxism. Joseph Berger, a former Communist official, quotes a Communist woman who, although deported to the gulag, retained her party membership and analysed the contradictions in this way:

> My generation of Communists ... accepted the Stalinist form of leadership. We acquiesced in the crimes ... We carry a stain on our consciences individually and collectively. How was all this possible? Did we all go crazy, or have we now become traitors to Communism? The truth is that all of us, including the leaders directly under Stalin, saw these crimes as the opposite of what they were. We believed that they were important contributions to the victory of socialism.[11]

It is curious that this atrocity has not been more fully explored. Stephane Courtois, in *The Black Book of Communism*, suggests that part of the problem is that we are reluctant to criticize violence if it is in the service of the greater good. The ideals of Marxism – brotherhood, equality, "to each according to his need, from each according to his ability" – are difficult to dismiss, even when they are accompanied with blind brutality and fanaticism. Khrushchev, in his 1956 "secret speech" criticized Stalin's perversions of the Marxist doctrine, but suggested that Soviet achievements, including the breakdown of the class structure and the establishing of collective farms, were worth the sacrifice of so many innocent lives.

How were the Russians able to use propaganda and manipulation to convince many Western writers and intellectuals to bear witness to the glorious successes of Soviet policies like collectivization and dekulakization? There is an element of religious fervour in the descriptions of people who put the progress of Marxism ahead of the individual lives of countless men, women and children. Sidney and Beatrice Webb, British apologists for the Stalinist regime, promoted the idea of the "class war" which could afford to take no prisoners – "Strong must have been the faith and resolute the will of the men who, in the interest of what seemed to them the public good, could take so momentous a decision."[12] That the decision involved the starvation of entire villages does not seem to enter into the equation. If the Russians were engaged in a philosophical war against Western capitalism, then they are guilty of war crimes for inflicting such cruel punishment on an innocent civilian population. But in their philosophy, no one was innocent.

In this period, the rise of fascism was a terrifying prospect for much of the world. When Hitler came to power in Germany, the world stood at a desperate precipice. The brotherhood and hope offered by Marxist doctrine, no matter what brutal and horrible means were employed to achieve it, was more positive a choice than the dark future of Nazism. That the Russians sacrificed so much to defeat German fascism fostered a feeling of indebtedness that made the West reluctant to take the Soviet regime to task for acts mirrored by the atrocities committed by the Nazis.

Was the "Holodomor" a genocide? The United Nations defines genocide as "acts committed with intent to destroy, in whole or in part, a national ... group [by] deliberately inflicting on the group conditions of life calculated to bring about its physical destruction in whole or in part".[13] The doctrinaire actions of the Stalinist government eradicated at least a quarter of the Ukrainian population in order to bring it to heel under the Russian boot. The successors to the Soviet regime in Moscow argue that other groups suffered in the same famine. In response, it is important to point out that all groups that fell victim to the 1932 famine had demonstrated determined resistance to the collectivization of agriculture. The starvation of the Ukrainians was, however, both politically and ethnically motivated.

I wonder if it is important to define the horror of the famine in legal terms. Will the woman who told fairy tales to her starving children benefit from this exercise? Can the homeless orphans who fled to the streets of Kiev to beg and who were shot by the GPU be given another chance at life? They cannot, but it is important to set history straight, nevertheless. The Russians refuse to accept responsibility for the Holodomor, but until they do, both they and Ukraine are hostages to the lies of the past. The truth is shameful – the brutality and cruelty, weakness and submission – all cause us to want to forget, to hide the truth under the forward rush to the future, but the truth must be told. Those who suffered and died must be acknowledged. Perhaps it is in the nature of human beings to repeat the horrible events of our history endlessly, but nevertheless, these events must be remembered. The suffering cannot be lost in the wind of the steppes.

NOTES

1 Vasily Grossman, *Forever Flowing* (London: Collins Harvill, 1986), pp. 164–65.
2 James E. Mace, *Communism and the Dilemmas of National Liberation: National Communism in Soviet Ukraine, 1918–1933* (Cambridge, Massachusetts: Harvard University Press, 1983), p. 285.
3 Nicholas Werth, et al, *The Black Book of Communism: Crimes, Terror, Repression* (Cambridge, Massachusetts: Harvard University Press, 1999), p. 147.
4 Victor Kravchenko, *I Chose Freedom* (New York: Garden City Publishing Co. Ltd., 1946), p. 91.
5 Vasily Grossman, *Forever Flowing*, pp. 143–44.
6 Nicholas Werth, *The Black Book of Communism*, p. 156.
7 Joseph Stalin, *Works* (Moscow: Foreign Languages Publishing House, 1955), pp. 197–205.
8 Petro Grigorenko, *Memoirs* (New York: W. W. Norton and Company, 1982), p. 41.
9 Victor Kravchenko, *I Chose Freedom*, pp. 113–18.
10 Ibid.
11 Stephane Courtois, *The Black Book of Communism*, p. 12.
12 Robert Conquest, *The Harvest of Sorrow* (Oxford: Oxford University Press, 1986), p. 317.
13 Wasyl Hryshko, *The Ukrainian Holocaust of 1933* (Toronto: Bahriany Foundation, 1983), p. 6.

10

The G-Word: Why Turks and Armenians Can't Talk

Karen DeVito

✧

"The question is," said Alice, "whether you can make words mean so many different things". "The question is," said Humpty Dumpty, "which is to be master – that's all".
Lewis Carroll

An elephant sat in the national living room of Turkey the night Orhan Pamuk, its best-known novelist, was awarded the 2006 Nobel Prize for literature. That elephant's name was "Genocide". The Nobel announcement met with mixed reactions in Turkey – some rejoiced at Pamuk's accomplishment and others denounced him. Pamuk had publicly spoken out about the Armenian genocide, as it is called outside Turkey, and without actually using the G-word had got himself indicted under Article 301 of the Turkish Penal Code for "crimes against Turkishness" which carries a possible imprisonment of six months to three years. Other writers had run afoul of this particular law and faced imprisonment, but Pamuk, the most known internationally, had put his country on notice that he would not remain silent. The charges against him were eventually dropped – the ensuing international attention may have led to subsequent acquittals of other writers charged for their mention of the Armenian genocide.

The "Armenian Question" came to the fore in the 1890s under the reign of Sultan Abdul Hamid II. At its centre was the fact that with the 1453 sacking of Constantinople and the dissolution of the Byzantine Empire, the Ottoman Turks designated Armenians alone as the "infidels" of the Turkish ethnic minorities. Thus began the policy of defining the

Armenians as "other". Abdul Hamid assembled an elite force comprised of another minority, Kurds, who resented the prosperity of the Armenians. This force was sent to roam the traditional lands of the Armenians, who were forced to quarter the often hostile and aggressive troops in winter. In addition, Armenians were submitted to double taxation: to the Ottoman regime and also to the Kurdish warlords who ruled parts of their lands. In 1894 Armenians in the Sasun area organized to protest double taxation and roughed up an Ottoman tax official – he sent back a report of armed rebellion. Ottoman troops intervened in the tense situation between local Kurds and Armenians, attacking and killing thousands of Armenians of all ages and sexes. Not even their priests were spared as they tried to shield their parishioners.[1] Word of the massacres blazed throughout Armenian communities and spread to Britain and America where relief efforts were undertaken. It was partly in the roots of the Suffragist movement in America that the Armenians found friends abroad. Participants in relief efforts would become witnesses in the massacres to come.[2]

With the ascendancy of the Young Turks in the early 1900s, and the Sultan's retreat into the background, came the hope in Armenian communities of a more liberal era. But it was the Committee of Union and Progress (CUP) that consolidated political power and, as World War I loomed, its program of Turkification precluded any notions of multiculturalism. Repressive laws were passed against the formation of ethnic organizations and new battalions created to specifically combat any rebellion, even if only perceived. And so it was in 1909 that several thousand Armenians were massacred in what was called an attempt to put down a counter-revolution. The British Vice-Consul and American missionaries were witnesses to the massacre. A show of an investigation was made, but there was no justice.

Enver, Talaat and Jamal emerged as leaders of the extreme nationalist movement and invested themselves with dictatorial powers, making it possible for them to instigate the elimination of the Armenians. Turkey's entrance into World War I and its animosity toward Russia gave a further opportunity to place blame on the Armenians. Not only were they portrayed as subversives who did not share the pan-Turkic vision, their men were conscripted into the military and then blamed for defeats at the hands of the Russians. They were now called "collaborators". In 1915 the Temporary Order of Deportation was proclaimed and what followed was a state-organized death march accompanied by mass murder. If this was indeed a state-sponsored or even state-condoned genocide, the instigators would need perpetrators, preferably disposable ones. Prisons were emptied and the criminal element was dispatched as killer bands called *chetes*, who worked with lower level officials to kill able-bodied Armenian men and deport the rest, town by town, village by village. Armenians were horribly abused as the deportations, forced death marches across Anatolia and mass killings progressed. Turkish officials used the railways, as Germany would later, to transport a mass of humanity crammed into boxcars like cattle, mainly women, the elderly and children, who were then marched into the Syrian desert. There were concentration-style camps and mass graves along the way. When it was over, Talaat asked US Ambassador Henry Morgenthau to obtain a list from American insurance companies of their Armenian policy holders, as there were few Armenians left, and abandoned assets should revert to the state. Morgenthau refused.[3] Under cover of war, the instigator and perpetrator groups had exterminated well over a million Armenians.

Talaat, Enver, and Jamal later fled and were tried in absentia – all three were eventually assassinated. It was the assassination of Talaat in 1920 by a young Armenian suffering from what we now call post-traumatic stress disorder that caught a Polish university student's attention. Rafael Lemkin, then twenty-one, questioned his professor why, if Talaat's assassin was being tried for one murder, Talaat could not have been tried for a million murders. He found the answer – that a state's sovereignty cannot be trespassed upon – unconvincing. By 1933 Lemkin had become a lawyer and drafted a law that would make it an international crime to attempt to eliminate any ethnic or religious groups like the Armenians.[4] Lemkin would later coin the word "genocide" with an eye toward galvanizing international action against instigators and perpetrators wherever they may attempt this crime against humanity.

Whether or not Lemkin's G-word is applied, why is it important for Turkey to acknowledge what happened in 1915 – it has been nearly one hundred years, so why not talk? Turkey has one foot in Europe and one in Asia – despite its Ottoman roots, Turkey has turned an eye toward Europe since its modernization by Mustafa Kemal Atatürk, a charismatic figure of near godlike stature in the national psyche. Turkey has applied for entrance into the European Union, which would be beneficial in obvious ways: Turkey would gain prestige and economic benefits and possibly more stability since the European Union has in the past helped settle border disputes of its members. The other members would benefit from Turkey providing stability, situated as it is among Muslim nations. But the Armenian Question has some members balking. France, for example, has passed a law against the denial of a genocide, including the 1915 Armenian massacres. Paradoxically, this measure might prove to be the obverse side of the coin from Article 301 as it may possibly discourage serious academic investigation into history – which does require questioning.

That Turkey's border with Armenia remains closed is painful to Armenians, since they can see Mount Ararat across the border but cannot visit it, nor other traditional landmarks and ancient churches in former homelands. The few Armenians left, mainly in Istanbul, are isolated from kin in Armenia and vice versa. But this isolation is not particularly beneficial to Turkey either, since it must build many extra miles of pipeline to skirt Armenia. While Armenia could be a welcome, if small, trading partner with Turkey, the Anatolia region would regain the economic benefit it once enjoyed if goods were once again exchanged across the border. An open border would also surely increase tourism across Anatolia and eastern Turkey to cultural sites Armenians have been longing to visit.

Most of all, Turkey has made overtures to become a nation among nations. Its geopolitical positioning may account for the tension between the glorification of Turkey's Ottoman roots in the sweeping out of the Byzantine Empire and the myth-making around the figure of Mustafa Kemal Atatürk, the visionary leader who modernized and secularized Turkey for a role in the twentieth century. On the one hand, Turks are proud of their culture and heritage. On the other, the figure of Mustapha Kemal straddles a dividing line between the Ottoman, Muslim ways and the modern secular ways, with the Young Turks as the new broom that cleared the way for his emergence. There has also been a resurgence of conservative Muslim thought with the election of Prime Minister Erdogan in 2003, perhaps a swing of the pendulum away from the westernization begun by Atatürk. The history of that transition and what happened to the Armenians is a history of national forgetting. It is a history somewhat like the airshaft between tall apartment buildings in Orhan Pamuk's novel *The Black Book* – it is meant to bring air and light to the windows that open onto it, but the windows have become grimy and the residents use the airshaft as a handy place to dispose of things they no longer want to see.

At the centre of this national amnesia may be the fact that many of the perpetrators of the 1915 massacres later fought together with Mustafa Kemal in the War of Independence against the Allied occupiers. Their success even gained some of them high positions in the military, the government, and in the National Assembly and therefore tacit immunity from accountability for their past actions.[5] This may be part of the reason the bureaucracy is steeped in secrecy and certain aspects of Turkish history are taboo. In Turkey, there is little scholarship done outside state-sponsored institutions, and scholarship on the subject of the 1915 massacres mainly consists of refutation of claims that they were anything other than ethnic conflict that got out of hand or the unfortunate circumstances of war, "collateral damage" in today's parlance.[6] Turkish governments have consistently maintained that no such policy of determined elimination ever existed – that it could not have existed. There is no mention of the events of 1915 in schoolbooks. Further, Article 301 has been used often to silence Turkish writers who dare contradict the official story.

Taner Akçam, a Turkish academic living in the United States, places his homeland on the couch and calls the denial of the Armenian genocide a defense mechanism. Further, he assesses Turkish claims that the Armenians murdered Turks and therefore had to be killed as the defense mechanism of projection.[7] After all, these atrocities took place in plain view of the rest of Turkish society, making for a large bystander group who did nothing as the killing proceeded. In fact, there may have been nothing these civilians could have done since the country was plunged into war and famine with plenty of suffering to go round. Eventually though, the former Armenian homelands were emptied of what was essentially Turkey's bourgeoisie and it may have been too painful for other citizens to consider how this came about. Still, modern Turks could be said to be the beneficiaries of the emptying of the Armenian lands. Turkey's Defense Minister Gönül recently said in Brussels that Turkey would not be the nation it is today without the deportations of Greeks and Armenians during its nation-building struggle.

Another factor in the continued denial of history is the Turkish "deep state" – the military, police, intelligence and bureaucracy are so interconnected as to provide a smoke screen for decision-making, interpretation and implementation of policy. One feature of Turkish lawmaking is that many statutes are passed and left to the lower levels of enforcement to interpret them. So there is an invisible power that cannot actually be traced to the source, making the workings of government as opaque as Pamuk's grimy windows on the airshaft. The opacity and paranoia of the deep state likely stems from the Turkish view of the Treaty of Sèvres after World War I as an attempt by the Allies to keep Turkey weak. It was later replaced by the Treaty of Lausanne which deleted all reference to the Armenians and solidified the Kemalist nationalist view of Turkey as a secular state with no class or ethnic distinctions. Subsequently, officials have denied that there ever were Armenian provinces.

But there were Armenian lands in today's Turkey, as the ruins of their churches silently attest. As rich as Ottoman history and culture is, Armenians also have a rich cultural tradition in arts, letters and architecture. Poets from Dante Alighieri to Byron to Walt Whitman have written paeans to its beauty. Byron was so entranced that he absented himself to an Armenian monastery on the island of San Lazzaro off Venice to learn the Armenian language and read Armenian literature. In Europe much of the remaining Armenian architecture now in Turkish lands is considered part of heritage sites worthy of being restored and protected. Armenians, like Turks, have much to be proud of in their heritage. And, as the Turks have done about their own leaders and heroes, they have engaged in myth-making, particularly around the bravery of Armenians who resisted oppression and fought to save their kin and fellows from the massacres. This myth-making is particularly evident in the Armenian diaspora in the United States where some groups use emotional and hyperbolic language when discussing the events of 1915. These appeals are often met with emotional and vehement Turkish denials and equally hyperbolic descriptions of the suffering of the Turkish people during those times. But reconciliation must involve getting beyond the conflicting grand historical narratives and shedding some light on a shared history.

Reconciliation cannot come without acknowledgement, yet it is hard to imagine Turkey stepping back from obduracy on the issue as well as throwing open the windows on its inner workings. But the European Union is seeking greater transparency in Turkey's government and also some acknowledgement of the Armenian genocide before awarding EU membership. Given Turkey's history of paranoia over sovereignty, there is little hope for reconciliation along the lines of an official Truth and Reconciliation Commission similar to South Africa's, especially if proposed by a western nation. There is neither the will nor the leadership at present. Further, Turkey is loathe to be told how to behave by western nations – after all, they as well have their own historical injustices.

It is more likely that incremental change may come through unofficial channels first, and there have been previous attempts, though timing is important. David L. Phillips gives an interesting account of the Turkish-Armenian Truth and Reconciliation Commission (TARC), a series of Track Two, or unofficial, diplomacy meetings in 2000–2001.The meetings had the goal of fostering a collaborative effort to view conflict as a shared problem worthy of joint cooperation. It began with separate seminars, then shared cultural events, confidence-building, and carefully drawn rules of engagement that still allowed for lively discussion. The meetings were not without controversy, and there were criticisms from outside the group from voices on either side. The account describes two groups, the Turks with their history of forgetting, and the Armenians with their history of constant remembrance, coming together to begin to construct shared history and build understanding. TARC faced many challenges, not the least being the attacks of September 11th. The United States' foreign policy interest in Turkish-Armenian reconciliation faded in the ensuing ramping up of plans to invade Iraq. American pressure on Turkey to open the Armenian border evaporated. It became impractical to apply pressure on a country whose co-operation and airspace was needed for military operations.

After some time, the TARC did agree to involve the International Center for Transitional Justice (ICTJ) in a study on whether "Lemkin's Law", the 1948 Genocide Convention, could be applied retroactively to the Armenian genocide, or the "so-called genocide" as the Turks preferred to call it. It was agreed that the Center's analysis would be provided confidentially to TARC. Unfortunately, despite the agreement of confidentiality, it was leaked to the press and support deteriorated, then crumpled.[8] Eventually though, the ICTJ did make a strictly legal determination as demanded by the Turks and declared that the Genocide Convention could not legally be applied retroactively to the events of 1915, a finding welcome to the Turks. But, it went on to say that the events did constitute genocide as described, which pleased the Armenians who already understood that retroactive application of the law, with concomitant monetary and/or land restitution, would not be possible.[9]

While the TARC did not produce official results, it was an important initiative that opened the door for further civil society discussions. For Turks, it is important to see re-opening history as an opportunity rather than a block to moving forward. For Armenians, whose very existence in Turkey is officially denied, recognition of their history is a first step toward achieving justice, even if that justice will be largely symbolic. The Turkish deep state is the custodian of the official story, and remains fearful that acknowledgement and recognition may lead to territorial claims and/or claims for compensation. Within the Turkish and Armenian nations, and among people of Armenian descent around the world, there is certainly a variety of voices and views. It may be time for space to be created where they can be brought together and heard.

The word "empathy" comes up in discussions of TRCs, but these efforts require more than mere fellow feeling. Since there was general suffering all round from war and famine during the events of 1915, productive discussions will need to recognize the tragic predicaments on both sides. Compassion is more active than empathy as it involves the engagement of the imagination rather than just "feeling bad" at the plight of another. It also takes courage to recognize that the perpetrators of the massacres were not an aberration in Ottoman history, as sometimes claimed, and not monsters, but that they were merely human. It will also take courage to acknowledge that the relatively small number of Armenians who committed political assassinations and acts of terror over the years did commit crimes. It is important to recognize that when life has done its worst to a person, or when a person has done the worst, they are still human. It is challenging to think of such events this way, but necessary if the goal is understanding rather than repetition of history.

If the G-word is to be used in discussions it will need to be as a descriptor of events, rather than a legal term, even though it was coined for legal use. Enough time has passed since the Armenians suffered that particular injustice that there are no instigators to put on trial, no perpetrators to punish. But recognition is possible. Relinquishment by Turkey of former Armenian homelands is likely out of the question, but granting of access through an open border is possible. Talk of the Armenian genocide is not going away and the time may have come, whether the Turkish government likes it or not, for it to allow more open discussion and freedom of speech for Turkish writers and academics.

World events continue to change the dynamics of relations between Turkey and western countries. While the European Union may earlier have feared Turkey's admittance as beginning the "Islamification" of Europe, it may now consider its entrance as providing a stable friend in the region, a buffer. In addition, the election of US President Barack Obama – with his message of hope and change – has been positively perceived in many Islamic countries, including Turkey. The new administration of the United States could use this period of good will to begin to mend relations between Turkey and Armenia. Obama himself has urged Turkey to acknowledge the *Medz Yeghern*, or Great Calamity, an Armenian expression for the atrocity – although he avoided using the G-word while in Turkey. The Armenian diaspora was disappointed that an earlier US House resolution to declare the 1915 events genocide fell by the wayside, opposed by the Bush administration in the early march to the "war on terror". Such a well-meaning declaration could possibly have hindered rather than encouraged more open discussion at that time, as the Bush administration prepared to invade Turkey and Armenia's neighbour, Iraq. The resolution has once again been quietly introduced in Congress, as the new US administration is finding its way and subtly changing its approach to its policies in the region. The US superpower's new president, Barack Hussein Obama, whose middle name is even cause for hope in the region, has committed to even-handed diplomacy and dialogue. On past Turkish relations with Europe and with the United States, one of Pamuk's characters states it well: "Can the West endure any democracy that is achieved by enemies that in no way resemble them?"[10] The Obama administration is yet young, and faced with sizable domestic and international problems, but that question remains to put it to the test.

The question now is, how can Turkish-Armenian relations change given the structure of Turkish government and in the face of laws like Article 301? There are signs that Turkey may be pushed to address the issue of transparency in government – things cannot remain hidden forever. Writers have publicly demonstrated for freedom of speech. The influence of the Turkish deep state is becoming more visible, like a stain beneath melting ice. It is woven through Pamuk's novels, where characters feel claustrophobia, that they are being watched, followed.

The assassination in 2007 of Hrant Dink, the editor of the Istanbul paper *Agos* was itself reminiscent of a scene from a Pamuk novel. Dink, an ethnic Armenian, was shot down outside his office after receiving threats that police ignored. He had worked with Taner Akçam on the Armenian-Turkish bilingual paper *Agos* promoting free discussion and reconciliation and he had contradicted the official version of 1915. At the time of his death he had been tried yet again under Article 301 for "insulting Turkishness" and given a suspended sentence. His seventeen-year-old Turkish alleged assassin admitted guilt, saying he objected to Dink's writings on Armenian history. Several other youths were later implicated, and since all were minors the trial was to be closed. Publicly, after the murder, officials have stated that Article 301 should be repealed, but there has been no such action and the trial continues. No one could have imagined that the Armenian genocide would be on the front page of the *New York Times* nearly ninety years after its occurrence, but Hrant Dink's murder placed it there. News later surfaced that a video exists of the assassin posing with police officers, leading some writers to speculate that the murder had the fingerprints of the deep state on it.

There are less sinister reasons to anticipate a shift in Turkish-Armenian relations. In September, 2008 as the first Turkish head of state to do so, President Gul visited Armenia with a stated goal of "normalizing relations" between the countries. In October, the Foreign Ministers of both countries attended a meeting of Baltic Foreign Ministers and hailed a beginning of new relations between the countries. In November 2008, the AGBU, the largest Armenian diaspora organization, held a conference in Brussels entitled "A Journey of Cultural Rediscovery: Armenian Heritage in Turkey" to highlight efforts in Turkey to reclaim the memory and preserve the cultural heritage of Armenians in Turkey. It was attended by Turkish and Armenian academics, writers and historians and members of the European Commission Parliament. This work was recognized as being important to the development of Turkish society, to Armenians in Turkey, to the diaspora, and to the improvement of Armenian-Turkish relations. It could also enhance the still-impoverished economy in eastern Turkey where it would promote tourism. The Minister of Culture has even expressed interest in building a museum to Armenian writer William Saroyan in his ancestral town. On a less official note, there have been ongoing discussions among Turkish and

Armenian academics and other interested parties as a result of joint conferences on reconciliation at universities around the world.

There are still Turkish journalists willing to risk arrest or worse for freedom of speech. Arat Dink has taken over his father's role as editor of *Agos* and continues to write. He published an immediate response to Defense Minister Gönül's comments about the benefits of past deportation of minorities entitled *Let My Non-Existence Be a Gift to the Turkish Nation*, a play on the words of the pledge school children recite, "Let my existence be a gift to the Turkish nation." Turkish academics and writers rapidly weighed in, pointing out that Turkey would indeed be different without the "deportations", that it would be a pluralistic, culturally and economically richer country. They further stated that before Anatolia was de-populated, no one talked about poverty there. The economy has never recovered, and an entire bourgeoisie was lost with the Armenians, along with a class of artisans, craftspeople and building experts. One wonders if Atatürk the reformer, who led his country out of occupation, were alive today he would approve of this discussion and dissent. It has been said that his leadership style was authoritarian, but he did, after all, secularize Turkey, showing that Islam and democracy can co-exist. His openness to western ideas was the hallmark of his reforms. He abolished the caliphate, allowed women the vote, reformed writing from Arabic script to the Roman alphabet, and limited Islamic dress.

The image of Mustapha Kemal Atatürk is still omnipresent in Turkey – stern portraits of the "Father of Modern Turkey" hang in virtually every café, public building and living room. His resolute face adorns the currency. His is revered with a devotion perhaps only seen in North Korea for the "Dear Leader" Kim Jong-Il. But in 2008 a Turkish journalist, Can Dündar, achieved what many felt was impossible – he released a film on the life of Atatürk. And, to the dismay of many, he portrayed him as human. Critics say that the film does not concentrate on his strength and bravery, but shows too much weakness – his fear of the dark, his admiration of women, his enthusiasm for whisky and cigarettes. Two professors in Istanbul filed a request for investigation of Dundar under Article 301 for "eroding Atatürk's respectability".[11] But, despite a popular conservative columnist's warning to avoid the film, more than a half-million viewed it in Turkey in its first two weeks.

It remains to be seen if Turkish society is ready to address historical collective memory and compare it with the official story. But if Turkey wishes to maintain her connections with western liberal democracy, it seems possible. Atatürk may have pushed his country westward, but now it appears that Turkey may be feeling a gravitational pull from the West. Nearly every other western democracy has recognized the Armenian genocide and it may be time to help Turkey confront its own history – but not by heaping opprobrium. There will be facilitator roles to be filled, and they may well be recruited best from outside Turkey. It is hard to imagine an entire democratic nation remaining in the dark in the twenty-first century, oft touted as the information age. Perhaps the words of Turkey's official story of the Armenian genocide have remained master for too long.

NOTES

1 Peter Balakian, *The Burning Tigris: The Armenian Genocide and America's Response* (New York: Harper Collins, 2003), pp. 40ff.
2 Ibid., p. 69.
3 Ibid., p. 261.
4 Samantha Power, *A Problem from Hell: America and the Age of Genocide* (New York: Harper Perennial, 2007), pp. 19–20.
5 Richard Hovannisian, ed., *The Armenian Genocide: Cultural and Ethical Legacies* (New Brunswick, NJ: Transaction Publishers, 2007), p. 358.
6 Taner Akcam, *From Empire to Republic: Turkish Nationalism and the Armenian Genocide* (London and New York: Zed Books, 2004), p. 208.
7 Ibid., p. 211.
8 David Phillips, *Unsilencing the Past: Track Two Diplomacy and Turkish-Armenian Reconciliation* (New York: Berghan Books, 2005), pp. 99–100.
9 Ibid., pp. 113–14.
10 Orhan Pamuk, tr. Maureen Freely, *Snow* (New York: Alfred A. Knopf, 2005), p. 228.
11 Ayşe Karabat, *Today's Zaman*, 18 November, 2008.

11

Syria: Hama Massacre

Omar Ilsley

✧

If you hate a person, you hate something in him that is part of yourself. What isn't part of ourselves doesn't disturb us.

Herman Hesse

In February 1982, Syrian government forces aggressively suppressed an uprising by the Islamic Front in the Syrian city of Hama. Thousands of civilians were killed along with rebel fighters. Accurate records of fatalities do not appear to exist and estimates vary widely. Government sympathizers allege that only around 3,000 people were killed,[1] while others put the figure as high as 30,000.[2] Amnesty International in its 1983 report mentions an unofficial death toll of 10,000.[3] There is uncertainty surrounding other details of the Hama incident as well – the official reporting by the Syrian government is vague and does little more than acknowledge that a confrontation occurred.[4] However, there is little doubt from the information that is available that there was a massacre of thousands of people, most of whom were civilians, in Hama in February 1982.

The Instigators

The animosity that led to this conflict has been apparent for centuries. It is essentially ethnic in nature, but has its roots in a religious schism which took place in the seventh century when the Shi'i faction of Islam broke away from other Muslims (now called Sunnis) in a dispute over the succession of leadership of the Muslims. One of the subsequent splits within the Shi'i gave rise to the Alawi sect. Traditionally, Alawis have been considered heterodox or heretical, especially amongst Sunnis. Even today some Sunnis do not consider Alawis to be Muslims.

The Syrian Government and its institutions are dominated by members of the Alawi minority. From the sixteenth century, during the Ottoman rule of what is now Syria, Alawis were marginalized, considered heretics, and excluded from positions of power. They lived in remote, rural areas in the northwest of the country, where they secluded themselves in an effort to avoid the domination of the Ottoman's hostile Sunni legal and administrative systems.[5] They were poor and often worked as labourers on the farms of wealthy Sunni landowners. In 1920, as the French replaced the crumbling Ottoman administration, the Alawis took advantage of the situation to align themselves with France against their traditional Sunni oppressors, who were resistant to French rule. By 1946, when France withdrew from the newly independent Syria, Alawis were well placed to participate in the governing institutions. In the succeeding years they consolidated their position, until a coup d'etat in 1970, when Hafiz Asad, then Defence Minister, seized power. Though the Alawis were just over ten percent of the Syrian population, they held effective control of the country.[6]

After World War I, aspirations for Arab independence, bolstered by the Allies during the war to encourage dissent against the ruling Ottomans, were frustrated by the French occupation of Syria. At that time Sunnis, traditional oppressors of the Syrian Alawis, enjoyed the privileges of the landowner and merchant classes, as well as of the indigenous political and social administration. However, the Alawis' favoured position with the French allowed for the erosion of Sunni influence. After Syrian independence in 1946, dissent amongst various Sunni factions grappling for political control of the country saw the further decline in Sunni power within the national institutions, while Alawis eagerly filled the vacuum. At the same time the spread of pan-Arabism and socialist ideas throughout the Arab world created a new threat to traditional Sunni society in Syria. Agitation amongst the farm labourers (many of whom were Alawi: the term Alawi was synonymous with peasant[7]) threatened the social stability and the economic viability of the landowners. Secularization and increased education also undermined the traditional and religious Sunni base.

By the spring of 1963 the Ba'ath Party, a secular, socialist organization with pan-Arab aspirations, had seized power in Syria. In the following years it attempted to consolidate its power base by purging Syrian institutions, particularly the military, of what were considered non-loyal elements. Many Sunnis were replaced by Alawis. As Asad came to power in 1970 through an internal coup within the governing Ba'ath party, the traditional relationship between the majority Sunnis and the minority Alawis was effectively reversed. The conservative and traditional Sunni establishment now saw itself marginalized from power by a group they despised. Continued resistance to the secular and socialist reforms of the Ba'ath government emerged in the form of the conservative Islamic Front, a loose organization of Sunni religious groups, like the Muslim Brotherhood, which advocated armed resistance and the establishment of an Islamic state. Especially in Hama "the once great landowners of the central Syrian plain", who had previously felt the impact of a socialist-inspired "peasant revolt, bore the Ba'ath a special grudge" and turned to the Muslim "Brothers' shock troops as a means of hitting back at their tormentors".[8] The Alawis, acting through the Ba'ath and very aware of their traditional subservient relationship with the Sunni, were alert to any type of dissent to their rule and became increasingly oppressive in eliminating it.

To consider both antagonists in this conflict to be instigators of the events that culminated in the Hama Massacre is perhaps unusual. It tends to be customary to distinguish victims from the oppressors, the oppressors being the side that dominates and prevails. However, both sides actively involved in this desperate struggle increasingly proved to be willing to resort to brutality and terror. In the twelve years from the ascension of Asad as President of Syria until the massacre in 1982, levels of violence and reactions to it escalated dramatically. Commentators have indicated that both sides were aware by the time of the open rebellion that the stakes were very high and that the fate of the country, the Ba'ath party, and the Islamic Front and an Islamic revolution were in the balance.[9] Asad is reported to have been alert to the precariousness of the situation for his government and the minority Alawis at the end of 1981, asserting that only one side or the other in the conflict would be able to survive.[10]

Prelude

The level of aversion developed between Sunnis and Alawis over centuries can be encapsulated by quickly reviewing pertinent events between 1970 and 1982. Islamic resistance to the new Asad regime was quickly apparent with uprisings in Damascus in 1972, again in Damascus and then in Hama the next year, and in Aleppo and Hama in 1975.[11] The Ba'ath put forward a new constitution in January 1973 which implied that the Syrian President didn't have to be a Muslim, a condition that outraged the more conservative Muslim sensibilities, especially in Hama. Seeking to placate the religious opposition, the constitution was revised to specify that the President had to be a Muslim, but it stopped short of recognizing Islam as the state religion. This issue re-resurrected the old, humiliating question of whether Alawis could actually be considered Muslims, forcing Asad to seek a ruling from Shi'i authorities that Alawis were considered part of Shi'i Islam.[12] Tensions continued to escalate, especially after the 1976 economic downturn that attracted more Sunnis to the Muslim Brotherhood and enabled and sustained a more persistent revolt against the Asad regime across a broader population.[13] Bombings, assassinations, and attempted assassinations of Ba'ath party officials, their families, and foreign advisers became common occurrences. Continued insurrections in Aleppo, Hama, and other towns challenged the government's authority.

On June 26, 1980, Asad narrowly escaped an assassination attempt, and the Ba'ath lashed out at their opponents. The next day 600 to 1,200 Muslim Brothers imprisoned in Tadmur prison were executed in their cells by Syrian soldiers[14] and the following month membership in the Brotherhood was made a capital offence. By this time hundreds if not thousands of political prisoners were in Syrian jails, and there were many reports of summary executions. A determination to defeat the opposition became entrenched within the Ba'ath, and images of Stalinist purges were rhetorically invoked to emphasize the type of action needed.[15] Amnesty International reported the execution of 350 Hama residents who were seized during house-to-house searches, dragged into the streets, and shot on April 23, 1981.[16]

The Islamic Front terror became more blatant and the government forces more desperate in their response. Journalist Robert Fisk, who visited Hama in the autumn of 1981, recounts talking with three very frightened foreign aid workers. "Dozens of senior Ba'ath party members had been murdered in their homes – some, though not all of them, Alawites – and in many cases their wives and children had been killed with them." In reprisal "200 executions had taken place since the previous

Easter. [...] In many cases the victims were related to wanted men; if an *ikhwan* [Brotherhood] member fled, then his father or brother would be murdered."[17]

It is useful to consider the events in other Middle East countries at this same time: the Islamic Revolution in Iran in 1979, the occupation of the Grand Holy Mosque in Mecca in November 1979 by religious extremists, the assassination of Anwar Sadat by members of the Muslim Brotherhood in October 1981. All these events must have affected the Ba'ath party and their assessment of the situation within Syria at the end of 1981. Syria was perilously close to an unrestrained civil war. There was a sense that the Islamic Front could not be suppressed and the survival of Hafiz Asad and the Ba'ath party in Syria was in doubt.

Massacre

There is no one definitive account of the Hama massacre. One author warns that most accounts of this incident appear to be very biased and employ unestablished details to support their biased position.[18] The versions that do exist all have very limited first-hand knowledge. The following account has been assembled from various sources[19] in order to establish only a general understanding of what happened.

In the early morning hours of February 2, 1982, a Syrian army unit, making its way on foot through the narrow winding alleys of the old city of Hama, unknowingly approached the hideout of one of the Islamic Front leaders, and was ambushed by his armed guards who killed many of the soldiers. As the army rushed in reinforcements, the Islamic Front responded by calling out through the speaker system on the mosques' minarets for a general jihad against the Ba'ath. Hundreds of armed fighters throughout the city emerged from their hiding places, repelled the Syrian forces, and took control of the city. Ba'ath officials were seized in their homes and executed, in some cases along with their families. Many young men who had previously not been associated with the Muslim Brotherhood or other subversive Islamic groups, rushed to assist the rebels because of their resentment towards the ruling regime. By the next day the city was "liberated" by the Islamic Front, with some reports claiming that they controlled all the territory within ten miles of Hama.

After an initial shocked hesitation the Ba'ath responded with ferocity. Reinforcing the local garrison with 12,000 troops under the direct command of Ri'fat Asad, the President's brother, the city was quickly sealed off from the rest of the country and the difficult task of re-taking the city began. Using tanks, artillery, explosives, and bulldozers, the Syrian forces penetrated into the warrens of the old city, engaging their tenacious opponent. Everyone they encountered was suspect and any association with the Islamic Front, or any indication of opposition to the Asad regime, was treated harshly. Families of reported suspects were executed. Many were directly killed in the fighting or bombardment, or when their hiding places were demolished before they could escape. Prisoners were interrogated and then executed, often buried in mass graves. The Syrian blockade effectively hindered escape and prevented the entry of any supplies including food. Those trapped within the city, both fighters and civilian non-combatants, began to starve.

The intense fighting lasted over a week. In order to maintain the loyalty of the regime's troops any soldiers who originally came from Hama were transferred to other units away from the fighting. Nevertheless, there were reports of some dissenting troops deserting to the rebels and other troops expressed discontent at fighting their fellow citizens when they could be fighting the Israelis. But the government forces prevailed, and the next couple of weeks were spent routing out any remaining insurgents. Some sources maintain that the majority of the fatalities occurred during mass executions after the main fighting ended. In particular, anyone with any role in the Muslim religious community was executed. Whole sections of the city were demolished, the ruins broken up, and compressed into the ground using heavy construction equipment. Many died in the demolition of their homes. Entire families were systematically sought out according to pre-prepared lists that may have been compiled from information obtained during tortuous interrogations, taken from their homes, and shot.

By the end of February, the situation was completely contained by the government forces. All resistance had ceased and the clean-up began. Robert Friedman, a *New York Times* correspondent, reports that when he visited the city in May he found three areas of the old city, each the size of four football fields, completely razed and flattened.[20] No one knows how many victims died on both sides of the conflict. In the absence of any firm evidence, most commentators seem to have settled on a figure of about 10,000 deaths. Some of the more extreme figures may reflect that many women and children who were allowed to escape from the city by Syrian troops and fled to safety were initially counted as fatalities.[21] It may be that after the battle up to 800,000 Syrians fled from throughout the country to safety[22] and it can be assumed that many of these would have been members of the Islamic Front or sympathizers of the more conservative religious perspective. The Islamic Front appeared to have been completely defeated through the brutal and outrageous actions of the Asad regime, and there was very little dissent from within the rest of the country. It is suggested that perhaps the Islamic Front's organizational capacity was not as strong as once believed, or that old divisions and divided loyalties within the Front impaired its ability to mount a country-wide insurrection.[23] A silence of consent seemed to envelope the country: nobody wanted to openly acknowledge that anything had happened. Perhaps Robert Friedman was able to capture the essence of the situation within Syria when he wrote:

> [...] if someone had been able to take an objective opinion poll in Syria after the Hama massacre, Assad's treatment of the rebellion probably would have won substantial approval, even among many Sunni Muslims. They might have said, "Better one month of Hama than fourteen years of civil war like Lebanon."[24]

Aftermath

There was only vague official acknowledgement from the Syrian Government of the events in Hama, and it reported only atrocities committed by the Brotherhood, characterized the Brotherhood as the "enemies of God and Islam", and associated it with both Zionism and American imperialism.[25] The Ba'ath regime rebuilt the destroyed sections of Hama, modernizing facilities and eliminating the old neighbourhoods, with their confusing alleyways, impassable to large vehicles and effective as a rebel stronghold. A hospital, schools, housing, sports facilities, training institutes, market facilities, mosques and a church were built, along with completely reorganized neighbourhoods. All evidence of the ruins of the battle was covered up.

A silence about the massacre fell over Syria. Lisa Wedeen, in her book *Ambiguities of Domination*,[26] discusses the control that the Asad regime was able to establish over the topics and vocabulary of public discourse. The permissible way of speaking of events was modelled for Syrians through the state-controlled media: they either adopted the official perspective and expressed it with the provided language, or they remained silent.

Even opinions expressed in private tended to respect the official position, or were resigned to them. Robert Fisk reports on a conversation he had with a minor government employee in Damascus over a decade after Hama. While acknowledging Fisk's own distress about the massacre, the employee goes on to say that the killings and executions had solved the problem of Islamic fundamentalism in Syria, and that the West should be grateful for that. "We are the only country in the Middle East to have totally suppressed fundamentalism,"[27] he emphasized. And in 2000, after Asad's death, Fisk talked to an old friend in Hama: "What happened, happened," the friend remarked. "The past is gone. We are children of the present – [19]82 is over with. Let's say no more."[28]

Initially, in 1982, there were a few reports in the international press about the events in Hama, but there was little detail, and interest was soon diverted by more visible concerns: the Falkland War; The Israeli invasion of Lebanon; expulsion of the PLO from Lebanon and the arrival of the US Marines; and the assassination of Bashir Gemayel. As the strength of the Islamic fundamentalist revival continued to grow in other parts of the Middle East and the impact it was having became more worrisome, criticism of Syria's "solution" for its religious rebellion became more muted. Fifteen years later, when Algeria was embroiled in a similar struggle with armed Islamic fundamentalists, there was little criticism of Algerian government atrocities. One incident, an assault on the Muslim stronghold at Ain Delfa by the Algerian army using artillery and tanks and the slaughter of up to 3,000 in December 1994, is remarkably similar to the Hama massacre.[29] It was as if the international community itself began to feel the implications of a spreading Islamic revolution and was ready to tolerate the extreme measures employed to contain it.

Since the spring of 1982, opposition to the Syrian government by Islamic groups within Syria has been almost non-existent. With the death of Hafiz Asad in 2000, his son Bashar became President. There are signs that there may be some changes in government policy concerning the Muslim Brotherhood, but Bashar himself stressed to American journalists that there would be no apologies for Hama. However, the Syrian ambassador to the United States did refer to the "tragic event" of Hama, and former members of the Muslim Brotherhood have been permitted to return to Syria with the condition that they "apologize for Hama". In the meantime there are signs of conciliation from Islamic religious groups, who appear to be softening their fundamentalist positions and adopting a more pragmatic stance in regards to the Syrian regime.[30]

While these developments may offer grounds for optimism, the historical antagonism between Sunni and Alawi, which in modern Syria has also been reflected in conflict between landowner and labourer, rural and urban, and socialists and conservatives, has roots that are over one thousand years old. Memories of humiliating injustices and atrocities, left unrecognized, can be expected to persist within the affected communities for generations. Suppressed collective memories of victim communities make acknowledgement and apology by the state extremely difficult and unlikely at this time. The massacre at Hama continues to be viewed as the culmination of a series of events and dynamics between ethnic communities stretching back centuries. As difficult as it is to establish the facts of what happened in Hama in 1982, each community has its own version, which is probably irreconcilable with the other's. Perhaps the best that can be expected for now is that Syrians concentrate on reconciling themselves to some sort of peaceful co-existence with each other. Perhaps once a measure of trust is established between the two communities, they may approach a shared version of this part of their history.

Conclusion

Atrocities are too often reduced to a series of incidents defined by "facts". The question of how many died, how they died and when they died, can overshadow the larger question of why they died. Viewed in this way, the fatalities tend to be nothing more than punctuation to a deadly conversation between adversaries, as if at some point the horror will cease to inspire revenge and requital, and one protagonist or the other will resign themselves to the futility of violence and acquiesce to the will of the other. Can one side persuade the other of its resolve by acting in inhuman ways? Perhaps atrocities are merely expressions of contempt for the other – killing, maiming, and humiliating as a means to demonstrate the inferiority and sub-humanity of the adversary. Or, perhaps, as appears in the case of the Hama massacre, the campaign is to eliminate rather than subdue the foe.

It seems that the Syrian regime was successful, at least temporarily, in eliminating their foe at Hama. Very little resistance to the Ba'ath regime from Islamic groups is evident over the last 25 years and religious life within Syria offers no challenge to the concerns of the government. The victims of the massacre included those who advocated the overthrow of the Ba'ath, but there is no way of establishing how many of the victims were directly involved in such political resistance. There are many instances where victims appear to have been family members of suspected Muslim Brotherhood members. It also appears that many were condemned simply by the location of their homes and the neighbourhood they lived in. In all the accounts of the massacre, there is little or no mention of another group of victims – the injured. It is possible that most of the "injured" were executed. As for the survivors, mostly women and children, we can only speculate that they escaped death by disassociating themselves from any connection to the Islamic Front. Their continued survival would have depended on their ability to maintain that disassociation. Any apparent connection to Hama, or to conservative Islam, would have been life-threatening. This ensured that any memory of Hama other than the "official version" was kept secret and well out of the public sphere.

And so, in understanding the victims of Hama, we must consider the thousands of lives that were extinguished, and perhaps the hundreds or thousands of families that were smothered. Traditions and memories stretching back hundreds of years have been silenced and suppressed. There may be efforts to nurture the stories by those that have inherited these family narratives, but the events of Hama will have a profound influence on how these stories are told. Will the memory, in the coming decades or centuries, inspire a continued divide between the old adversaries of Sunni and Alawi, or will the conflict be redefined as one between socialism and tradition, religion and secularism, Ba'ath and the oppressed Syrian people? Some may wish that collective amnesia would descend on the whole episode, and that Syrian society could be redefined to eliminate the old divisions. However, this appears unlikely, and recent efforts by the new President, Bashar Asad, to improve relations between the government and conservative religious groups supports the view that the Hama massacre will not be forgotten, but will at some time need to be dealt with at the national level.

The violent Islamic challenge to the Hafiz Asad regime three decades ago was resolved through a brutal and inhumane response. That solution perpetrated on the citizens of Hama now has the potential of causing further division and dissent within Syrian society. Is it possible to prevent the suppressed legacy of the Hama massacre from reigniting a violent struggle? Unfortunately, public recognition of victims of this historical dispute, restitution, and reconciliation appear unlikely. More probable are efforts to assimilate members of the conservative religious community back into Syrian society with opportunities for education, jobs and prosperity. There are indications that Bashar may be prepared to make concessions to conservative religious elements, causing speculation that the Ba'ath in Syria could retreat from its ideology of secularism.[31] If so, this may open the possibility of accommodating conservative Muslims within Syrian public life without compromising their beliefs. Consistent with Ba'ath practice during its four decades of rule in Syria, it is not expected that this would lead to any toleration of dissent, but it would allow greater participation and inclusion of those who have been excluded since 1982.

NOTES

1 Patrick Seale, *Asad of Syria: The Struggle for the Middle East* (London: Tauris, 1988), p. 334.
2 Umar F. Abd-Allah, *The Islamic Struggle in Syria* (Berkeley: Mizen, 1983), p. 192.
3 *Amnesty International Report 1983* (London: Amnesty International Publications, 1983), p. 331.
4 Lisa Wedeen, *Ambiguities of Domination: Politics, Rhetoric, and Symbols in Contemporary Syria* (Chicago: University of Chicago Press, 1999), pp. 46–47.
5 Oded Haklai. "A Minority Rule Over a Hostile Majority: The Case of Syria", *Nationalism & Ethnic Politics*, Autumn 2000, Vol. 6, Issue 3, p. 31.
6 Patrick Seale, *Asad of Syria: The Struggle for the Middle East*, p. 78.
7 Oded Haklai, "A Minority Rule Over a Hostile Majority: The Case of Syria", p. 31.
8 Patrick Seale, *Asad of Syria: The Struggle for the Middle East*, pp. 92–93.
9 Lisa Wedeen, *Ambiguities of Domination: Politics, Rhetoric, and Symbols in Contemporary Syria*, p. 8; Patrick Seale, *Asad of Syria: The Struggle for the Middle East*, p. 333; Umar F. Abd-Allah, *The Islamic Struggle in Syria*, p. 192; Thomas L. Friedman, *From Beirut to Jerusalem* (New York: Farrar Straus Giroux, 1989), p. 82.
10 Moshe Mo'az, *Asad: Sphinx of Damascus: A Political Biography* (London: Weiden & Nicolson, 1988), p. 155.
11 Flynt Leverett, *Inheriting Syria: Bashar's Trial by Fire* (Washington: Brookings, 2005), p. 232, note 36.

12 Patrick Seale, *Asad of Syria: The Struggle for the Middle East*, p. 17.
13 Flynt Leverett, *Inheriting Syria: Bashar's Trial by Fire*, p. 232, note 36.
14 Thomas L. Friedman, *From Beirut to Jerusalem*, p. 79.
15 Patrick Seale, *Asad of Syria: The Struggle for the Middle East*, p. 329.
16 *Amnesty International Report 1982* (London: Amnesty International Publications, 1982), p. 347.
17 Robert Fisk, *Pity the Nation: The Abduction of Lebanon* (New York: Thunder's Mouth Press, 2002), p. 182.
18 Kathrin Nina Wiedl, *The Hama Massacre – Reasons, Supporters of the Rebellion, Consequences* (Munich: Grin Verlag, 2006).
19 The version of the massacre presented here is derived from accounts presented by Umar F. Abd-Allah, Robert Fisk in *Pity the Nation* (above) and *The Great War for Civilisation: The Conquest of the Middle East* (London: Fourth Estate, 2005), Thomas L. Friedman, Moshe Ma'oz, Patrick Seale, and Carstan Wieland, *Syria at Bay: Secularism, Islamism and 'Pax Americana'* (London: Hurst, 2006).
20 Thomas L. Friedman, *From Beirut to Jerusalem*, p. 86.
21 Patrick Seale, *Asad of Syria: The Struggle for the Middle East*, p. 334.
22 Moshe Mo'az, *Asad: Sphinx of Damascus: A Political Biography*, p. 163.
23 Umar F. Abd-Allah, *The Islamic Struggle in Syria*, pp. 193–94.
24 Thomas L. Friedman, *From Beirut to Jerusalem*, p. 101.
25 Lisa Weeden, *Ambiguities of Domination: Politics, Rhetoric, and Symbols in Contemporary Syria*, pp. 46–47.
26 Lisa Wedeen, *Ambiguities of Domination: Politics, Rhetoric, and Symbols in Contemporary Syria*.
27 Robert Fisk, *The Great War for Civilisation: The Conquest of the Middle East*, p. 1006.
28 Ibid., p. 1014.
29 Ibid., p. 672.
30 Flynt Leverett, *Inheriting Syria: Bashar's Trial by Fire*, pp. 106–08.
31 Carstan Wieland, *Syria at Bay: Secularism, Islamism and 'Pax Americana'* (London: Hurst, 2006), p. 107.

12

Israel: Stillborn Nation

Dale Darychuk

✧

The struggle of man against power is the struggle of memory against forgetting.
Milan Kundera

Western literature, art and history are replete with stories of birth, death and rebirth. The creation of the state of Israel in 1948 is the most recent significant example of this archetype. After the Holocaust and the rejection of Jewish refugees by western countries, Jews were given a haven in what the Zionist ideology defined as their ancient homeland where they were supposed to be able to live in peace and security. The labour pains of this rebirth were felt mostly by the Palestinian people who occupied the lands destined to belong to Israel. They suffered massacres, rapes, and wholesale destruction of hundreds of villages that preceded their mass exodus. These events are collectively called *al-Nakba* in Arabic, which translates as "the catastrophe". The fundamental moral question surrounding the creation of the state of Israel that has remained largely unasked and certainly unanswered for 60 years is, "How can one condone the expulsion of one people from its homeland to make room for another?"[1] After setting out the historical background surrounding the *Nakba*, I will discuss the reasons why the telling of the stories of the *Nakba* has been so slow in coming and why even when the stories are told, their full moral weight is either ignored or marginalized.

Historical Background

The *Nakba* had its beginnings in the late 19th century. In 1895, Theodor Herzl, one of the founders of the Zionist movement, described a two-part plan to remove the Palestinians from their land to establish the state of Israel. "We shall try to spirit the penniless population across the border by procuring employment for it in the transit countries while denying it any employment in our country... Both the process of expropriation and removal of the poor must be carried out discreetly and circumspectly." As for the rich, his plan was to buy them out. "Let the owners of immovable property believe that they are cheating us, selling things for more than they are worth. But we are not going to sell them anything back."[2] Despite this bold statement, the land holdings of the Jewish community and Zionist institutions in Palestine were estimated to be only between 5.6 and 7 percent at the end of the British Mandate (1921 to 1948).[3] The Zionist vision was encouraged by the Balfour declaration of 1917 which spoke of a national home for the Jewish people. British Foreign Secretary Balfour anticipated that western public opinion would favour the establishment of the Jewish state over the human rights of the Palestinian people when he stated:

> In Palestine we do not propose to go through the form of consulting the wishes of the present inhabitants of the country... Zionism, be it right or wrong, good or bad, is rooted in age-old traditions, in present needs, in future hopes, of far profounder import than the desires and prejudices of 700,000 Arabs who now inhabit the ancient land."[4]

On November 29, 1947, the United Nations General Assembly passed a resolution calling for the partition of Palestine into two states: a Jewish state and an Arab one. The Jewish state was to be established on 56 percent of Palestinian territory with a slight Jewish majority of 499,000 Jews to 438,000 Palestinians. The Arab state was to be comprised of 43 percent of the country and would include 818,000 Palestinians and fewer than 10,000 Jews.[5] In the proposed Jewish state, Jewish holdings were 11 percent compared to 80 percent of land then owned by Palestinians. In the proposed Arab Palestinian state, Jews owned only 1 percent of the land.[6] The ownership of over half of Palestine was not enough to satisfy the colonization goals of one of the leaders of the Zionist movement, David Ben-Gurion, who "saw partition as a stepping stone to further expansion and eventual takeover of the whole of Palestine."[7]

In a letter to his son Amos, Ben-Gurion declared,

> [A] Jewish state in part [of Palestine] is not an end, but a beginning... Our possession is important not only for itself... through this we increase our power, and every increase in power facilitates getting hold of the country in its entirety. Establishing a [small] state... will serve as a very potent lever in our historical efforts to redeem the whole country.[8]

Despite the vote for partition, the United Nations took no steps to implement the two-state proposal. The Palestinians opposed partition and supported the establishment of a political system that would reflect the wishes of the majority. The Palestinian position is summarized by the historian Walid Kahlidi:

> The Palestinians failed to see why they should be made to pay for the Holocaust..., and recalled that Zionism was born in the 1880s, long before the advent of the Third Reich. They failed to see why it was not fair for the Jews to be a minority in a unitary Palestinian State, while it was fair for almost half of the Palestinian population—the indigenous majority on its own ancestral soil—to be converted overnight into a minority under alien rule in the envisaged Jewish State.[9]

After the United Nations partition resolution, skirmishes broke out between the *Yishuv* (pre-Israel Jewish population) and the Arabs, resulting in civil strife. Worried about the developing Cold War between the Soviets and the Americans and not wanting to upset the Americans, the British prepared to evacuate Palestine. The planned date was originally set for August 1, 1948 but then moved up to May 15, 2008. Fearing that the Americans would withdraw support for partition in favour of an international trusteeship, the *Haganah*, the main Jewish military force, began a large-scale offensive called Plan D, the aim of which was to capture all of the land allocated to the proposed Jewish state, as well as areas of Galilee and on the highway between Tel Aviv and Jerusalem that were part of the proposed Palestinian state.[10] The plan, as quoted in Morris,[11] was to create "operations against enemy settlements which are in the rear of, within or near our defence lines, with the aim of preventing their use as bases for an active armed force." Morris points out that the effect of the plan in such a small country was to place most Palestinian towns and villages within this category. Brigade commanders were given discretion to destroy the villages or leave them standing.[12]

In the execution of Plan D, the Zionist forces expelled people from their towns and villages, committed rapes and other acts of violence, massacred civilians, and executed prisoners of war. These acts have been widely documented, most forcefully by Israeli historians using military and state archives.[13]

It was not until May 15, a month and a half after the implementation of Plan D, that neighbouring Arab states sent in armed forces to attempt to halt the Zionist actions. But by then, many acts of expulsion and atrocities had already occurred. The massacre of civilians at Deir Yassin was especially brutal. This village had signed non-aggression agreements with adjacent Jewish settlements and the *Mukhtar* (village leader) not only rejected proposals by Arab militias to station themselves in the village but also passed information to the *Haganah* regarding the movement of Arab forces in the area. It was attacked by a joint *Irgun*-LEHI force that by conservative estimates slaughtered about 115 men, women and children and stuffed their bodies down wells.[14] The massacre was widely publicized through mobile loudspeaker units in cities such as Jaffa[15] and Haifa and through Arab radio, creating tremendous fear in the civilian Palestinian population and hastening their exodus. Following the massacre, future Nobel Peace Prize winner and Israeli Prime Minister, Menachem Begin sent a letter to his commanders saying, "Accept congratulations on this splendid act of conquest... Tell the soldiers you have made history in Israel."[16] Saleh Abdel Jawad has documented sixty-eight massacres of Palestinians in 1948 by Zionist and Israeli forces.[17] Between Haifa and Tel Aviv, 58 out of 64 of the Palestinian villages were wiped out.[18] The 1948 War led to the destruction of 420 Palestinian towns and the expulsion of at least 750,000 Palestinians. This was more than one-half of the Palestinian population and 80 percent of the Palestinians who lived in the territories upon which the Jewish State was established.[19]

Israeli Rationalization

The mainstream Israeli narrative of the events of 1948 emphasizes the glorious rebirth of an ancient people after tremendous suffering, redeemed by the establishment of their own modern nation-state complete with sovereignty, a flag, an anthem, a history and a future. The Jewish diaspora could come home to safety after wandering the world for two millennia. What is missing from this narrative is the presence of the Palestinians, whose fate could only be an embarrassment to the colonizers. The eminent Israeli historian, Benny Morris, has taken a special interest in the events of 1948 and has written several books on this topic. In 1988, he published a comprehensive history of the events of 1948 entitled *Birth of the Palestinian Refugee Problem.* Following its publication, an enormous amount of Israeli archives became available to Morris which led him to publish a second edition. From the Israeli side, Benny Morris has devoted more research and thought to the *Nakba* than any other historian, so it is profitable to review his position. Morris acknowledges the propaganda value of the meta-narratives arising out of the events of 1948 for both Israel and the Arab states. The general Arab claim is that the Palestinians were expelled by the Jews in a pre-planned and pre-determined systematic, grand political design. The official Israeli narrative is that the Palestinians fled "voluntarily" without any Jewish compulsion, or that they were asked or ordered to do so by their leaders or by the leaders of the Arab states. Morris adopts a middle position denying that there was an agreed, systematic policy of expulsion, but acknowledging that:

> At the same time, largely as a result of Arab belligerence and the Yishuv's sense of siege, fragility and isolation, from early April 1948 on, 'transfer' was in the air and the departure of the Arabs was deeply desired on the local and national levels by the majority of the Yishuv, from Ben-Gurion down. And while this general will was never translated into systematic policy, a large number of Arabs were expelled, the frequency of expulsions and the expulsive resolve of the troops increased following the pan-Arab invasion of mid-May 1948 that threatened the Yishuv with extinction.[20]

From the summer of 1948, there was a policy, often applied with brutality, towards those who had been displaced and those who were yet to be displaced, that they should not return at all costs. "In this sense, it may fairly be said that all 700,000 or so who ended up as refugees were compulsorily displaced or 'expelled'."[21]

While premeditation is denied, opportunistic *realpolitik* is acknowledged. Morris believes that as more military and state archives become open to the public, there will be further revelations of atrocities. Morris's historiography has been the subject of considerable controversy among Israeli academics. Morris has shown courage in writing about the atrocities of 1948. He relates a conversation over lunch with a colleague who claimed to know far more about the atrocities of 1948 than was described in the *Birth*, but who would never have written about them.[22] Despite his intimate knowledge of these atrocities and his status as a leading Israeli historian, Morris does not call upon the Israeli leadership to acknowledge the immorality of the past and to address the plight of the Palestinian refugees. Instead, he has written that Ben-Gurion should have cleansed the whole country of Palestinians and, in so doing, he would have stabilized the State of Israel for generations:

> The need to establish the state (Israel) in this place overcomes the injustice that was done to the Palestinians by uprooting them... Even the great American democracy could not have been created without the annihilation of the Indians. There are cases in which the overall, final good justifies harsh and cruel acts that are committed in the course of history.[23]

Political expediency trumps basic human rights. Morris writes at a time when Israeli society is terrified by the potential of Palestinian suicide bombers and Iranian aggression. His present need to feel secure overshadows his knowledge of the truth of the *Nakba*. We can view Morris' stance as an example of the importance of creating and maintaining a powerful myth to explain away "minor details".

Another instance of Israeli moral blindness can be seen in the enactment of the Law of Return which was passed by the Knesset in 1950. It declares that Israel constitutes a home not only for the inhabitants of the State but also for all members of the Jewish people everywhere, regardless of their personal circumstances. The purpose of the Law of Return was to re-establish a home for the entire Jewish people in *Eretz Yisrael*, the Land of Israel. The law gives the right of return to Israel to all those born Jewish (having a Jewish mother or grandmother), those with Jewish ancestry (having a Jewish father or grandfather) and those who have converted to Judaism. It is the embodiment of a spiritual idea coupled with the practical goal of providing security and refuge for those facing anti-Semitic persecution. The effect of the law of return is that a Jew whose ancestors had not set foot in Palestine in 2,000 years could move to Israel and live there as a full citizen while a Palestinian who now lives only miles away from the property that his family had occupied from time immemorial could not return. The expediency of protecting one's own people, no matter how tenuous their connection to the land, trumps the injustice done to one's neighbour.

Western Complicity

European notions of enlightenment and civilization also figure prominently in the birth story of Israel. A popular slogan used to justify the establishment of Israel in Palestine was "a land without people for a people without land". The Zionists were aligned with western cultural and political values and democratic, rational institutions while the Palestinians belonged to the autocratic, feudal Arab systems. Decades of living under a British Mandate that discouraged the development of national institutions and their own failure to train an elite to take over after the departure of the British left the Palestinians vulnerable to a determined colonizer. The creation of Israel was viewed as enlightened colonialism with the kibbutz as the socialist ideal bearing fruit on virgin soil. Some Americans viewed the Zionist settlers in the same light as the first American settlers.[24]

The *Nakba* came in the wake of the Holocaust in central Europe, the heart of western civilization. How could enlightened western governments atone for this most disturbing act of inhumanity? The calming of the Western conscience could be achieved by having the Jewish people reborn with their own ethnic state. Ben-Gurion understood western guilt well when he referred to the west's support for the partition of Palestine as "western civilization's gesture of repentance for the Holocaust".[25] The suffering of the Palestinians was rendered irrelevant in the greater context.

The effect on the Palestinians was either disregarded or made into a refugee story akin to that of people who wandered in Europe after World War II. The Palestinians were relegated to the backwaters of human history, as is so elegantly described by Elias Sanbar, a Palestinian historian and writer in his essay, *Out of Place, Out of Time*:

> The contemporary history of the Palestinians turns on a key date: 1948. That year, a country and its people disappeared from maps

> and dictionaries… 'The Palestinian people does not exist,' said the new masters, and henceforth the Palestinians would be referred to by general, conveniently vague terms, as either 'refugees' or in the case of a small minority that had managed to escape the generalized expulsion, 'Israeli Arabs.' A long absence was beginning.[26]

In order for the stories of the *Nakba* to be told, there have to be listeners willing to hear them. Western nations have not wanted to hear the stories of the *Nakba*. Settler societies such as Canada, Australia and the United States have yet to come to terms with their own histories of colonization and its adverse effects on indigenous peoples. A society that does not recognize its own failings in its relationship with its indigenous peoples is unlikely to be sympathetic to indigenous groups in an "exotic" part of the world.

Palestinian Reaction

The creation of Israel generated a Palestinian diaspora dividing the Palestinian population into numerous groups – including those remaining in the newly created Israel (estimated to be between 60,000 and 156,000), those in the West Bank who came under the harsh regime of the Hashemites – the rulers of Jordan, and those who resided in the Gaza Strip, who were subjected to an uncaring Egyptian administration. The effect was to fracture Palestinian collective life into distinct parts with very limited communication between the groups. Divided families would send heart-breaking greetings across airwaves without any expectation of a response or even knowledge of its reception on the other end. Only after the 1967 War, when Israel brought the Gaza and the West Bank under military occupation, was there the opportunity for the different Palestinian communities to construct a collective narrative of their experience.

Palestinian society has not been able to go through the cycle of grieving[27] that is required to mourn the losses suffered in the *Nakba*. For a long time after 1948, the *Nakba* was known as *sanat-al-hujayi* – the act of escaping from a grave danger, or *sanat al-hijra* – the year of migration, a term carrying with it the heavy symbolism of the Prophet Muhammad's flight from Mecca to Medina, a migration that carried with it the promise of triumphal return. As time went on and the prospect of return became more hope than reality, the use of the term *Nakba* prevailed. Despite the acknowledgement that they had suffered a catastrophe, Palestinians did not actively tell their stories of dispossession and loss. There are several factors that have hindered both the telling of individual Palestinian stories and the creation of a Palestinian collective narrative of the *Nakba.*

1. The victory of the Zionists demonstrated the inability of Arab military and political forces to unite in a common defence. The Arab population was humbled by their defeat and ashamed of their vulnerability making it difficult for them to acknowledge the facts of the Nakba.
2. The military tactic of raping of women and girls is viewed as particularly horrific in Arab and Muslim societies. The victims were reluctant to discuss their ordeals and their male kin were rendered powerless by their inability to protect their female relatives. The loss of honour was so great that rather than suffer further trauma, memories of rape were submersed. Warnock characterizes this aversion to rape among Palestinians as "the Achilles heel of national resistance".[28]
3. In many ways, the *Nakba* is not over for the Palestinian people. They have suffered further occupation as a result of the 1967 war, military bombardment in the refugee camps in Shatila and Sabra in Lebanon, and the daily humiliation of checkpoints and further Israeli settlement of their lands. Victims of trauma need time to do the "memory work" to articulate their stories. They need to have a detached presence in order to relate to the past. Although the actual physical events of the *Nakba* took place over a few months in 1948, the *Nakba* is not over yet:

   > The *Nakba* became a constituent of Palestinians' sense of identity not only because of the scale of their loss, but also because it generates new catastrophes that scar each succeeding generation afresh. It cannot be separated from what happened afterward; to view it as an event, recorded and classified, would be to mask its meaning as a continuing predicament.[29]

   For many Palestinians, the exigencies of daily life preclude the luxury of emphasizing the past. Freud teaches us that memory is the root cause of trauma but also the key to the gradual return to normality. "Revealing is healing." Mourning is crucial to the return to the normal life. Those who are not able to mourn may lapse into a pathological state such as melancholia. The experience of the *Nakba* and the subsequent catastrophes has thrown a large shadow over the Palestinian collective psyche. There is a sense of *Nakba* time, where the *Nakba* is the baseline for the history of the Palestinian people and for individual Palestinians as well. Time stands still for the Palestinians as they have not yet been able to mourn their loss. Many live in a state of melancholy unable to move forward with hope.

4. Palestinians have been denied the process of memorialization of the *Nakba*. A Palestinian equivalent to Yad Vachem does not exist. Plaques reminding of the destroyed villages, placed by sympathetic Jews, are often quickly removed. Only in the past few years have Israeli dissidents invited Palestinians to return to areas where their villages once stood to give tours to Israeli Jews to teach them about the *Nakba*. In fact, the Israeli efforts to memorialize the Holocaust in Israel complement the prevailing Zionist view denying the former presence of the Palestinians. To commemorate victims of the Holocaust, whole forests of European fir trees not native to Palestine have been planted in areas formerly occupied by destroyed Palestinian villages and towns, including an area now called "Canada Park". These trees hide the Mediterranean ground cover, removing both the memory of the natural environment and of the people who once inhabited the land.
5. In researching and discussing the events of 1948, Israeli historians have had the advantages of writing from the winning side and with the basic tools of western historiography – written documents. On the Palestinian side, there were never any official archives. The reliance on oral histories has its weaknesses as their reliability decreases with time. The generation that directly experienced the *Nakba* is rapidly disappearing. The phenomenon of post-memory – the experience of having one's everyday reality overshadowed by the memory of a much more significant past that one's parents lived through – affects both children of Holocaust survivors and of the *Nakba*.[30] The difference is that the Holocaust has been recognized and denounced but the *Nakba* remains unacknowledged.

Conclusion

Present-day Israel is obsessed with issues of security and defence. Most of these concerns have their roots in the *Nakba*. Despite the mythical quality of the official Israeli narrative of the events of 1948, the *Nakba* casts a shadow over the collective identity of Israelis as a moral community, as a people who face responsibility. In this sense, the state of Israel remains stillborn. Barthes tells us that "myth does not deny things... simply it purifies them, it makes them innocent, it gives them a natural and eternal justification... it abolishes the complexity of human acts, it gives them the simplicity of essence, it does away with all dialectics."[31]

Until the myths surrounding the creation of Israel are deconstructed and the stories of the *Nakba* as documented by historians such as Benny Morris and as told by survivors penetrate the moral consciousness of the Israeli people, they will continue to deny the tainted genesis of their nation. With this denial, Israelis fail to show empathy and are not able to move to an understanding and an equitable resolution of the conflict, particularly the vexatious question of the return of refugees. Unlike Elie Wiesel, who defends Israel, including its mistakes, enlightened Israelis must come to terms with their past and make the necessary amends in order to move forward in security and peace.

NOTES

1 Ahmad H. Sa'di & Lila Abu-Lughod (eds.), *Nakba, Palestine, 1948 and the Claims of Memory* (New York: Columbia University Press, 2007), p. 295. For an excellent and thorough discussion of the *Nakba* from the Palestinian point of view, this compilation of essays is highly recommended.

2 Theodor Herzl, *The Complete Diaries of Theodor Herzl*, Vol. 1 (Edited by Raphael Patai) (New York: Herzl Press and Thomas Yoselov, 1960), p. 88.

3 Sami Hadawi, *Palestinian Rights and Losses in 1948* (London: Al-Saqi, 1988); John Ruedy, "Dynamics of Land Alienation in Palestine" in Ibrahim Abu-Lughod (ed.), *The Transformation of Palestine* (Evanston: Northwestern University Press, 1971), pp. 119–38; Walid Khalidi, *Before their Diaspora: A Photographic History of the Palestinians 1876–1948* (Washington, DC: Institute for Palestine Studies, 1991).

4 Sir Anthony Nutting, *Balfour And Palestine: A Legacy of Deceit* (London: The Council for the Advancement of Arab-British Understanding, n.d.), p. 5.

5 Walid Khalidi, "Revisiting the UNGA Partition Resolution", *Journal of Palestinian Studies* 27, no. 1 (1997), p. 11.

6 Ibid., p. 13.

7 Benny Morris, "Revisiting the Palestinian Exodus of 1948", in Eugene Rogan and Avi Shlaim (eds.), *The War for Palestine: Rewriting the History of 1948* (Cambridge: Cambridge University Press, 2001), p. 138.

8 Ibid.

9 Walid Khalidi, *Before their Diaspora: A Photographic History of the Palestinians 1876–1948*, pp. 305–06.
10 Simha Flapan, *The Birth of Israel: Myths and Realities* (London: Croom Helm, 1987), p. 42.
11 Benny Morris, *The Birth of the Palestinian Refugee Problem Revisited* (Cambridge: Cambridge University Press, 2004), p. 164.
12 Ibid., p. 165.
13 Ahmad H. Sa'di & Lila Abu-Lughod (eds.), *Nakba, Palestine, 1948 and the Claims of Memory*, p. 292.
14 Charles Smith, *Palestine and the Arab-Israeli Conflict*, 5th ed. (Boston: Bedford/ St. Martin's, 2004), p. 194.
15 Before its surrender, Jaffa had been one of Palestine's largest and wealthiest cities, with a population of over 100,000. In the 1947 UN partition plan for Palestine, the city was given to the Palestinians even though it lay in the heart of the planned Jewish State. As soon as the British Government had announced its intention to pull out of Palestine, Jaffa became the scene of some of the most vicious fighting between poorly armed Palestinian irregulars and the *Haganah*, more particularly *Irgun* militias. When it surrendered on on May 13, 1948, Jaffa was a ghost city with only three to four thousand inhabitants.
16 Michael Palumbo, *The Palestinian Catastrophe: the 1948 Expulsion of a People from Their Homeland* (London, Boston: Faber and Faber, 1987), p. 55.
17 Saleh Abdel Jawad, *Why the Palestinians "Left" Their Paradise? Rewriting the Creation of the Palestinian Refugee Tragedy* (Forthcoming).
18 Ilan Pappé, *A History of Modern Palestine: One Land, Two Peoples (*Cambridge: Cambridge University Press, 2004), p. 137.
19 Ahmad H. Sa'di & Lila Abu-Lughod (eds.), *Nakba, Palestine, 1948 and the Claims of Memory*, p. 297.
20 Benny Morris, *The Birth of the Palestinian Refugee Problem Revisited*, p. 589.
21 Ibid.
22 Benny Morris, *1948 and After: Israel and the Palestinians* (Oxford: Clarendon Press, 2003), p. 47.
23 Benny Morris, "Mikhake la-barbarim" [Waiting for the Barbarians], *Ha'aretz*, January 6, 2004.
24 Ahmad H. Sa'di & Lila Abu-Lughod (eds.), *Nakba, Palestine, 1948 and the Claims of Memory*, p. 296.
25 Benny Morris, *Righteous Victim: A History of the Zionist-Arab Conflict, 1881–2001* (New York: Vintage, 2001), p. 186.
26 Elias Sanbar, *Mediterranean Historical Review*, 16, no. 1 (2001), p. 87.
27 Elizabeth Kubler-Ross's cycle of grief with its five stages of denial, anger, bargaining, depression and finally, acceptance.
28 Kitty Warnock, *Land Before Honour: Palestinian Women in the Occupied Territories* (New York: Monthly Review Press, 1990), p. 23.
29 Ahmad H. Sa'di & Lila Abu-Lughod (eds.), *Nakba, Palestine, 1948 and the Claims of Memory*, p. 153.
30 Ahmad H. Sa'di, "Catastrophe, Memory and Identity: Al-Nakbah as a Component of Palestinian Identity", *Israel Studies 7*, no. 2 (2002), p. 177.
31 Roland Barthes, *Mythologies* (London: Vintage, 2000), p. 143.

13

THE 2002 MASSACRE OF GUJARATI MUSLIMS: THE VIOLENT FACE OF HINDU NATIONALISM

Vinit Khosla

✧

We have no orders to protect you.
Gujarati police officer

Background

From February 28, 2002, until mid-June that year, thousands of Gujarati Muslims were killed, beaten or raped by Hindu mobs. Muslim homes, businesses and places of worship were destroyed. These incidents have been described as "communal violence" or "Hindu-Muslim riots". While it is true that both sides rioted and committed acts of violence, such terms are speciously neutral – they mask the nature and size of the carnage inflicted upon the Muslim minority. At the time, a state government spokesman described the killings as "spontaneous". However, almost every independent investigation has concluded that the invasion of Muslim neighbourhoods in Gujarat was carefully planned and efficiently executed, and, further, that the state government and police force were integral to this coordinated effort. The Central Government did not provide active support for the attacks, but it did nothing to stop them when they were at their worst. Since the massacre, government support or compensation for victims has been reprehensibly weak. There has been no official apology. The identities of many of the perpetrators of crimes remain unknown, and of the people arrested, few have been convicted. More significantly, none of the Hindu nationalist leaders or senior government officials who acted as instigators have been brought to justice for their complicity and criminal negligence. When there is such a dark cloud hanging over the role of the state, we must turn to the accounts of eyewitnesses, journalists and independent human rights groups to get a true picture of what happened.

This atrocity is intimately linked to the relatively recent rise of Hindu nationalism, or *Hindutva* (meaning "Hindu-ness"). The major exponent of this ethos is the RSS (Rashtriya Swayamsevak Sangh), a sprawling organization with religious, educational and political arms, one that writer Pankaj Mishra describes as "dedicated to establishing a Hindu nation by uniting Hindus from all castes and sects and by forcing Muslims, Christians and other Indian minorities to embrace Hindu culture."[1] A primary effect of this unification effort has been the instilling of hatred of Muslims among Hindus. The RSS has been particularly successful in doing this in Gujarat. Moreover, the fact that the BJP (Bharatiya Janata Party, the political arm of the organization) was the ruling party in Gujarat allowed RSS members to infiltrate important positions of authority in government and law enforcement agencies. These conditions allowed Hindu nationalists, both plain citizens and officials, to carry out a pogrom against Gujarati Muslims in 2002, all the while presenting their actions as a spontaneous retaliation.

The fact that the RSS is a movement with national aspirations should cause Indians to worry. A movement based on the presumed ethnicity of the majority directly contradicts the vision of a secular, democratic and pluralistic society – not just in Gujarat, but across India.

A Brief Account of the Gujarat Massacre

The events in 2002 have a direct link to another episode of communal violence a decade earlier. On December 6, 1992, a huge crowd of Hindus destroyed the Babri Masjid in Ayodhya, as police watched. The destruction of the mosque was inspired by the belief that the mosque had been erected on the site of a Hindu temple and the birthplace of the deity Ram. The campaign to destroy the mosque was led by BJP politician L.K. Advani. The BJP also led the charge to build a new Hindu temple on its ruins, in defiance of a Supreme Court injunction. On February 27, 2002, a trainload of volunteers for this project, members of the VHP (the Vishwa Hindu Parishad, the religious arm of the RSS), was returning to Gujarat from Ayodhya on the Sabarmati Express. When their train stopped in the town of Godhra, they were met by a mob of angry Muslims. Two train cars were set on fire, and 58 Hindu passengers were burned alive. There is controversy about whether the fire was pre-planned or an accident. What was clearly untrue was what Gujarat Chief Minister Narendra Modi immediately claimed – that the fire was the work of the Pakistani ISI. This was only one of the ways Modi turned the train burning incident to his political advantage. He also supported the VHP's call for a state-wide strike on February 28. The ostensible purpose of the strike was to allow for funeral processions to take place in Ahmedabad. However the strike was more importantly a call to action among the VHP cadre, especially since most of the victims did not come from Ahmedabad. Given that the state government did not take preventive measures against the chaos that had to be expected, Modi's endorsement of the strike made "violence virtually inevitable",[2] as senior police officials later admitted.

On the day of the procession, and in the weeks that followed, thousands of Hindu militants descended on Muslim neighbourhoods. The attacks began in Ahmedabad and spread to 151 towns and 1993 villages in Gujarat. They occurred between February 28 and March 3, and restarted on March 15, continuing until June. Muslims were shot, stabbed, clubbed or hacked to death; they were made to watch the burning of their children before being burned themselves. The official death toll is 1004 (790 Muslims and 254 Hindus), but independent reports, such as the one from Amnesty International,[3] claim it is over 2000, mostly Muslim. The treatment of women was particularly horrific. An international women's committee concluded that "sexual violence was being used as a strategy for terrorizing women belonging to a minority community in the state."[4] Eyewitnesses report that "mobs gathered round and raped women. Then they poured kerosene down their throats and the throats of their children and threw lighted matches onto them."[5] Human Rights Watch reports that "in some cases, pregnant women had their bellies cut open and their fetuses pulled out and hacked or burned before the women were killed."[6] The attacks also resulted in massive destruction of property. The *New York Times* reported that "more than 20,000 homes and businesses were damaged or destroyed, along with 360 Muslim places of worship."[7] As Muslims fled their communities, mobs burned and looted their homes.

As a result, most of the 100,000 displaced Muslims currently living in refugee camps are completely dispossessed of all their belongings.

What needs emphasis is the systematic nature of the attacks. The militants all wore white shirts, khaki shorts and saffron scarves, identifying them as members of the Bajrang Dal, the youth wing of the RSS. Indian rights activist Arundhati Roy writes: "They were armed with petrol bombs, guns, knives, swords and tridents... They had trucks loaded with thousands of gas cylinders, hoarded weeks in advance, which they used to blow up Muslim commercial establishments."[8] Other empty trucks were on hand to carry away the loot. Mob leaders were equipped with voter and business lists obtained from government sources, enabling them to target Muslim homes and even Muslim shops with Hindu names. The Godhra incident provided the militants with the go-ahead for actions for which they were well–prepared; it was a pretext, rather than a provocation.

The Role of the Authorities

The Gujarat Government

Roy writes that "the pogrom ... has at best been conducted under the benign gaze of the State and, at worst, with active State collusion."[9] The "benign gaze" is encapsulated in Modi's remark, on March 1: "Every action has an equal and opposite reaction... The ... 50 million people of Gujarat have shown remarkable restraint under grave provocation." In a high profile case documented by the Indian National Human Rights Commission (NHRC),[10] former Muslim MP Ahsan Jaffrey pleaded with the Police Commissioner for police reinforcements to protect him and other Muslims he was harbouring from the mobs surrounding his house. The Commissioner assured him help was on its way, and that Modi was aware of the situation. The help never arrived. Jaffrey, his family and 37 others were burned alive. But the state did not merely stand by and watch. Independent reports suggest an active alliance between political power – the BJP – and religious power – the VHP, both members of the same Hindu nationalist family. Senior police officials told the *New York Times* that workers and officials of the party and the council were complicit in the attacks and, in some cases, instigated the mobs.[11] They also confirmed the truth of another report – that "a key BJP state minister ... [took] over police control rooms in Ahmedabad on the first day of the carnage, issuing orders to disregard pleas for assistance from Muslims."[12] A witness deposing before a state commission investigating the riots testified that the mobs were led by Bajrang Dal leader Babu Bajrangi, accompanied by the BJP MLA for the district, Maya Kodnani.[13] There is speculation, based on reports from intelligence officials, that the state government deliberately delayed the deployment of national paramilitary troops until March 1 to give the Hindu militants a free hand.[14]

The Police

Human Rights Watch states that the police "at best were passive observers, and at worst they acted in concert with murderous mobs and participated directly in the burning and looting of Muslim shops and homes and the killing and mutilation of Muslims."[15] There are accounts of attacks occurring adjacent to police posts, of police leading mobs and of police leading victims into the hands of attackers. On February 28, when at least 155 Muslims were killed, not a single arrest was made. During the next three days, police killed more Muslims than Hindus, while ostensibly containing Hindu violence. In many cases, police reportedly refused to record or investigate complaints (First Information Reports), or to include the names of attackers in FIRs, making arrests and convictions impossible.

Perhaps the conduct of the police should not come as a surprise – the Gujarat Police Commissioner admitted his men "were equally influenced by the general sentiment".[16] Furthermore, the police were under extreme pressure from the state. Several police officers who actually enforced the law to quell the violence were removed from their positions. But the accounts of the transferred officers demonstrate that the police could be extremely effective in mob control – if they so desired. Their testimonies undermine the state government's claim that the crowds were overwhelming, and that "the police had done the best they could".[17]

The Central Government

While the Central Government has not been accused of direct involvement in the massacre, its response was grossly insufficient. It must be remembered that then Prime Minister A. B. Vajpayee and Home Minister L. K. Advani also belonged to the BJP. They steadfastly resisted demands to fire Modi, and they were almost successful in defeating a parliament motion to censure him. Vajpayee did not visit the site of the tragedy until a month after it began. Shortly thereafter, he declared: "Let us not forget how the whole thing started. Who lit the fire? How did it spread? Wherever Muslims are, they tend not to want to live peacefully with others." By drawing people's attention to the train incident, he sought to diminish their recognition of what followed it. To the extent that the central government ensured that Modi's government would not pay a price for its complicity, it played a supportive role.

Since the Riots

Refugee Camps

Over 100,000 Muslims are estimated to be still living in refugee camps in Gujarat. Rights groups have condemned the inadequacy of state provision of food, medicine, sanitation facilities and shelter. One camp is located on the site of a Muslim graveyard, with its 6000 residents sleeping among graves. Observers also note the absence of government officials in many camps. In fact, NGOs and Muslim volunteer groups, such as the Islamiya Relief Committee, have been the ones building schools and shelters, even as their efforts are obstructed by officials.

Ghettoization

Gujarati Muslims not displaced by the attacks have not been unaffected. Those living in Muslim neighbourhoods are afraid to leave their enclaves; those living in mixed communities are afraid to leave their homes. Such restrictions have impacted their ability to find employment and provisions. The resulting impoverishment has been exacerbated by boycotts. In their December 2003 report, the International Initiative for Justice in Gujarat wrote: "In many cases, Muslims face an economic boycott, despite claims to the contrary. They remain unable to farm their fields, operate commercial vehicles, or return to their businesses. They are no longer allowed to rent stalls in public markets or fairs, and are being fired from their jobs including in the public sector."[18] Although the VHP did not claim responsibility for the leaflets promoting the boycotts, their spokesman said he was "in complete agreement with whatever is propagated through them".[19]

Compensation

The Indian government recently offered a relief package of about $66 million (US), to supplement the much smaller amount offered by the state government. This money was to go the next of kin of people killed in the riots (both Hindu and Muslim), to people with injuries, and towards damaged residential and commercial property. Apart from the small size of the amount offered, and the fact that it is based on casualty and damage figures that are seriously disputed, the package has another flaw: The payments are "ex-gratia"; the victims are not *entitled* to anything, but rather will receive money out of the good graces of government. At least the central government did not repeat the injustice of the Gujarat government, which was to initially offer Hindu victims of the train carnage twice as much as Muslim victims of the riots, on the grounds that the Hindus were victims of terrorism. One hopes that the central government will deliver on its promise – NGOs report that many victims have still not received any money from the state government.

The Justice System

According to Amnesty International, "the processes of seeking redress by victims of communal violence in Gujarat have raised concerns about the impartiality of institutions of the criminal justice system in the state, including the police, prosecution service and elements of the judiciary."[20] The lack of information from police in the First Information Reports allowed the state's judiciary to close half of the 4000 riot-related cases. Some of these were reopened as a result of a directive from the Indian Supreme Court, which was highly critical of the Gujarat government's handling of the riot cases. The irony is that the reinvestigation of the cases, and the police's role in them, was carried out by the very ones accused of complicity in the attacks – the Gujarat police. More arrests were made, but to date there have been only a handful of convictions. And not a single senior politician, police officer or RSS member has been charged with a criminal offence – let alone convicted – for their role in the massacre. The partiality of the state's judiciary is well-exemplified by the Best Bakery case. A Gujarat court initially acquitted all accused of burning 14 people alive inside the bakery. Acting on a petition, the Indian Supreme Court ordered a retrial outside the state, which produced nine convictions. This was the first time a retrial had been ordered outside the state, underlining the lack of credibility of its judiciary. Another case was ordered "shifted to a competent court in Mumbai".[21] It involved Bilkis Bano, a woman who was gang raped while pregnant, and then forced to witness the massacre of her daughter and 13 other family members. Apparently she could not get justice in her home state.

There is gross injustice to the Muslims who have been illegally and arbitrarily detained, tortured or denied access to lawyers. Also, Muslims were arrested and detained under the provisions of the Prevention of Terrorism Act (POTA), while Hindus were subject to normal Indian criminal law. Journalist Edward Luce writes that, as of 2006, "more than 200 Muslims remain incarcerated without trial"[22] under POTA provisions.

The state government's investigation into Godhra and its aftermath has been tainted by its lack of independence. The two members of the Nanavati Commission were handpicked by Modi; Justice Shah was known for his proximity to the BJP. Several organizations withdrew from the process in 2003 when the Commission, without even having held hearings in a number of affected areas, was uncritical of the way the Gujarati government had handled the communal clashes. In September 2008, the Commission determined that the train fire was a pre-planned conspiracy, and that there "is absolutely no evidence to show that either the Chief Minister and/or other Minister(s) in his Council or Police officers had played any role in the Godhra incident or that there was any lapse on their part in the matter of providing protection, relief and rehabilitation to the victims of communal riots… there is no evidence of any definite religious or political organization in the conspiracy." The report almost ignores the "post-Godhra" incidents, except, amazingly, to "not find anything therein establishing any connection between them and the burning of S-6 of Sabarmati Express train at Godhra".[23] Such statements completely contradict both independent reports and common knowledge.

Lack of Recognition

It would be unfair to say the Gujarat massacre has been forgotten. Many individuals, groups and sections of the Indian media have given their support to the affected Muslims and continue to demand justice. Moreover, the memory of Gujarat is kept alive by new episodes of communal violence in other parts of India. But the role of the state in the massacre is clearly unrecognized. The fact that no state authorities have been held to account more than six years later is depressing evidence of lack of official acknowledgement. The current non-BJP central government, which does not want to offend its Hindu constituency, helps to bury the truth through delay and the relegation of responsibility to the state government. Modi's re-election in a landslide victory at the end of 2002 and his continuing rule in Gujarat make it almost impossible to formally recognize the Gujarat government's culpability. They also indicate widespread acceptance of the actions of Hindu militants and their collaborators in government. It seems the fires of Hindu nationalism still burn brightly.

Hindu Nationalism

If the train burning was the trigger for the attacks, Hindu nationalism laid the groundwork for them; they were almost a disaster waiting to happen. To understand Gujarat, we need to place it in the context of religious nationalism.

Hindu nationalists are proud of their ancient heritage, but their organization's roots are actually quite recent. The RSS was founded in 1925 by K. B. Hegdewar, partly to assert the traditional power of upper-caste Brahmins fearful of democratization, but largely to forge a new national identity based on the Hindu religion and culture. In the organization's manifesto, Guru Golwalkar writes: "The foreign races in Hindustan must either adopt the Hindu culture and language… must entertain no other idea but those of the glorification of the Hindu race and culture, i.e. of the Hindu nation and must lose their separate existence to merge in the Hindu race, or stay in the country wholly subordinated to the Hindu nation, claiming nothing, deserving no privileges, far less any preferential treatment – not even citizens' rights."[24]

Luce writes: "Most people think of their nation as a natural entity awakened by history, oppression, or revolution. But this view overlooks the way in which nations seek to establish their identity by defining themselves against other nation-states. One of the principal tools of nation-building is the selective rummaging through history for events that can provide rallying stories or myths."[25] The Hindu nationalist image of a pure, unified country that was corrupted by foreign forces is belied by India's pluralist past. As Mishra notes, "The bewildering diversity of people that inhabited India before the arrival of the Muslims hardly formed a community, much less than a nation, and the word "Hinduism" barely hinted at the almost infinite number of folk and ethnic cultures, religious sects, and philosophical traditions found in India."[26] The often-cited tolerance of other religions and cultures is not the "Hindu heritage", it is the Indian heritage. And most of India's Muslims are not descendants of "foreigners" – their ancestors were low-caste Indians seeking to improve their status.

But for religious nationalists, *Hindutva* was an empowering doctrine that restored former glory and challenged Muslim and Christian narratives. It conflicted with the principles of India's secular nationalist movement, and the rift between the two deepened with partition of the country in 1947. For Hindu nationalists, their sacred country was being broken up, and they held Gandhi responsible. Gandhi was assassinated in 1948 by N. R. Godse, a member of the RSS. The partition of the country along religious lines has had dire consequences – the creation of an Islamic state on one side, and the fostering of a Hindu nation on the other. Hindu nationalism feeds on suspicion of the more than 140 million Muslims who have remained in India, forming 15% of the population. Indian Muslims are the "other" – no wonder, then, that they feel a deep sense of isolation and anxiety.

Hindu nationalism gained strength in the 1980s as the popularity of the Congress Party's brand of secular socialism began to wane. The RSS derived support from upper-caste Hindus enraged by governmental affirmative action programs, but it was also able to draw in the lower castes by appealing to the common bond of Hinduism and the need to restore the Hindu nation. The Ayodhya campaign, begun in 1987, was central to the forging of this bond. History was rewritten to demonstrate how Hinduism had been violated. It did not matter that Ram, whose birthplace was to be reclaimed, had largely been a mythical figure, or that Emperor Babar, who presumably erected the mosque, is not known to have visited Ayodhya, or that there was no proof of the existence of an ancient temple there – the movement's use of myth mobilized millions of Hindus, including many from Gujarat.

Gujarat has been described as "the country's laboratory for Hindu nationalism".[27] The RSS was able to capitalize on the desperate lot of Gujarati Dalits ("untouchables") and Adivasis (tribal groups), offering them Hinduism as a source of pride. Roy writes: "How else can you explain the project of trying to disenfranchise, drive out or exterminate the second-poorest community in this country, using as your foot soldiers the very poorest (Dalits and Adivasis)?"[28] In the years before 2002, thousands of Gujarati "foot soldiers" were indoctrinated in *rakshas* (RSS schools) and given paramilitary training. They were primed to join the mobs that attacked Muslims.

Gujarat was also the first large state where the BJP formed government, in 1995. The stage was set for the alliance of religious and political power. The religious movement, the VHP, benefited from having members of its "family" in prominent government positions, and BJP politicians like Modi could tap religious sentiments to their advantage.

The BJP duplicated its success at the national level in 1998, and in the six years of its rule, proved successful at adapting Hindu nationalism to the modern era. It continued the liberalization and economic reforms begun in 1991. Hindu nationalists lost earlier reservations about the corrupting influence of western civilization as they embraced new technologies and free-market consumerism. As Mishra notes, these reforms attracted India's relatively wealthy and expanding urban middle class; it also "attracted a generation of rich Indians who live in the United States and the United Kingdom and were eager for cultural and economic links with their ancestral land, a desire that turned nonresident Indians into the BJP's most devoted followers and sponsors and helped the BJP itself evolve rapidly, despite its Hindu nationalism, into a keen advocate of economic globalization".[29]

Modernity is often associated with secularism, but the new face of Hindu nationalism shows there is no inherent contradiction between the new forces of globalization and religiosity. Mishra observes that we got a glimpse of "the profound modernity of religious nationalism" in Gujarat, "as Benetton-clad young Hindus carted off the loot of digital cameras and DVD players in their new Japanese cars."[30]

Broader Implications of the Massacre

Given the size and power of the RSS, probably India's largest political movement, its project to create a nation founded on a constructed and imagined Hindu heritage is an enormous threat to India's pluralistic heritage and democratic aspirations. The damage to pluralism has been evident in the destruction of mixed communities in Gujarat as a result of the attacks. Refugee camps and boycotts separate Hindus and Muslims in a blatant fashion. The 2002 attacks have increased ethnic tensions across India. In a cycle of retaliation, many Hindus see the attacks as just retribution for the train burning. On the Muslim side, revenge has taken the form of terrorist attacks. In September 2002, Muslim terrorists from Pakistan murdered 35 Hindus in a Gujarati temple in response to the massacre. The following year, two bombings in Bombay killed fifty people, but this time the terrorists were home-grown. The Hindu nationalist-led massacre helped breed mutual brutalization. Luce quotes the owner of a Gujarati Muslim charity: "It is bitterly ironic that young Muslim men who had no radical instincts before the riots, came out of the riots very radicalized."[31] The cycle of retaliation has cast a pall on Hindu-Muslim relations across the country.

The challenge to secularism arises because *Hindutva* treats members of religious minorities as unequal citizens who exist only because of the "good will" of the majority, and who need to understand their place in society. Extreme Hindu nationalists enforce this message in a brutal form.

There is interdependence between pluralism and democracy in India. Luce writes: "The most important reason India has remained intact as a country is because it is a democracy. And perhaps the most important reason that India has remained a democracy is because it is so diverse."[32] India's diverse traditions require democracy and secularism to sustain them, and diversity is incompatible with the notion of nationhood founded upon the religion of the majority. The ability of Hindu nationalists to attack Gujarati Muslims with the knowledge and backing of the state is an attack on the institution of democracy. How else can one interpret the NHRC's conclusion that "there was a comprehensive failure on the part of the State Government to control the persistent violation of the rights to life, liberty, equality and dignity of the people of the State"?[33]

Because the Gujarat massacre was the result of a national movement, Indians should be concerned not just about the plight of Gujarati Muslims, but also the plight of minorities across the country, and about the state of the institutions that are meant to protect and uphold them. The capacity of Hindu nationalism to adapt to the times presents an ongoing challenge to India's relatively young and multi-ethnic democracy.

If the Indian government wants to repair the long-term damage caused by the Gujarat massacre and its aftermath, it needs to officially recognize the massacre and the state's complicity in it. A formal apology, adequate compensation for both Muslim and Hindu victims, and support for rebuilding Gujarati Muslim communities are all measures that would assist in communal reconciliation. It is also vital that the major instigators of the violence, including state government officials with a command responsibility, be brought before impartial courts or tribunals. Only then might massacre victims begin to have faith in their country's system of justice.

NOTES

1 Pankaj Mishra, *Temptations of the West* (New York: Picador, 2007), p. 89.
2 Celia W. Dugger, "Religious Riots Loom Over Indian Politics", *New York Times*, July 27, 2002.
3 "India/Abuse of the Law in Gujarat: Muslims Detained Illegally in Ahmedabad", *Amnesty International*, September 6, 2003.
4 "Intl. experts spoil Modi's party, say Gujarat worse than Bosnia", *Express India*, December 19, 2002.
5 Edward Luce, *In Spite of the Gods* (New York: Anchor Books, 2008), p. 159.
6 "'We Have No Orders to Save You', – State Participation and Complicity in Communal Violence in Gujarat", *Human Rights Watch*, April 2002, Vol. 14.
7 Celia W. Dugger, "Religious Riots Loom Over Indian Politics".
8 Arundhati Roy, "Democracy: Who is she when she's at home?", *Outlook (India)*, May 6, 2002.
9 Ibid.
10 "Report on the visit of NHRC Team headed by Chairperson, NHRC to Ahmedabad, Vadodra and Godhra", National Human Rights Commission, March 22, 2002.
11 Celia W. Dugger, "Religious Riots Loom Over Indian Politics".
12 "'We Have No Orders to Save You', – State Participation and Complicity in Communal Violence in Gujarat", *Human Rights Watch*, April 2002, Vol. 14.
13 "Riot witness names MLA, says she led Naroda mob", *Times of India*, September 30, 2003.
14 Rahul Bedi, "Soldiers 'held back to allow Hindus revenge'", *The Telegraph*, March 4, 2002 (http://www.telegraph.co.uk/news/worldnews/asia/india/1386725/Soldiers-%27held-back-to-allow-Hindus-revenge%27.html).
15 "'We Have No Orders to Save You', – State Participation and Complicity in Communal Violence in Gujarat", *Human Rights Watch*, April 2002, Vol. 14.
16 Celia W. Dugger, "Religious Riots Loom Over Indian Politics".
17 Celia W. Dugger, "Hindu Rioters Kill 60 Muslims in India", *New York Times*, March 1, 2002.
18 "Final Report of the International Initiative for Justice in Gujarat", *onlinevolunteers.org*, December 10, 2003.
19 "Drive for boycott of Gujarat Muslims", *Dawn*, March 22, 2002.

20 "India/Abuse of the law in Gujarat: Muslims detained illegally in Ahmedabad", *Amnesty International*, November 6, 2003.
21 "Second Riot Case Shift", *The Telegraph*, August 7, 2004.
22 Edward Luce, *In Spite of the Gods*, p. 60.
23 "Godhra, post-Godhra: Nanavati failed to see Newton's law", *Times of India*, September, 27, 2008.
24 Guru Golwalkar in Pankaj Mishra, *Temptations of the West*, p. 90.
25 Edward Luce, *In Spite of the Gods*, p. 149.
26 Pankaj Mishra, *Temptations of the West*, p. 87.
27 Celia W. Dugger, "Religious Riots Loom Over Indian Politics".
28 Arundhati Roy, "Democracy: Who is she when she's at home?", *Outlook (India)*, April 28, 2002.
29 Pankaj Mishra, *Temptations of the West*, p. 109.
30 Ibid., p. 112.
31 Hanif Lakdawala, in Edward Luce, *In Spite of the Gods*, p. 162.
32 Ibid., p. 332.
33 "Report of National Human Rights Commission on Gujarat", National Human Rights Commission, May 31, 2002.

14

Shadow Play: Political Mass Murder and the 1965 Indonesian Coup

Elaine Brière

✧

No one cared, so long as they were communists that were being butchered.

Howard Federspeil, Indonesian expert, US State Department

In the early morning hours of October 1, 1965, Indonesia plunged into the darkest period of its history. A group of army officers calling itself the September 30 Movement kidnapped six top Indonesian generals, including the commander of the army, General Yani. Within a few hours, all six were dead. While an atmosphere of Cold War intrigue and mystery still surrounds the perpetrators of the coup and their motives, there is no mystery about the results. By the next morning, General Suharto, a relative unknown, gained control of the army, blamed the Indonesian Communist Party (PKI) for the aborted coup, and, confining Indonesian President Sukarno to his quarters, proceeded to conduct what the CIA describes as "one of the worst mass murders of the 20th century, comparable to the atrocities of Hitler, Stalin, and Mao... certainly one of the most significant events of the 20th century."[1]

The victims of the massacres were members of the Communist Party (PKI) and scores of peasant and worker organizations associated with the party. The PKI was large and well-organized. It had a membership of 3 million and support base of some 30 million. It was the third largest Communist party in the world after those in China and the

Soviet Union. The PKI had won 27% of the vote in the last elections and though the party had no armed wing, it posed a serious ideological threat to the political ambitions of the army.

Indonesia became a republic after gaining independence from the Netherlands in 1946. Its popular president, Sukarno, a war hero imprisoned by the Dutch, was head of the Partai Nasional Indonesia, a key player in the liberation struggle. He was an outspoken opponent of imperialism and colonialism. Sukarno was also a founding member of the 118-member Non-Aligned Movement, along with Nehru of India, Nasser of Egypt, Tito of Yugoslavia, and Kwame Nkrumah of Ghana. In 1959 Sukarno dissolved the elected Constituent Assembly in favour of an appointed assembly which proclaimed him "President-for-Life" the following year. He believed western-style democracy would not work in Indonesia and preferred a system called "Guided Democracy", built on consensus amongst parties which were elected. Sukarno was a popular leader. Many Indonesians referred to him affectionately as Bung Karno, meaning brother or friend. He supported the Communist Party as a way of empowering peasants and workers after decades of colonial oppression and as a counter-balance to the power of the army. The Cold-War neutrality, anti-imperialism and friendly relations of the Indonesian President with the Sino and Soviet bloc countries were very worrisome to the United States.

There were serious political divisions within the armed forces and a power struggle among the top generals in the army. This power struggle is what many believe paved the way for the putsch by the September 30 Movement against those suspected of plotting a coup against President Sukarno. Carmel Budiardjo, former economist in the Sukarno government and winner of the Right Livelihood award, claims that Suharto turned attention away from the fact that the coup attempt reflected deep divisions within the leadership of the armed forces by blaming the PKI as the mastermind of the coup. There remains the question of why Suharto, then a major-general, was not among the kidnapped generals even though he commanded Kostrad, the only rapid deployment force capable of crushing a rebellion. The truth is that with these troops at his command, Suharto was quickly able to thwart the September 30 Movement the morning after the kidnappings and assume de facto control of the armed forces, replacing the murdered General Yani. This was the real beginning of the Suharto coup.

Under the pretext of protecting the president, Suharto isolated Sukarno in his palace, turning him into little more than a figurehead and marginalizing his repeated pleas to stop the killings. Sukarno kept calling for calm and railed against what he saw as absurdities in the press aimed at stirring up hatred within the country. Suharto was careful not to move against the popular president too quickly – the ousting of Sukarno took two-and-a-half years to complete.

Suharto quickly took control of the press, TV and radio. An intense anti-communist propaganda campaign accompanied one of the most extensive and brutal mass slaughters in human history. From October 1965 till March 1966 the army kept the country in a perpetual state of political and economic turmoil, using army-backed student fronts, partly paid for by the United States, to demonstrate in the streets, whipping up public sentiment against the PKI and denouncing President Sukarno. A series of media fabrications, done with a sophistication suggestive of outside expertise, set the stage for the killings. Photographs of the mutilated bodies of the dead generals were featured in all newspapers and television broadcasts, with texts claiming that the generals had been castrated and their eyes gouged out by communist women. However, later official medical autopsies completely negated these fabrications. After show trials of five core leaders of the coup, they were summarily executed, thus removing any chance of a more detailed and accurate account of the event. When the remaining coup leader, General Latief, was put on trail in 1978, he testified that he had informed Suharto of the impending coup beforehand.

The kidnapping, or "communist coup" as labelled by Suharto, gave a convenient pretext for political mass murder on a scale hitherto unrivalled in the Cold War period. The killings were organized in a military fashion and proceeded as paratroopers spread out across the country. In mid-November of 1965, the army ordered a series of "cleaning out" operations and set up special military teams to supervise the details of the killings. The massacres were particularly severe in Central and East Java, Bali and North Sumatra. Like German Jews rounded up by Nazi authorities, many dutifully appeared when called to report to army headquarters, with no idea of what was about to take place. Intellectuals, teachers, civil servants, peasants, workers and even children of suspected PKI members were slain with bullets, knives, and *parangs* (a curved Indonesian machete). Many were forced to dig their own graves. Decapitated and impaled heads were put on grisly display to instil fear and terror in the population.

Some of the most extensive series of massacres occurred as Colonel Sarwo Edhie's Army Para-commando Regiment moved from Jakarta to Central and East Java, and finally to Bali. Civilians assisting in the massacres were either recruited and trained by the army on the spot, or were drawn from groups such as army- and CIA-sponsored trade unions and student organizations which had collaborated for years with the army on political matters. Lists compiled by the military were given to right-wing Muslim groups armed with *parangs*, and transported in army trucks to villages, where they killed and mutilated. Schoolchildren were asked to point out "communists" and many so identified were shot on the spot by the army. Many were denouncements made to settle personal disputes and "on the basis of one word or the pointing of a finger, people were taken away to be killed".[2] According to former senior CIA officer Ralph McGehee, "the killing was on such a huge scale as to raise sanitation problems in East Java and Northern Sumatra, where the smell of decaying flesh was pervasive and rivers were impassible because of the clogging by human bodies."[3] In Aceh, as many as 40,000 workers in the palm oil plantations were killed and some 200,000 deaths occurred across Sumatra. The massacres in Bali were particularly extensive as many peasant, artisan and trade union organizations in Bali were affiliated with the Communist Party. Because of the extensive killings, it was difficult to buy Balinese wood carvings or musical instruments on the island for many years following the massacres.

President Sukarno, powerless as the carnage engulfed large areas of the country, repeatedly pleaded for a return to sanity. He refused to comply with Suharto's demands that the PKI be outlawed. He tried in vain to restore unity between the nationalist, religious-based and communist parties. In December, when the massacres were in full swing, Sukarno commissioned a nine-man team to investigate the scale of the slaughter. It came up with a figure of 78,000 dead but US journalist John Hughes believed the figure to be much higher:

> You mustn't forget that when we talked to officials and village headmen, they were trying to downgrade the figures of people they'd killed. On Bali they gave us a figure of 10,000. I believe it was nearer 100,000. There was covering up elsewhere, too. So I calculate that about ten times as many people were killed as we actually reported.[4]

Estimates by human rights groups range from 500,000 to 1,000,000 killed. The Amnesty International estimate for people arrested is 750,000.[5] Of these, only about 800 were brought to trial, mostly by military tribunals, and usually receiving death sentences. Amnesty International estimated that in 1977 there were still between 55,000 and 100,000 political prisoners. Many of those arrested simply disappeared. Tens of thousands were shipped to remote islands in the Indonesian archipelago where they died of malnutrition and untreated diseases. The son of the Deputy Director of the island prison of Nusakembangan, off the coast of Central Java, revealed that some 30,000 prisoners were transported to the island after 1 October 1965. He said that "prisoners were dying at a rate of twenty a day from malnutrition and disease. Every night dozens were taken... shot dead and buried in mass graves by special police brought to the island from the mainland."[6] Many thousands more were taken to the notorious Buru Island prison, where Indonesia's foremost writer and novelist, Pramoedya Toer, was imprisoned for fourteen years. The efforts of Amnesty International turned Pramoedya into a famed prisoner-of-conscience and he was eventually released. Most of the killings and arrests took place within six months of the initiation of the Suharto coup. However, massacres continued to occur sporadically as late as 1969 when army and local civic guards in Central Java "were said to have killed some 3,500 alleged followers of the PKI by means of blows of iron staves to the neck".[7]

When US investigative journalist Kathy Kadane interviewed former US Ambassador Green in 1989, he claimed the US Embassy provided lists of some 5000 names of prominent PKI activists to the army. Ambassador Green: "I know that we had a lot more information than the Indonesians themselves... My guess is that once this thing broke, the army was desperate for information as to who was who in the PKI."[8] It is likely that the US-provided lists were used to target key activists in the PKI and members of the armed forces loyal to Sukarno most likely to oppose Suharto's coup. In the Air Force, in particular, many officers were supporters of the Communist Party. Several thousand members of the Air Force, army, marines and navy were tortured and killed as the armed forces were "cleansed" of PKI sympathizers.

About five months after the initiation of the coup, on March 11, 1966, Sukarno was forced to sign a paper giving special powers to General Suharto. Although the paper was vague in its wording, Suharto used it to ban the PKI and numerous other organizations, to arrest fifteen cabinet ministers and to begin to reshape government policy. When the country's Supreme General Assembly was convened in March 1966, more than half of its members had been purged or killed. The result of the purges was to effectively disenfranchise the entire population and to turn the political parties into loyal supporters of the government. Golkar, the party of the army, gained control of a majority of seats in the general assembly, giving the army effective veto power and control over all aspects of government. Civil society in Indonesia had come to an end.

The killings provoked no international outcry or condemnation in the western press and on the contrary were warmly greeted by a leading editorial in *The New York Times* as "a gleam of light in Asia",[9] and by the *Toronto Globe and Mail*: "It is both encouraging and remarkable that responsible leaders have emerged in Indonesia."[10] Most western media reports downplayed the responsibility of the army for the killings and played up the role of civilians. Orientalist stereotypes came to the fore as Indonesians were betrayed as primitive, savage and backward. A *New York Times* headline on one of C. L. Sulzberger's editorials read "When A Nation Runs Amok". It describes the killings as almost normal in "violent Asia, where life is cheap".[11] *Life* magazine meanwhile stated: "Nowhere but on these weird and lovely islands... could affairs have erupted so unpredictably, so violently, tinged not only with fanaticism but with blood-lust and something like witchcraft."[12] In a lengthier article in the *New Yorker*, Robert Shaplen repeated the same storyline. It was unfair for what he called "the rest of the 'rational' world" to expect the Indonesians to feel they had done anything wrong because "the Indonesians were able to explain the bloodbath, at least to their own satisfaction, in ancient terms of catharsis and the eradication of evil."[13] Instead of bureaucratically organized state violence, the massacres were largely portrayed as spontaneous popular pogroms against a political minority that had lost all claims to humanity. An article by Far Eastern correspondent George McArthur that appeared on November 15, 1978 in the *Los Angeles Times – Boston Globe* completely reverses the roles of the actors in the 1965 events: "The Indonesians broke relations with the US in 1965, when the Mao-inspired Communist Party, now outlawed, attempted to seize power and subjected the country to a bloodbath."[14] The victims had now become the perpetrators.

The removal of Sukarno and the installing of the "New Order" regime of General Suharto accomplished a dramatic reversal of US fortunes in Indonesia. Before the 1965 coup the US Embassy routinely faced PKI-led anti-imperialist demonstrations at its gates. Workers were seizing plantations and oil wells owned by US companies and the government was threatening to nationalize US assets. According to Indonesian scholar John Roosa, in *Pretext for Mass Murder*, "The loss of Indonesia would have been a very large loss for the United States, much costlier than the loss of Indochina."[15] In a 1965 speech President Nixon justified the bombing of North Vietnam as a means to safeguard Indonesia's "immense mineral potential". He called Indonesia "the region's richest hoard of natural resources... by far the greatest prize in Southeast Asia".

Indonesia was coveted by the United States because of its immense resources and strategic location. Repeated attempts were made to bring Indonesia into the US sphere of influence before the events of October 1, 1965. John Roosa claims that between 1958 and 1965 the United States trained, funded, advised and supplied the army so precisely that it could turn itself into "a state within a state".[16] Under the command of General Nasution (who later openly demanded the extermination of all three million Communist Party members with all their followers and sympathizers) and Chief of Staff General Yani, the army gradually expanded its powers, consolidated its officer corps, created a political party, Golkar, and made itself a government-in-waiting.

A tactic of the Eisenhower administration and the Dulles brothers in the late 1950s was to sponsor rebellions led by army colonels in north and west Sumatra and parts of Sulawesi with the intention of breaking Indonesia into smaller states. These covert action campaigns failed as Sukarno moved against the dissident colonels and re-established his authority in the rebel areas. In May 1958 Sukarno forces captured CIA operative, Allan Pope, an American pilot who was shot down after a bombing raid on the city of Ambon, killing about seven hundred civilians. President Sukarno emerged more popular than ever from this attempt by the United States to undermine Indonesian sovereignty. However, the rebel colonels emerged from the rebellions flush with cash and guns from the CIA and more ambitious than ever in terms of moving from regional rebellions to overthrowing the government in Jakarta.

While the annihilation of the Communist Party and its supporters was still in progress, the Suharto regime ushered in the institutionalized persecution of hundreds of thousands of "communist suspects". Nearly 1½ million people had the initials E.T. (meaning ex-*tapol*, political prisoner) stamped on their identity cards, marking them out for special treatment. They were excluded from many kinds of employment such as teaching, that might enable them "to exert an influence" on public opinion. Many were required to report regularly to the local military commander, renew their identity cards annually and needed special permission to travel, even within the country. They were often summoned to attend indoctrination courses. Tens of thousands of ex-*tapols* were prohibited from voting in general elections, from standing for election, and from playing an active role in any parties or organizations permitted to exist by the regime. They had to prove that they came from "a clean environment", meaning that there were no ex-PKI amongst their siblings, parents, grandparents and in-laws. This so-called litmus test was used when people applied for jobs in designated sectors and when applying to enrol in state universities. Today, even after the death of Suharto, few of the restrictions put in place in 1966 have been repealed and the situation of ex-*tapols* in Indonesia remains very uncertain.

Several organizations representing "1965 victims", with the assistance of the Legal Aid Institute in Jakarta, have filed a class action suit against five Indonesian presidents on behalf of all the men and women who have since 1965 borne the stigma of being alleged members of the banned Indonesian Communist Party. The class action focuses on political rights and the principles laid down under the United Nations International Covenant on Economic, Social and Cultural Rights. The action also calls for the defendants to erect monuments to the victims of the 1965 massacre and calls on President Yudhoyono to include the history of the persecution in the national school curriculum.

Presently, in Lubang Buyana, where the bodies of the murdered generals were taken, a monument called the Sacred Pancasila Monument (Pancasila being the official state doctrine of Indonesia), depicting the October 1965 incident, is still standing. It contains life-size bronze statues of the deceased generals and gruesome bas-relief sculptures of "Communist" women defiling the bodies of the generals, despite the fact that such allegations were proven false many years ago. During his 32-year reign Suharto used this monument to fetishize the 1965

"Communist coup", requiring all school children to visit the monument and all members of parliament to take the oath of loyalty to Pancasila at the monument every five years. Also on September 30 all television stations were required to broadcast a four-hour film about the kidnapping and murder of the generals and the "heroic" rescue of the country by General Suharto. This was mandatory annual viewing for schoolchildren. Under Suharto the crimes of the official enemies were imprinted on the public consciousness with a systematic regularity reminiscent of China's Mao Tse Tung.

The 1965 coup initiated a brutal army rule that was to claim many more victims. For over three decades, the terror tactics of the Suharto regime went unchecked in Java and across the archipelago. After the numbing experience of the massacres of 1965–66, political dissent in Indonesia virtually disappeared for some years, but resurfaced again in pro-democracy student demonstrations in the mid 1970s. These were violently repressed, student councils banned and military officers put in charge of rebellious campuses in "normalization" operations. In September of 1984 hundreds of Muslims demonstrating against the regime were massacred. In the mid-1980s para-military death squads, composed mostly of off-duty officers, became a salient feature of the "law and order" regime. Thousands were taken out of their homes in the middle of the night and shot, their bodies left on public display in the streets and marketplaces. Suharto later claimed responsibility for these "mystery killings", writing in his memoirs that they were "shock therapy" against "criminal elements" in society.[17] Human rights groups like Amnesty International have documented at least 200,000 killed in West Papua since the 1970s, 150,000 or more deaths during the 24-year occupation of East Timor from 1974 to 1999, and thousands killed and "disappeared" in rebel Aceh province in Sumatra since the mid-1980s. The wholesale transfer of indigenous populations from the outer islands into "model villages" to make way for development projects also became a key feature of the regime.

Despite his record, Suharto enjoyed the full support of western countries, including Canada, during his 32 years of military rule. On a state visit to South Africa, even Mandela decorated the Indonesian dictator for his alleged support. With the overthrow of the nationalist government of Sukarno, Indonesia was transformed into "a paradise for investors".[18] The children of Suharto and his wife became involved in a wide variety of business ventures. According to *TIME-Asia* (24 May 1999), the six Suharto children owned between them significant equity in at least 564 companies, ranging from oil and cloves (used in kretek cigarettes) to land, toll roads, airlines, hotels, TV stations and real estate. Tommy Suharto, the youngest son, owns many companies, including the Lamborghini sports car company, and 22 luxury apartments in Ascot, Britain. A year after Suharto's forced resignation on 20 May 1998, the STAR (Stolen Assets Recovery) initiative, an agency set up by the World Bank and the United Nations, put him at the very top of their list of corrupt heads of state for stealing between $15–35 billion during his term as president of Indonesia.[19]

Before the 1965 massacres, Canada had negligible investments in Indonesia. After the ascendancy of Suharto, Canada became a major investor along with the United States and Australia. Indonesia also became a top recipient of Canadian aid and credits from the Export Development Corporation. The crimes of Suharto received scant attention by politicians or the media in Canada. According to Sharon Scharfe in *Complicity: Human Rights and Canadian Foreign Policy*, "Canada's official interest in Indonesia was shaped by Prime Minister Pierre Trudeau."[20] He formally visited Indonesia in 1971 and again in 1983. Suharto made a state visit to Canada in June of 1975. It is widely believed the Suharto visit had a decisive impact on Canada abstaining from the UN General Assembly vote condemning the Indonesia invasion of East Timor in December of 1975. Successive Canadian governments voted against the withdrawal of Indonesian troops from East Timor at the UN Decolonization Hearings, until Suharto was removed from power. Canadian cultural institutions such as The Museum of Civilization in Ottawa received numerous gifts from the Suharto regime. Universities across Canada were regular recipients of CIDA funding for various projects that gave a veneer of "normality" to a corrupt and brutal dictatorship. Simon Fraser University in British Columbia was the recipient of two 20-million-dollar CIDA grants for collaborating with Indonesian institutions of higher learning, and in the course of the process indirectly helping legitimate the Suharto regime's presence in rebel areas in the outer islands. Canadian business did particularly well in Indonesia in the Suharto years, gaining extensive concessions in oil, gas and mining. INCO, Canada's Sudbury-based giant nickel company, with the aid of Canadian taxpayers, set up the world's largest and most profitable nickel mine in the early 1970s on land confiscated from the indigenous people of Southern Sulawesi. Suharto was a featured guest at the APEC summit in Vancouver in November 1997.

The fear of being publicly identified as a former communist is still very much a part of life in Indonesia even after Suharto was forced to resign at the behest of Secretary of State Madeleine Albright during the Indonesian economic collapse in the spring of 1998. The Americans had lost confidence in Suharto's ability to run the country. There was dissent within his own Golkar party and riots thoughout Indonesia demanding his resignation. However, the memories of the victims of the 1965–66 massacres still haunt Indonesian society and recur repeatedly as a theme in Indonesian cultural and literary expression. Following Suharto's downfall, several writers took advantage of the greater press freedom to publish accounts critical of the official version of what happened in 1965. Amongst these was Soebandrio, first deputy prime minister under Sukarno, imprisoned for most of Suharto's reign and Omar Dani, a former commander in the Air Force. However, reaction by Indonesian censors to *Lastri*, a love story released by Indonesian filmmaker, Eros Djarot, set in the backdrop of 1965, was swift. It is banned from theatres for "promoting communism".

Current efforts by groups of citizens in Indonesia to uncover the past, exhume remains, and bring charges against the current Indonesian government of President Yudhoyono receive little attention in the international press outside of Australia. Since 2003, many groups of former political prisoners have made representations to the National Human Rights Commission and to the DPR, the national parliament, seeking redress and compensation for their unlawful arrest and detention. This is a result of changes in the Indonesian Criminal Code since the resignation of Suharto, recognizing a number of crimes as gross violations and crimes against humanity. In late 2000, a law was passed providing for the setting up of human rights courts. This legislation restored the principle of retroactivity in contradiction to a constitutional amendment passed a year earlier by the People's Consultative Assembly (MPR) which invoked the principle of non-retroactivity, protecting perpetrators of crimes from prosecution. Several military officers who are responsible for serious crimes still hold high office within the armed forces or in government. In 2000, an organization set up by former political prisoners with branches in many parts of the country exhumed the bodies of two dozen victims in Central Java, for reburial by their families. However, the families involved became the target of a vicious attack by an anti-communist group, which halted the removal of the bodies. The National Human Rights Commission has not had the courage to deal with the massacres of 1965, and still refuses to set up a commission of inquiry.

Much to the displeasure of the Indonesian government, in 1998 *Dateline* (ABC Australia) screened a film by Mike Carney called *Indonesia's Killing Fields*, following Sulami, a woman in her seventies, who is devoting the remainder of her life to investigating the massacres. The film is a damming exposure of Suharto's role in the events of 1965. It interviews Muslim leaders who participated in the killings and an army officer who boasts of his role in "cleaning up" the communists. Declassified Australian, British and American documents reveal that western powers not only knew about the killings, but were accomplices in the atrocities.

With the continued military control of government in Indonesia and absence of international pressure, progress in investigating the 1965 massacres is slow. However, in spite of enormous resistance, light is gradually being shed on the perpetrators of the killings. Light is also being shed on those who orchestrated and supported the killings from behind the scenes, much like an unseen puppet-master manipulates puppets from behind a screen in a traditional Indonesian *Wayang Kulit* shadow play.

NOTES

1 CIA, Directorate of Intelligence, "Intelligence report column, Indonesia, 1965, the coup that backfired", Washington, 1968.
2 Amnesty International, *Indonesia AI*, 1977, p. 21.
3 Cited by Noam Chomsky and Edward S. Herman in *The Washington Connection and Third World Fascism* (Boston: Southend Press, 1979); Malcolm Caldwell, "Lest We Forget", *Ten Years' Military Terror* (Spokesman Books, 1975), p. 14.
4 John Hughes, *The End of Sukarno* (Angus and Robertson, 1967), p. 185.
5 Amnesty International, *Indonesia AI*, 1977.
6 Carmel Budiardjo, *Surviving Indonesia's Gulag* (Cassell, 1996), p. 51.
7 "Indonesian Communism Since the 1965 Coup", *Pacific Affairs*, Spring 1970, pp. 35–36.
8 Kathy Kadane, "After 25 years, Americans speak of their role in exterminating Communist Party", *Washington Post*, 21 May 1990.
9 Cited by John Roosa, *Pretext for Mass Murder* (The University of Wisconsin Press, 2006), p. 16.
10 Brière and Susan Gage, *The Indonesia Kit*, 2nd Edition (International Center for Human Rights and Democratic Development, 1995, p.7.
11 Ibid., p. 27.
12 Ibid., p. 27.
13 Ibid. p. 28.
14 Cited by Noam Chomsky and Edward S. Herman in *The Washington Connection and Third World Fascism* (Southend Press, 1979), p. 216.
15 John Roosa, *Pretext for Mass Murder* (University of Wisconsin Press, 2006), p. 13.
16 Jacques Decornoy, *Le Monde*, 11 November 1972, cited by John Roosa, *Pretext for Mass Murder* (University of Wisconsin Press, 2006), p. 15.
17 *Ucapan dan Tindakan Saya* (Suharto: My Thoughts, Sayings and Deeds).
18 John Roosa, *Pretext for Mass Murder* (University of Wisconsin Press, 2006), p. 185.
19 "The British Campaign for Political Prisoners in Indonesia", *TAPOL Bulletin*, March 2008.
20 Sharon Scharfe, *Complicity: Human Rights and Canadian Foreign Policy* (Montreal: Black Rose Books, 1996), p. 130.

15

Comfort Women: Sexual Slaves of the Imperial Japanese Military

Linda Elaine Vogt Turner

✧

The bandits of the Eastern Sea…
Are the same shameless ones who have tampered with the history books.
Three hundred thousand wronged souls surround Japan,
Wanting only to report the facts around the world:
Their blood has not dried in sixty years.

Joseph Lo, *The Rape of Nanking*, tr. Bernard Cleary

Thirty million Chinese were brutally killed during the Japanese occupation of China that began in 1931 and officially ended with the surrender of Japan on August 15, 1945. But little had been written and published about the atrocities the Japanese military committed as it forced Japan's neighbours to surrender sovereignty. With the 1996 publication of James Yin and Shi Young's collection of shocking photographic evidence, public pressure mounted for the Japanese government to admit and accept responsibility for the human rights violations it committed against its neighbours, especially women and non-combatants, during its 14-year occupation.[1] This historical evidence, combined with testimonies of survivors, demonstrates that the Japanese military systematically dominated, abused and denigrated women as sex slaves in organized brothels during this period. The atrocity of recruiting and holding women as sexual slaves was a gross human rights violation that remains unresolved. The Japanese government has apologized to these women and their communities for enslaving them as "comfort women". However it has not assumed legal responsibility, nor has it made any effort to prosecute the perpetrators or provide compensation. The story of the "comfort women" will remain a dark chapter in Japanese history until the government fulfils its obligations.

Comfort Women

Surviving comfort women, not active participants in war, were nevertheless its tragic victims. The personal testimonies of these victims, forced into sexual slavery during Japan's invasion and occupation of Asia, especially Korea, were suppressed for complex reasons until the early 1960s. First, it was almost impossible for these women to speak out. Upon liberation in 1945, they returned to their home communities where sexual chastity and fidelity in marriage were expected virtues. Speaking out would have sullied their reputations further by bringing dishonour to the instigators and to any others who could have corroborated their story. Next, government documents that might implicate the military were destroyed or censored until the early 1960s. Finally, bystander members of the United Nations looked the other way while the United States and its allies lessened Japan's war reparations in order to enlist it as a capitalist ally in the Cold War. This necessarily involved burying the comfort women's stories.

In 1962, Senda Kako, a Japanese journalist researching the war, came across a previously censored photograph of women whom he was told were "P" women, a vulgar designation for persons who provided sexual comfort. In 1969, Ito Keiichi published a document from the late 1930s detailing the regulations of comfort stations in Shanghai. In 1976 Senda Kako published a book, verified by comfort woman survivor Kim Ilmyŏn, that also substantiated Keiichi's publications with further documentary evidence and her personal testimony. As international awareness grew so did the confidence of the women. Three women filed a lawsuit in Tokyo in 1991 which in turn prompted a United Nations investigation after the lawsuit was deemed hopeless. Japanese law provided many loopholes, including a 20-year Civil Code statutory limitation preventing victims of torture from suing perpetrators.[2]

Without including the thousands of girls and women raped by Japanese soldiers incidentally, it is estimated that between 139,000 and 200,000 were held captive as comfort women. From those numbers it is estimated that 116,000 survived the war and that 58,000 were still living in the early 1990s.[3] Yet only a brave few came forward to offer their often horrific personal testimonies, most of which were published in the 1990s. One Korean woman testified that she and 40 others in her village received draft notices from the Japanese government. Little did the women know that their names were only a few in a book compiled for conscripting women into sexual service for Japanese soldiers. This woman and others testified that they endured endless lines of Japanese soldiers relentlessly forcing themselves upon them. The women had little time to eat or sleep and little regard was paid if the women were bleeding, sick, pregnant, or recovering from a drug-induced miscarriage. Their testimonies[4] describe some of the indignities they endured and the long-lasting after effects they suffered. Many women and girls entered this service with feelings of betrayal since collaborators of both sexes had signed them up using a combination of coercion and an appeal to the women's sense of duty. And so, the girls and women signed up for "hospital" or "factory" work having been told that if they refused, mothers needed at home would have to go in their stead. Once they arrived at a comfort station, the women were allotted a small mattress in a four-by-six-foot cubicle in a sea of identical cubicles. They would faint from exhaustion, only to be revived and further abused. Fainting allowed only momentary escape and many women attempted flight and even suicide, but were caught or revived only to endure worse treatment. One woman reported that she was brought to by a lit cigarette placed under her nose, and when she regained consciousness, the lit cigarette was forced into her vagina. Many became sterile after contracting venereal diseases and after receiving "medical treatments" concocted from arsenic. The women who survived returned home physically disfigured and psychologically damaged, bringing home with them feelings of shame and violation, and the inability to love, marry and have children.

While relatively few women have spoken out, their testimonies have brought forth an abundance of investigation and documentation. Because the Japanese military kept meticulous records, photographing every comfort woman, and established regulations governing comfort stations,[5] it is now known that stations existed wherever the troops served, including Japan. Military records confirm that although the majority were Korean women, Japanese, Taiwanese, Chinese, Filipina, Indonesian, Vietnamese, Burmese and Dutch girls and women were also recruited and then forced into sexual slavery. The Japanese command had its own reasons for establishing comfort stations.[6] It claimed they would prevent the outrage that would be caused by the rape of Chinese wives, thereby fostering better relationships with conquered populations. The service would grant soldiers some respite from the battlefield and maintain their morale while precluding the danger of possible espionage that unregulated sexual relations could bring. Another practical rationale was that the stations would prevent the spread of venereal disease.

It is also important to note that the imperialist Meiji system of that time, with fascist overtones, imposed a patriarchal social structure – in the family, women were subordinate to men. In order to reinforce and protect the imperial family structure, the government legalized prostitution to satisfy the lust of men. The military comfort system was a variation of the legal system, but this military system coerced and deceitfully recruited women. An estimated 80 thousand of these women died during allied counter attacks.[7]

According to military records, the first confirmed comfort stations were established in Shanghai, following the Manchurian incident, the staged street fight between five Japanese monks and Chinese workers, triggering the invasion. After the Japanese Chief of Staff received reports of sexual assaults committed by his soldiers, comfort stations were established, ostensibly aimed at "preventing unregulated rape", but in reality meant to serve as institutions for legalized rape. The Chinese were understandably outraged. After the invasion of Nanking and the news of mass rape spread from China to the international community, the expansion of the comfort station system increased steadily and rapidly even though reports of raping and looting continued.[8]

Rape of Nanking

The Japanese invasion was termed the Rape of Nanking because of the widespread atrocities committed by the military – rape, looting, mass murder and arson. Yet the chief instigators and perpetrators of the crimes against humanity were never charged, as allied prosecutors looked the other way.[9] General Douglas MacArthur, Supreme Commander of Allied Powers, struck a secret deal with Shiro Ishii. Emperor Hirohito had established a biological warfare program, with Ishii in command. In exchange for his immunity and that of all his subordinates and superiors, including the Imperial Household, Ishii agreed to turn over all records detailing the biological program to General MacArthur.

Following this "top secret deal" some Japanese men were rounded up, tried and hanged as war criminals. General Iwane Matsui was one such man, falsely accused and tried as the "Butcher of Nanking".[10] He commanded the forces of Nanking for a mere three days, but was relieved of his command when he expressed anger toward Prince Asaka for allowing mass brutality, against his, Matsui's, orders. The Emperor then transferred General Matsui to a figurehead position in China, and subsequently appointed Prince Asaka in his place for the remaining five and a half weeks of the Nanking Expedition. General Matsui was old and sick, yet spoke out forcefully against the atrocities. Sadly he was ridiculed and later tried as a war criminal while the actual instigators and the perpetrators of the Nanking Massacre received immunity. Evidence corroborating Matsui's innocence was suppressed during the Cold War. From military documents unsealed after Emperor Hirohito's death, it is clear that Matsui was telling the truth and that the Emperor, the Imperial Family and their closest collaborators were the chief instigators and perpetrators but were granted immunity in exchange for their secret biological warfare program – under the guise of preventing the spread of communism.[11]

Chinese journalist accounts and photographs of Japanese atrocities were published by western news agencies in 1937 and 1938. In 1995 these accounts, together with personal testimony of the survivors of Nanking and photographs and military documents of the comfort stations, were published to mark the 50th anniversary of the end of World War II. The documents and photographs published in 1995 and after reveal a brutality that cannot simply be attributed to lack of democracy, or the military actions of fascist soldiers, or the Emperor's fear of communism – four hundred historical photographs speak of an attitude of power and intimidation.[12]

A 1937 picture of a howling baby covered in blood, sitting alone amid the rubble of a Shanghai railway station after Japanese bombing, tragically illustrates the vulnerability of the non-combatant. Another photograph depicts the beheading of civilians while Japanese soldiers cheer and take pictures for souvenirs. Another shows a Japanese soldier exposing the breasts of an elderly woman. And another reveals the looming shadow of a soldier as he forces three nude spread-eagled female rape victims to pose for the camera. Several photos show lone female victims forced to pose spreading apart their own genitalia. Still others reveal how officers instructed new recruits to learn and practise proper bayonet procedure on live prisoners tied to poles. A diary of a Japanese corporal reveals how he and other soldiers, out of sheer boredom, sought out Chinese civilians and either buried them alive, pushed them into fires, or beat them with clubs for entertainment. Another account details that burial alive often meant that victims were bound hand and foot then planted neck deep with their heads exposed. Some were then crushed by passing horses or tanks, jabbed with bayonets or soaked with boiling water.[13]

It is tempting to blame Japan's military abuses in Nanking on its lack of democracy at the time. But this explanation does not account for the fact that western democratic nations engaged in the "war on terror" continue to commit abuses against women. And, misogyny and brutality are still taught and reinforced in military academies of democratic countries today. New recruits who fail to measure up are called sissies, wimps, faggots, cunts or lays.[14] The Rape of Nanking is one of the most dramatic examples of the wartime abuse of women, a phenomenon that occurs across cultures and political systems – the abuse of women in militaristic and wartime contexts.

Human Rights

During the 1990s the United Nations Human Rights Commission conducted several investigations for the purpose of establishing whether or not the Japanese government was liable for the comfort system it reportedly established and systematized prior to and during World War II. Gay J. McDougall, appointed Special Rapporteur, submitted formal reports, one in 1996, and another in 1998. In these reports McDougall recommended the government of Japan accept and admit legal liability for the victims of the comfort stations it managed during the Second World War. According to McDougall, those who systematically recruit women for sexual slavery or slavery-like practices, or those who commit acts of rape during armed conflict, commit crimes against humanity. Moreover, McDougall reminded Japan that slavery for any purpose has been recognized internationally as a crime against humanity since the end of the 19th century.[15] Japan argued that it had never ratified the 1926 treaty prohibiting slavery and looked for loopholes in international law. Nevertheless, McDougall's report concluded that the Japanese government was liable for crimes against humanity. In addition, she rejected the Japanese government's argument that the peace treaties and reparation agreements signed between Japan and Asian governments following World War II exempted Japan from further prosecution and liability. She further argued that the failure of Japan to admit legal liability for the mass rapes and its institutionalized comfort station system has prevented other nations from admitting and accepting liability for crimes of a sexual nature committed more recently.[16]

However, Japan has not fully accepted McDougall's recommendations. Japan only established an Asian Women's Fund and issued apology letters to the comfort women. But opposition groups in Japan feared that even these largely symbolic gestures would make the government appear too apologetic, especially the placing of a "comfort women" reference in middle school text books. The objectionable reference was the simple statement that "women were made to accompany the military as comfort women and were treated horribly".[17] Meanwhile, private donations supported the Asian Women's Fund. And the official letters to the women employed the least sincere wording to convey apology and were carefully worded to avoid liability.[18] The fund, the apology letters and the absence of restitution have angered comfort women and their advocates, who view the government as having shrugged off responsibility. Adding insult to injury, a recently published Dutch government report reveals that the comfort women issue was deemed a war crime – but that only those Japanese who perpetrated crimes against women of *European* descent were tried; furthermore, only their Dutch victims were compensated.[19]

In 1980, human rights activists petitioned the Japanese government to take responsibility for 81,222 victims suffering ill-health due to pollution. The government ceded to their demands and admitted liability for these victims and future victims and has entitled them to government financial aid.[20] In contrast, financial compensation for 50,000 surviving comfort women was shrugged off in 1998 as a personal matter for the consciences of private citizens. Therefore, it is not surprising that many comfort women were infuriated with the government's failure to set up social programs or financial aid programs to alleviate their suffering, which has not diminished with time.

Where Responsibility Lies

The Japanese government has a responsibility to disclose the truth surrounding the issue of the comfort women. The government's failure so far to accept legal responsibility for the crimes of the Imperial Japanese military not only bestows impunity on those responsible for the crimes but also sets a terrible precedent. With its acknowledgement, Japan can increase its moral standing among other nations. Remembering the atrocities and identifying the actors involved will take courage but may stand to prevent such atrocities in the future.

The Japanese Government would be well advised to accept the United Nations Special Rapporteur's recommendations. Japan's claim that it has paid war reparations and that those responsible have been prosecuted and hanged is insufficient. As mentioned, the reparations that Japan made were minimized and chief instigators and perpetrators were granted immunity in a secret deal. In addition recent documentary and photographic evidence gives reason to re-examine the actions of the Japanese military in World War II.

Prosecuting the long line of soldiers who used the comfort stations would not be practical or particularly helpful. But prosecuting the military personnel and their civilian collaborators who established the comfort stations, and forced women into them would send a clear signal to Japanese society and the rest of the world – women, as full persons, are protected under international law. They are not at men's disposal for comfort and pleasure, nor are they to be abused.

The rights of women transcend the culture they live in, whether that of Japan in World War II or that of a western democratic nation today. Japan's culture did and does not absolve Japan of its responsibility for the atrocities against the comfort women between 1931 and 1945. Modern societies, too, need to be vigilant of women's rights, especially in the context of war.

The Japanese government has taken legal responsibility for the victims of environmental pollution but has taken only moral responsibility for the comfort women, and that too only in symbolic fashion. One reason the Japanese government has not acceded to compensation for comfort women is that people looked the other way during the war crimes trials, making justice for the victims elusive. Unfortunately, the cost of prosecuting the real instigators, perpetrators and collaborators today may be prohibitive. Moreover, evidential documents that could convict the criminals have most likely been lost, destroyed, or tampered with, and those with first-hand knowledge may have been murdered or falsely accused and executed like Iwane Matsui. There simply may not be enough evidence for trials.

However, this legal quandary should not prevent the Japanese government from providing social programs and financial aid to ensure that surviving comfort women wherever they reside spend the rest of their lives in dignity. Nor should it prevent the Japanese government from admitting that a secret agreement was made between Shiro Ishii and Douglas MacArthur, and putting that fact in school textbooks, along with historical pictures, testimonies and diaries of the comfort women.

NOTES

1 James Yin and Shi Young, *The Rape of Nanking: An Undeniable History in Photographs*, ed. Ron Dorfman and Shi Young (Chicago: Innovative Publishing Group, 1996), p. xiii.

2 Keith Howard, ed., *True Stories of the Korean Comfort Women: Testimonies Compiled by the Korean Council for Women Drafted for Military Sexual Slavery by Japan and the Research Association on the Women Drafted for Military Sexual Slavery by Japan* (New York: Cassell, 1995), pp. v–vii; 2–11, 193.

3 George Hicks, *The Comfort Women: Japan's Brutal Regime of Enforced Prostitution in the Second World War* (New York: W.W. Norton & Company, 1995), p. 19.

4 Sangmie Choi Schellsted, ed., *Comfort Women Speak, Testimony by Sex Slaves of the Japanese Military* (New York: Holmes & Meier Science and Human Rights, 2000), pp. 7–105.

5 George Hicks, *The Comfort Women: Japan's Brutal Regime of Enforced Prostitution in the Second World War* (New York: W.W. Norton & Company, 1995), pp. 72, 83, 107.

6 Yoshimi Yoshiaki, *Comfort Women: Sexual Slavery in the Japanese Military during World War II*, tr. Suzanne O'Brien (New York: Columbia University Press, 2000), pp. 65–75, 94, 180.

7 Keith Howard, ed., *True Stories of the Korean Comfort Women: Testimonies Compiled by the Korean Council for Women Drafted for Military Sexual Slavery by Japan and the Research Association on the Women Drafted for Military Sexual Slavery by Japan* (New York: Cassell, 1995), pp. 15–23.

8 Yoshimi Yoshiaki, *Comfort Women: Sexual Slavery in the Japanese Military During World War II*, tr. Suzanne O'Brien (New York: Columbia University Press, 2000), pp. 43–51.

9 Ibid., p. 162.

10 James Yin and Shi Young, *The Rape of Nanking: An Undeniable History in Photographs*, ed. Ron Dorfman and Shi Young (Chicago: Innovative Publishing Group, 1996), p. xi.
11 Ibid., pp. 282–302.
12 James Yin and Shi Young, *The Rape of Nanking: An Undeniable History in Photographs*, ed. Ron Dorfman and Shi Young (Chicago: Innovative Publishing Group, 1996), pp. xi, 10.
13 Ibid., pp. 2, 138, 139, 158, 159, 168, 170, 178, 192, 194, 202, 203.
14 Karen J. Warren, *Ecofeminist Philosophy: A Western Perspective on What It Is and Why It Matters* (Maryland: Rowman & Littlefield Publishers, Inc., 2000), p. 207.
15 Sangmie Choi Schellsted, ed., *Comfort Women Speak, Testimony by Sex Slaves of the Japanese Military* (New York: Holmes & Meier Science and Human Rights, 2000), p. 141.
16 Ibid. pp. 151–52.
17 Yoshimi Yoshiaki, *Comfort Women: Sexual Slavery in the Japanese Military During World War II*, tr. Suzanne O'Brien (New York: Columbia University Press, 2000), p. 24.
18 Ibid.
19 Ibid., pp. 175–76.
20 Yoshiro Hoshino, "Japan's Post-Second World War Environmental Problems" in *Industrial Pollution in Japan*, ed. Jun Ui (Tokyo: United Nations University Press, 1992), pp. 65–75.

CONCLUSIONS

Why Atrocities Remain Unacknowledged

Beyond simply chronicling horror stories, what common lessons can we draw from these diverse events regarding political violence, ethnic conflict and collective memory? All authors sketched the historical context of why the atrocity occurred and why it has remained unacknowledged. These unique cultural conditions of a specific time and place hardly lend themselves to meaningful comparisons. Nonetheless some commonalities can be discerned as to why massacres remain unacknowledged.

In the 15 cases sketched, neither were trials instituted nor did truth commissions shed light on the traumatic events. Yet over thirty different Truth and Reconciliation Commissions (TRC) are currently in session or have operated since the Latin American military dictatorships were overthrown during the 1980s. The subsequent South African TRC (1996–99) with its unique features of political education, amnesty upon full disclosure and a political motive for perpetrators became the template for many similar exercises around the world (Adam et al, 1987). Therefore the question why certain societies forego this option in favour of a "forget and forgive" alternative remains puzzling, although we know little empirically about the healing effects of truth commissions. Three conditions would seem to block truth processes.

First, when power-holders or their ideological heirs are themselves implicated in gross human rights violations, they obviously shun the process of historical accountability. Revealing the truth about past atrocities always impacts politically. Truth processes are usually given official blessings after a regime change. The new rulers aim at discrediting their predecessors with revelations of previous brutality. Sometimes ruling parties want to score points against political rivals and carry favour with victims, as happened in Australia and Canada with regard to indigenous minorities. Thereby a government, irrespective of its ideological leanings, elevates itself to a model of virtue and "progressiveness". Yet genuine truth processes also produce unintended consequences. For example, the South African TRC accused not only the apartheid regime of gross human rights violations, but also the ruling ANC in its "armed struggle" of carelessly harming civilians or abusing combatants in its camps. This led the then South African president Thabo Mbeki to complain bitterly about the commission "criminalizing" the liberation movements and equating perpetrators with victims. The five-volume Commission report did neither. The TRC elaborated the important distinction between "just war" and "injustices in war". Even during a just war of liberation, human rights conventions should apply. However, would the ANC have as wholeheartedly supported the exercise had its outcome been known beforehand?

Second, a truth process is eschewed when opening the wounds of the past perpetuates ongoing divisions in a split society. After bitter civil wars end without clear victors, it may be wiser to focus on peaceful co-existence than publicly blaming each other for mutual atrocities. Lebanon is a case in point. Ideologically divided Japan and Spain opted for forgetting. Since both are formal democracies it cannot be argued that "coming to terms with the past" is a precondition for a well-functioning democracy. When it is a question of re-integrating combatants of the other side into divided communities, reconciling local rituals may be preferable to retribution or public shaming. After a vicious proxy war between Frelimo and Renamo during the 1980s, Mozambicans reconciled through a cleansing ceremony of burning the clothes of former enemies before accepting them back into their communities. Only a few leading instigators of the 1994 Rwandan genocide appeared before the special UN tribunal in Arusha. The country dealt with the more than 100,000 imprisoned "ordinary" perpetrators through re-integrating village courts several years later. Zimbabwe, Namibia, Angola and the Democratic Republic of Congo still have not even contemplated how they should approach their recent atrocities.

The varied practices should caution against a Western temptation to impose a uniform model of restorative justice on transitional societies. As the now global International Center for Transitional Justice (ICTJ) acknowledges, its noble universal norms only work once they are welcomed by local actors, adjusted to local circumstances and negotiated with all the parties concerned. In short, while upholding the value and necessity of officially acknowledging, our analysis does not pronounce on what form is the appropriate one. Warnings against impunity and a fundamentalist advocacy of retribution could be as problematic as the plea for forgiveness and amnesty. Whether relative peace trumps justice remains an unresolved question. Justice without peace is rarely realized. On the other hand, letting the Mugabes of the world go unpunished deeply offends a liberal human rights consciousness, as the International Criminal Court (ICC) indictment of Sudan's President Bashir demonstrates, a decision not shared by a majority of fellow autocrats of the "African Union" (AU).

Third, recognition or apologies for past crimes often carries legal implications for redress. Governments avoid responsibilities for compensation to damages done by predecessors, even if they were ideological foes. The new ANC government barely heeded the recommendations of its TRC for reparations to recognized apartheid victims. The ANC even opposed suits to extract redress from multinational companies that profited from apartheid, brought under the "Alien Tort Claims Act" in the United States. The reasoning advanced concerned damage to the investment climate.

Causes and Implications of Mass Atrocities

Nowadays human rights advocates are keen to detect early warning signs of mass atrocities. The "international community", whatever that notion means, is asked to engage with such situations preventively rather than post-facto. These laudable calls for intervention and action, however, are often not grounded in a realistic understanding of the origins of ethno-national and ethno-racial violence. While we now have a vast literature on post-conflict reconstruction, on how to repair a broken social order, on how to fix institutions and constitutions, strengthen civil society – and even how to deal with the crimes of the past – we lack comparable knowledge, let alone consensus, on what caused the strife in the first place. These reflections on the fifteen cases are meant to highlight some selected insights and startling common features.

Ethnicity often acquires a deadly dimension when a state or empire unravels. During these uncertain transitional periods of social breakdown, collective grievances are more easily aired and scores are settled. That situation prevailed after the collapse of the Ottoman empire in Turkey, after World War II in Eastern Europe, post-colonial

Nigeria, the disintegration of the Soviet Union, and Yugoslavia in the aftermath of Tito's death. Previously enforced "brotherhood and unity" is revealed as an empty slogan. People fall back on their own tribal affiliation for safety and security. Calls for revenge for long-forgotten humiliations are heard, scapegoats for general misery are easily discerned and genocide looms. Ethnic targeting can also take place under strong totalitarian systems, such as Nazism and Stalinism, in the process of reorganizing their state to secure dictatorial rule and establish a new order. The stigmatization of Jews and other diasporic minorities provides the classical example. Both regimes were prone to designate scapegoats as obstacles for national renewal; both portrayed themselves as threatened and requiring loyalty for mobilization against a host of enemies.

Without an effective deterrent, in the form of a standing United Nations intervention force, the international community is reduced to a bystander role in such conflicts. Global citizenship is paralysed by the veto of national interests in the Security Council. Noble resolutions as to the "responsibility to protect", when a failed state is unable or unwilling to prevent gross human rights abuses, have been discredited by US unilateral actions for national selfish interests. Laudable attempts at globalizing justice through the ICC have so far not acted as a deterrent, but have often instead entrenched intransigent abusers, who fear arrest outside their borders (see Marchak, 2008).

Atrocities can also occur when an ethnic minority of a multi-nation state strives for secession, putting thousands of lives at risk, as the cases of Pakistan and Biafra demonstrate. During the second half of the 20th century intra-state, rather than inter-state wars predominated. Civil war along ethnic lines, be it in Bosnia, Chechnya, Sri Lanka, Northern Ireland or Lebanon, knows few constraints. Only a very few successful partitions occurred peacefully in recent history, such as the Czech-Slovak separation or the Norwegian-Swedish split earlier. Therefore, a constitutionally regulated "moral right to secede" (Buchanan, 1991) is to be welcomed, although it provides no guarantee for the desired outcome.

In 1998, the Supreme Court of Canada laid down such conditions for a legitimate secession. The Court ruled that "a clear majority vote in Quebec on a clear question in favor of secession would confer democratic legitimacy on the secession initiative which all the other participants in confederation would have to recognize" through "principled negotiations". However, the Court deliberately did not clarify what a "clear majority" and "a clear question" concretely means, but left this "for political actors to determine … in the circumstances under which a future referendum vote may be taken". Since separatists claim the sovereign right to determine the process of secession themselves, the ambiguous Court decision as well as a subsequent federal "Clarity Act" are unilateral shots in a legal battle that is ultimately decided by the political power constellation. Fortunately for a non-nationalist Canada, tanks in the streets of Ottawa or major atrocities over Quebec secession are difficult to envisage in a country where dissent is traditionally pacified with co-optation rather than subdued by force.

Our case studies challenge a conventional wisdom about the origins of racism: racist aggression is not confined to European colonialism. Blacks can be as racist as whites and engage in similar crimes. Europe merely systematized and ideologized racism as a pseudo-scientific doctrine of biological superiority to legitimize colonial expansion and slavery. However, a "civilizing mission" also equips the Chinese in colonizing "backward" Tibet. Arabs used Zanzibar on the African East coast in similar ways for slave trading as Europeans treated their captured commodities on Goree island off Senegal's west coast. Imperial Japan's brutalization of Koreans and Chinese testifies to an Asian variant of racism as does the semi-fascism of India's BJP Hindutva towards the country's 14 percent disadvantaged Muslim minority. In short, persecution of constructed "others", based on stereotyping and dehumanizing, is a human, not a specific national trait that can be found in all societies. Ethnocentrism – the glorification of one's in-group – at least seems universal, although the closely related racism, i.e. the perceived link between phenotype and biology, developed as a historically more recent phenomenon.

Religion and Bigotry

Nowadays acts of mass atrocities are usually attributed to religious zealots. However, avowedly secular regimes have engaged in the same behaviour with the same fervour as indoctrinated believers in divine designs. Identification with a secular dogma, such as Nazism or Stalinist communism, has produced mass murder on a grand scale. Pol Pot's urban cleansing of Cambodian cities was rooted in a secular ideology. Victor Zaslavsky (2008) has coined the term "class cleansing" in his book with the same title, describing the execution of thousands of imprisoned

Polish officers by the Soviet Secret Police at Katyn in 1940, a massacre for which the Nazis were falsely blamed. The German invasion of the Ukraine was welcomed by large sections of the local population because of Stalin's "class cleansing" of kulaks in the preceding Holodomor. Ironically, the thoroughly secular Syrian Ba'ath Party unleashed its forces against the rival Muslim Brotherhood with religious ruthlessness. Hitler's national socialism substituted traditional religion with aggressive secular mobilization and genocide. In short, secular dogmatism engenders the same fanaticism as religious fundamentalism.

Religious communalism can facilitate strife by isolating people from each other through endogamy and notions of exclusive salvation. It legitimizes demonizing non-believers. It makes pragmatic compromises difficult through absolutist claims to holy places and incompatible interpretations of doctrine. Therefore, sharing education in integrated schools and fostering optimal contact between different people in a multicultural setting immunizes more against stereotyping than the parochialism of communitarian homogeneity. However, the limits of this so-called "contact hypothesis" also have to be recognized. Contact alone is insufficient as differences can always be constructed. As Harvey Weinstein has summarized, the contact hypothesis involves four components: equal status, cooperative activity, personal interaction and social norms, mediated by a respected authority. Equal status ranks first. In short, increased intermixing, social contact, same religion, intermarriage and assimilation provide no guarantee against collective punishment. The Hutus and Tutsis of Rwanda shared the same Catholicism and had frequently intermarried, but were not of equal status. The vast majority of German Jews were totally assimilated, secularized and indistinguishable from non-Jewish Germans in all virtues and vices. Jews constituted 0.3 percent of German society and were no threat. Yet the Nazis singled them out for industrialized genocide on the basis of ancestry just as Rwandan Hutus went for killing orgies, including even their closest neighbours and friends. What matters in inter-group relations in divided societies is the artificial labelling and the values attached to difference by instigating demagogues.

Religious leaders on both sides often reinforce nationalism. When Israeli settlers "redeem" land as fulfilment of biblical prophecy and Islamist preachers inveigh against infidels on sacred soil, they apply a logic of divinely ordained destiny, crusades against evil and collective redemption that is foreign to secular truth seeking. Sanctified land and holy places are not easily given up or even shared in a spirit of historical justice or expedient compromise in Jerusalem or Ayodhya in India. Historical factual truth hardly affects the believer if it contradicts doctrine. Herein lies the limits of truth commissions and trials. In the competing narratives and myth-making, corpses are paraded for ideological legitimation, demonstrating the "barbarity" of the adversary and unique "victimhood" of one's own people. Suffering and violation is marshalled as a weapon.

Victims as Victimizers of Collective Punishment

In the aftermath of conflict, ethnic or otherwise, victims can easily change into victimizers, once they have gained power themselves. They use their past suffering and heroic struggles for survival to create empathy and to justify their own acts of aggression. Only two years after Mugabe had defeated the racist Rhodesian Smith regime, he let his tribal blood hounds loose on his Ndebele allies. Lately this autocrat asserts that a cross on a ballot cannot be allowed to wipe out his anti-colonial revolution. Similarly, the arbitrary brutality with which the victorious Algerian FLN dealt with rural fellow citizens who supported the French mostly out of self-protection, exceeded the horrors that the colonialist employed in subjugating resistance. No special sensitivity develops among formerly oppressed victors who almost seem to apply their own experience of victimization to their adversaries. Right-wing members of the Israeli Knesset threaten militant Palestinians with the Jewish experience under the Nazis. Some Israeli politicians self-righteously claim immunity from any criticism by labelling any challengers anti-Semitic or self-hating traitors, even well-meaning critics from within. Palestinian activists in positions of power within both the Fatah and Hamas factions brutally killed and tortured fellow countrymen in their struggle for domination. Barely liberated from apartheid, poor blacks turned against right-less fellow African migrants in massive xenophobic violence (Hassim, 2009; Crush, 2008). In short, historical victimhood does not immunize against repeating abuses of others. There is no people that by history or nature would be exempt from inflicting harm onto others.

Much of the violence in ethno-national conflicts is administered as collective punishment. Some of the grossest human rights violations occur in the name of teaching whole populations a lesson, regardless of the attitudes of individuals. Revenge for past crimes by the collectivity is supposed to justify collective punishment. The indiscriminate Allied bombing of German cities in revenge for the prior Nazi attacks on London and Coventry was intended primarily to demoralize civilians, not merely to destroy the military capacity of the enemy. In the words of the celebrated Arthur ("Bomber") Harris, the Chief Marshall of the Royal Air Force Bomber Command, quoted in the chapter on Dresden:

> The aim is the destruction of German cities; the killing of German workers; and the disruption of civilized life throughout Germany. It should be emphasized that the destruction of houses, public utilities, transport, and lives; the creation of a refugee problem on an unprecedented scale; and the breakdown of morale both at home and at the battle fronts by fear of extended and intensified bombing, are accepted and intended aims of our bombing policy. They are not by products of attempts to hit factories.

Yet even in a "just war" of defence, the deliberate murder of civilians is a violation of Article Three of the Geneva Conventions of legitimate warfare (see Adam, 2005). Moreover, collective punishment is counter-productive. Intended to undermine enemy morale and encourage insurrection against rulers, indiscriminate terror often reinforces a problematic patriotism. Just as Churchill succeeded in mobilizing British public opinion for all-out warfare against Nazi Germany after the "Blitz" against London, so most of the German population blamed the Allies for their suffering rather than turning their ire against the real cause. Israeli "targeted assassinations" of Palestinians in Gaza with the usual "collateral damage" only strengthens Hamas. Likewise, NATO's "regrettable" allowance for increasing civilian casualties in Afghanistan, provides increased support for the Taliban. In short, a population is not turned against its local oppressors by being punished by foreign forces.

While atrocities may be collectively administered, the drama is played out at a personal level as well. Today's Islamist suicide bomber is a good example. What is dismissed as an irrational glorification of martyrdom had its predecessors on a much larger scale in European or Japanese nationalism. Nationalism can best be perceived as politicized ethnicity. Nationalist Japanese kamikaze fighters also employed suicide as a weapon. The social psychologist Richard Koenigsberg (2009) in his book *Nations Have the Right to Kill* has persuasively outlined the central notion of sacrifice as the core of European nationalism. The Nazis were not unique in arguing that the best people have to sacrifice themselves in order for the nation to survive. Internalized sacrifice made both German and Allied soldiers go singing to their deaths during two World Wars. In the trench warfare of the First World War, millions of soldiers literally dug their own graves. Conscientious objection to conscription was minimal and also frowned upon as traitorous cowardice. Dying for one's fatherland was the height of devotion.

Theories of Ethnic Hostility

The widespread notion of sacrificing oneself for the nation raises the broader question of what underlies the phenomenon of ethnocentrism? Four broad strands of different explanatory foci are offered in the academic literature: 1. Leadership mobilization focuses on scheming elites to heighten their status and power; 2. Instrumentalist, interest-based foci of ethnic solidarity, highlight competition for scarce resources, or a split labour market between indigenous and migrant workers; 3. Socio-biological explanations of preferential kin selection and nepotism, conditioning the human species through evolutionary advantages; and 4. Psychological, particularly psychoanalytic accounts of hostility, entail projecting onto others what socialization suppresses in each individual. The four approaches are not mutually exclusive, but have different explanatory clout.

Leadership mobilization designates enemies and enhances the status of ethnic elites in competition with rivals. A heterogeneous constituency is united behind a common cause; the leader instils a sense of superiority among followers and thereby attracts support and often blind loyalty. Laboratory experiments have demonstrated that even fictitious adversaries can generate intense hate. Formerly amiable groups, for example school classes, can be divided easily into hostile camps that are ready to harm each other. A manipulative leader dehumanizes the outgroup with derogatory labels ("cockroaches, snakes, bloodsuckers, parasites") and sets them up for being attacked as a patriotic duty. Research on xenophobic violence in South Africa has dismissed the notion of a faceless crowd spontaneously attacking foreigners, but has shown that community leaders organized the riots (Crush, 2008; Hassim, 2009). They levied "protection fees" against shop owners or rented shacks that provided lucrative "employment opportunities" for themselves. Leadership manipulation arguably amounts to the most popular social science explanation of ethnic hostility, as the work of Paul Brass on Indian ethnic entrepreneurs or Benedict Anderson's account of "imagined communities" testifies. However, the sole focus on leadership mobilization falls short of explaining why followers are so susceptible to the calls of demagogues.

A typical situation in which competing material interests can trigger pogroms is a split labour market. An indigenous working class resents foreign migrants who are prepared to work for less and are therefore preferred by employers. Immigrants "stealing jobs", consorting with local women, "overcharging and exploiting" or "importing foreign diseases" constitute the usual rationalizations for xenophobia (Nyamnjoh, 2006). In such contexts, interest-focused explanations of ethnic antagonisms make sense. Yet the implicit economic reductionism misses other elements that make ethnicity lethal. It is neither the high ratio of perceived strangers nor the degree of difference that triggers ethnic conflict. While discrimination obviously benefits some and shortchanges others, it would be misleading to reduce ethnic mobilization to material privileging alone. Collectivities murder on account of values. The killing is part of a belief system – nationalism, identity, religion, status – with which perpetrators interpret the world and give meaning to their situation. These "ideal interests", as Max Weber calls them, are as real as material motivations. Ideologies of hate and dehumanization, propagated by influential leaders, are independent motivators that cannot be reduced to greed or numbers.

For example, former East Germany experienced many more incidents of violent xenophobia despite a relatively small number of resident foreigners (100,000), compared with West Germany with a 45 times greater population of foreigners (4.5 million) competing for scarce jobs. Laboratory experiments proved that invented groups can elicit as intense antagonism as real ones. A Polish saying suggests that there can be virulent anti-Semitism without any Jews left in a country. Different state ideologies and different economic systems would also seem to make little difference in the manifestation of bigotry. African students in the former Soviet Union experienced as much, if not more racism, than their counterparts in the West. Nor does official multiculturalism, as opposed to assimilationist pressure, shape different inter-group attitudes. The late American historian George M. Fredrickson (1999:37) concludes:

"Despite the myths that Canada is a 'mosaic' and the United States a 'melting pot', racial prejudice and xenophobia exists to about the same extent in both countries."

Such comparative evidence would seem to minimize social conditions in influencing collective antagonism. It would seem to validate the socio-biological explanation. According to its proponents, particularly the notable scholar Pierre van den Berghe (1987), ethnicity is deeply rooted in the human condition, because it is "kinship writ large". In this view we are genetically conditioned to favour kin over non-kin, because such nepotism bestowed an evolutionary advantage to cohesive, endogamous groups. Van den Berghe rejects the criticism of genetic determinism. He does not consider ethnicity as a fixed, rigid and unchangeable concept, but also allows for situational variables and opportunistic behaviour. "Selfish maximizers" in an ever changing environment intelligently use, manipulate and redefine common markers of descent. Therefore ethnic relations are shaped by the interplay of biological descent as well as the subjective perception of this objective reality.

However, this rather sweeping definition by socio-biologists explains everything and nothing. Similar to the economic reductionism, socio-biologists obscure the vast intra-group differences in ethnocentric attitudes through a biological reductionism. If putative descent, the "imagined community" of fictional, delusional common origin serves the same function as genuine relatedness, why elevate the one over the other as the basis of solidarity? How does the socio-biological paradigm explain cases of non-related groups being given legal preference over related kin? That was the case when the Afrikaner apartheid regime enfranchised European immigrants but discriminated against Cape Coloureds, their own related offspring.

The psychoanalytic perspective focuses on socialization for an explanation of the striking individual differences in the same ethnic group. Starting from the empirical evidence assembled in this collection, that all people are potentially capable of inflicting harm on others, we have to look at the social conditions that restrain the aggressive potential in humans as well as the incentives that trigger solidarity and reciprocity. A vast literature deals with the crucial correlation between early socialization, ego-development and subsequent attitudes towards collective attachment. This research ranges from Adorno's et al 1950 account of "The Authoritarian Personality" to Tom Pettigrew's focus on "conformity pressure"; the famous Milgram experiment on obedience to legitimate authority, to Vamik Volkan's (2006) "bigotry as a syndrome".

The Indian psychoanalyst Sudhir Kakar's analyses the Hindu-Muslim riots in this tradition of "othering". Kakar reminds us that the community in which we are socialized is always part of our personal identity. Its myths, history, rituals and symbols are idealized by the young child "in the enhancement of self-esteem for belonging to such an exalted and blessed entity" (Kakar, 1996:189). However, the internalization of necessary social rules (culture) also clashes with a person's natural drives. This conflict is solved through projection of "bad representations" onto others. "First projected to inanimate objects and animals and later to people and other groups – the latter often available to the child as a pre-selection by the group – the disavowed bad representations need such 'reservoirs' as Vamik Volkan (2004) calls them. These reservoirs – Muslims for Hindus, Arabs for Jews, Tibetans for Chinese, and vice versa – are also convenient repositories for subsequent rages and hateful feelings for which no clear-cut addressee is available. Since most of the bad representations arise from a social disapproval of the child's animality, as expressed in its dirtiness, and unruly sexuality, it is pre-eminently this animality which a civilized moral self must disavow and place in the reservoir group" (Kakar, 189).

Kakar's account explains why in every ethnic hostility the other group is ascribed sexual licentiousness, drunkenness and other forbidden behaviour. We project onto others what we have to suppress in ourselves. When this stigmatization is accompanied with dehumanization of the outgroup, the stage is set for the massacres described in this collection. The body politics is "cleansed" from "parasites", "vermin", "infidels" and other threatening viruses as a hygienic duty. Empathy for the suffering of other humans is suspended, because they are simply not perceived as humans.

Ego-weak characters in search of identity are attracted to such glorifying behaviour in exalted groups. Because of the common socialization experience, associated with early childhood security and comfort, individuals in a crisis fall in easily with "my people" at the expense of solidarity with other humans. Difference is never the cause of strife. Indeed, the greater the similarities between groups, the more intense the antagonism often displayed. In fact, in the absence of visible difference, imagined pseudo-differences are magnified to reinforce an uncertain identity, as Freud's theory of "narcissism of small difference" pointed out. While the victims are blamed for their fate, their behaviour is largely irrelevant indeed. The bigoted mind is prejudiced not only against one minority. Scapegoats are interchangeable.

"Lawfare": What is to be Done?

While there are commonalities in our case studies, their complexity and diversity also defy a simple answer to the question of "What is to be done?" If the psychoanalytic paradigm is correct, strengthening the self-concept and critical autonomy of adolescents points to a crucial educational route. Many policymakers on the other hand clamour for a more immediate intervention and stress the deterrence of universal jurisdiction. In the wake of the Holocaust and post-Nuremberg jurisdiction, a "globalization of justice" has advanced through legal visions of a "responsibility to protect". Leading violators of universal human rights laws are also targeted through the International Criminal Court (ICC) when states themselves or the Security Council refer them to the court for possible indictment.

Universal jurisdiction allows for arrest and trials of violators of international humanitarian law by those states that decide to enforce it after a charge has been lodged. Pinochet was arrested in Britain under this principle. However, what constitutes violations is open to diverse interpretations. Progressive and reputable legal bodies could be the intellectual leaders in further developing, clarifying and applying international humanitarian law. Engaging in "lawfare", as the use of law as a weapon of war has been labelled by the US military judge Charles Dunlap, is bitterly contested. The Israeli case as well as the March 2009 indictment of Sudanese President Omar al-Bashir illuminate the problems of a globalized justice. Both cases demonstrate that universal jurisdiction is taken seriously by potential offenders, but needs to be extended and clarified.

On the one side of the lawfare, Amnesty International and Human Rights Watch insist with substantial documentation on Israel's (and Hamas') human rights violations in Gaza. The international and local Israeli NGOs threaten to hold IDF commanders responsible. On the other side the Israeli army prepared itself. During its 2009 Gaza invasion a special unit was set up to advise on "humanitarian warfare". Critics charge that rules were drafted how civilians could be killed "lawfully". So serious was universal jurisdiction taken that a ban on names and pictures of commanders was instituted and military personnel was assured the full protection of the Israeli state should they ever be held accountable abroad. The Israeli government took great care to present the high number of civilian deaths and destruction as collateral or unintended in what amounted to an attempt to pre-empt accusations of violating the principle of proportionality. For example, before a house or neighbourhood in densely populated Gaza was bombed, the inhabitants of the house were usually warned to evacuate. If the women and children did not hear or heed the warning or returned to their home after a while, they were then considered legitimate "enemy combatants". With a sense of legal entitlement commanders could now bomb without concern about proportionality. They were given the green light to employ new "humanitarian munitions" (white phosphorus). They spoke of "humanitarian co-ordination" and how to achieve smaller "kill ratios". The Israeli behaviour has yet to be tested in an impartial court. The thorough but much maligned Goldstone inquiry, initiated by the UN Human Rights Council and boycotted by Israel, blamed both Israel and Hamas for gross human rights violations in its lengthy September 2009 report.

The 2009 indictment of Sudan's Bashir by the ICC has brought other problems of a globalized justice to the fore. The ICC has never investigated western involvement and complicity in war crimes under the pretence that western democracies are willing and capable of enforcing human rights laws themselves. (The same is argued by Israel.) However, the virtual legalization of torture, rendition and indefinite confinement without trial of hundreds of suspects by the Bush administration has put a lie to this claim. Moreover, the United States has opposed establishing the ICC and pressed various signatory states into bilateral agreements, guaranteeing immunity for US citizens. It is ironic and hypocritical that the United States now supports and celebrates the indictment of an enemy dictator (Bashir), but tolerates its own friendly violators. The accusation of political bias by African states is therefore to be expected, although the charge of a new legal colonialism is false when most African states have signed on the ICC Rome treaty. However, major states such as Russia, China and India, like the United States, did not, and therefore more than half of the world population still lives outside the jurisdiction of the ICC. On the other hand, the 300,000 victims of ethnic cleansing in Darfur call for a forceful response, if only to deter similar atrocities in other war-torn countries. Arguing that such outside interventions jeopardize potential peace negotiations and reinforce intransigence (as is said to have happened in the case of the Ugandan Lord's Resistance Army) are as unpersuasive as the warning of retaliation against NGOs by Bashir. The expulsion of the aid agencies on which most of the Darfur population depends for survival, amounts to genocide by other means and confirms the ICC indictment of "extermination". It merely demonstrates that such regimes do not care about its own African victims, as Desmond Tutu has pointed out. If international human rights law is truly universal it must apply everywhere and enforcement should be stepped up rather than be delayed. The African Union and the Arab League defending Bashir as a victim of Western imperialism shows an astonishing disregard for universal human rights laws.

The blatant defiance of ICC indictments by state elites, who have voluntarily signed on to the ICC treaty, demonstrates the limits of international law. Instead of arresting Bashir, which governments are legally obligated to do, they court the perpetrator during his travels in Africa. In similar vein, the dictator Mugabe receives long ovations when he visits South Africa and rants against British imperialism or gay cabinet ministers. What does that reveal about the collective mindset and the security of civil liberties in Mandela's democratic model state? Equally telling is the silence of international institutions and leaders in the face of ICC treaty violations. Commercial interests of trade and investments and the anxiety not to be replaced by more opportunistic competitors (China) prove stronger than the rhetorical commitment to ethical behavior and responsible government. Unfortunately, on the whole, power politics trumps justice, whether in the developed North or the struggling South. The "rule of law" is always embedded in a specific socio-political environment. Human rights law triumphs only in the rare instances when the interests of power-holders coincide with the normative stipulations or the risks of unlawful behaviour outweigh compliance. Fearing delegitimation may at best restrain some brutality when regimes need to sell themselves as "democratic".

It would therefore be naïve for minorities to place their security and well-being solely on the existence of progressive laws. Time and again constitutions have been torn up and international treaties ignored, as our case studies have shown. Trust in the law can turn out to be deadly even under globalized justice, as Srebrenica proved not long ago in July 1995. In the special UN protection zone 400 armed Dutch UN peace-keepers did not intervene when Serb para-military forces singled out 8,000 Muslim men and boys for the worst European massacre since the Second World War. Although Srebrenica is now memorialized in Bosnia it could also have been added to the long list of unacknowledged atrocities as it is still mired in fierce controversy among Serbs, and some leading perpetrators (Ratko Mladic) have still not been apprehended.

Apart from being alert to the many obstacles preventing ongoing mass atrocities one lesson needs to figure prominently: we need to create political literacy in order to reflect upon and understand the various manifestations of political violence. Without political literacy and understanding, the quest for public acknowledgement of past atrocities is stillborn. Our collection will hopefully contribute to such an awareness.

SELECTED BIBLIOGRAPHY

✧

Chapter 1

Alexander, Jocelyn. "Dissident Perspectives on Zimbabwe's Post-Independence War." *Africa: Journal of the International African Institute* 68, no. 2 (1998): pp. 151–76.

Catholic Commission for Justice and Peace and Legal Resources Foundation. "Breaking the Silence, Building True Peace: A Report on the Disturbances in Matabeleland and the Midlands 1980–1988, Summary Report." (April 1999): pp. 1–35, http://www.sokwanele. com/pdfs/BTS.pdf.

Chatham House: Royal Institute of International Affairs. "Zimbabwe's Gukurahundi: Lessons from the 1980–1988 Disturbances in Matabeleland and the Midlands." http://www.chathamhouse.org.uk/publications/papers/view/-/id/549/

Hill, Geoff. *The Battle for Zimbabwe.* Cape Town: Zebra Press, 2003.

Hope, Christopher. *Brothers Under the Skin: Travels in Tyranny.* London: Macmillan, 2003.

Sané, Pierre. "Zimbabwe: Open Letter from Amnesty International to His Excellency the President Robert Mugabe." Amnesty International, http://asiapacific.amnesty.org/library/print/ENGAFR46031997.

UNHCR Refworld. "Assessment for Ndebele in Zimbabwe." UN Refugee Agency, http://www.unhcr.org/refworld/docid/469f3aeb14.html.

US Department of State. "Background Notes: Zimbabwe." Bureau of African Affairs, http://www.state.gov/r/pa/ci/bgn/5479.htm.

Wetherell, Iden. "The Matabeleland Report: A lot to hide." *AfricaFiles* 12, no. 3 (1997): pp. 1–4. http://www.africafiles.org/printableversion.asp?id=3843.

Chapter 2

Bang, Anne. "Cosmopolitanism Colonised? Three Cases From Zanzibar 1890-1920", in Simpson, Edward and Kai Kresse (eds), *Struggling with History, Islam and Cosmopolitanism in the West Indian Ocean.* New York: Columbia University Press, 2008.

Bennett, Norman R. *A History of the Arab State of Zanzibar.* London: Methuen & Co Ltd., 1978.

Clayton, Anthony. *The Zanzibar Revolution and its Aftermath.* London: C. Hurst & Company, 1981.

Cohen, John (text), and Gualtiero Jacopetti and Franco Prosperi (film); *Africa Addio.* New York: Ballantine Books, 1966.

Lofchie, Michael F. *Zanzibar: Background to Revolution.* Princeton: Princeton University Press, 1965.

Martin, Esmond Bradley. *Zanzibar, Tradition and Revolution.* London: Hamish Hamilton, 1978.

Okello, John. *Revolution in Zanzibar.* Nairobi: East African Publishing House, 1967.

Petterson, Don. *Revolution in Zanzibar: An American's Cold War Tale.* Colorado: Westview Press, 2002.

Web Sources

Lucas Lukumbo. "Zanzibar Revolution Commemorated 44 Years Later." *Pan-African News Wire.* http://panafricannews.blogspot.com/2008/01/zanzibar-revolution-commemorated-44.html. Accessed 2008-11-13.

Zanzibar Net. Zanzibar History. http://www.zanzibar.net/zanzibar/history. Accessed 2008-11-09.

Zanzinet Forum, History. http://www.zanzinet.org/zanzibar/history/historia.html. Accessed 2008-12-06.

ZanzibarMagic.com, British Period. http://www.zanzibarmagic.com/english/indexb%20egl.htm. Accessed 2008-11-12.

Helen Hunter. "Zanzibar Revisited." *CIA Historical Review Program,* released as sanitized 18 September 1995. https://www.cia.gov/ library/center-for-the-study-of-intelligence/kent-csi/docs/v11i2a01p_0001.htm. Accessed 2008-11-09.

Making Our Mark Org.UK: The Slave Market. http://www.youtube.com/watch?v=NBTErUDIcz8&eurl=http://www.zanzibarmagic.com/english 2nd/british%20period.htm. Video clip from February 2007; accessed 2008-11-14.

Chapter 3

Anderson, David. *Histories of the Hanged.* London: Weidenfeld & Nicholson, 2005.

BBC News Kenya. "Call for Kenyan truth commission." http://news.bbc.co.uk/2/hi/africa/7227112.stm. Accessed 2008-03-12.

Clough, Marshall S. *Mau Mau Memoirs: History, Memory & Politics*. Boulder, Colorado: Lynne Rienner Publishers, Inc., 1998.

Elkins, Caroline. *Britain's Gulag: The Brutal End of Empire in Kenya*. United States: Henry Holt and Company, LLC, 2005.

Finke, Jens. "Kikuyu—the Mau Mau Uprising and Independence." http://www.bluegecko.org/kenya/tribes/kikuyu/maumau.htm. Accessed 2008-07-11.

Kennedy, Dane. "Constructing the Colonial Myth of Mau Mau." *The International Journal of African Historical Studies* 25, no. 2 (1992): pp. 241–60. http://www.jstor.org.proxy.lib.sfu.ca/stable/219387.

Kyle, Keith. *The Politics of Independence of Kenya*. New York: St. Martin's Press Inc, 1999.

Lonsdale, John. "Constructing Mau Mau." *Transactions of the Royal Historical Society* 40, (1990): pp. 239–60. http://www.jstor.org.proxy.lib.sfu.ca/stable/3679170.

———. "Mau Maus of the Mind: Making Mau Mau and Remaking Kenya." *The Journal of African History* 31, no. 3 (1990): pp. 393–421. http://www.jstor.org.proxy.lib.sfu.ca/stable/182877.

Maloba, Wunyabari O. *Mau Mau and Kenya: An Analysis of a Peasant Revolt*. Indiana: Indiana University Press, 1998.

Robbins, Richard H. *Global Problems and the Culture of Capitalism*. Fourth ed. United States: Pearson Education, Inc., 2008.

Rosberg, Carl G., Jr. and John Nottingham. *The Myth of "Mau Mau": Nationalism in Kenya*. New York: Frederick A. Praeger, 1966.

Sabar-Friedman, Galia. "The Mau Mau Myth: Kenyan Political Discourse in Search of Democracy (Le Mythe Mau Mau: Le Discours Politique Kenyan à La Recherche De La Démocratie)." *Cahiers d'Études Africaines* 35, no. 137, La démocratie déclinée (1995): pp. 101–31. http://www.jstor.org.proxy.lib.sfu.ca/stable/4392578.

Tarus, Isaac. "Taxation, Migration and the Creation of a Working Class in Kenya." CODESRIA. http://www.codesria.org/Archives/ga10/Abstracts%20Ga%206-11/Migration_Tarus.htm. Accessed 2008-08-11.

Waweru, John F. , Major. "The Bitte Struggle to Independence." http://www.globalsecurity.org/military/library/report/1988/WJF.htm. Accessed 2008-09-11.

Chapter 4

Aluko, Mobolaji. "Oputa Panel Commission Timeline." 2006. http://www.nigerianmuse.com/nigeriawatch/oputa/?u=commission_timeline.htm.

Human Rights Violations Investigation Commission. *Oputa Panel Report: Volume One*. 2005. http://www.kwenu.com/record/2005/ndm_oputa. htm. Accessed 2008-11-16.

Human Rights Watch. *Criminal Politics: Violence, "Godfathers" and Corruption in Nigeria*. October 8, 2007. http://www.hrw.org/en/reports/2007/10/08/criminal-politics-0. Accessed 2008-12-08.

International Committee of the Red Cross. *People on War; Country Report Nigeria*. Greenberg Research, Inc, 1999.

Kirk-Greene, A. H. M. *The Genesis of the Nigerian Civil War and the Theory of Fear*. (Research Report No. 27). Uppsala, Sweden: The Scandinavian Institute of African Studies, 1975.

Kymlicka, Will. *Multicultural Odysseys: Navigating the New International Politics of Diversity*. Oxford: Oxford University Press, 2007.

Stremlau, John. J. *The International Politics of the Nigerian Civil War, 1967–1970*. Princeton, New Jersey: Princeton University Press, 1977.

Uzokwe, Alfred. *Surviving in Biafra: The Story of the Nigerian Civil War*. Lincoln, NE: Writers Advantage, 2003.

Additional Sources

O'Connell, James. "The Scope of the Tragedy." *Africa Report* 13:2 (1968): p. 8.

Ojukwu, C. Odumegwu. *Biafra; Selected Speeches and Random Thoughts*. New York: Harper and Row Publishers, 1969.

Proclamation of the Republic Of Biafra. Enugu: Government Printer, 1967.

Chapter 5

Adam, Heribert and Moodley, Kogila. *Seeking Mandela: Peacemaking between Israelis and Palestinians*. Temple University Press, 2005.

Boualam, B. *Les Harkis au Service de la France*. Paris: Éditions France-Empire, 1963. Excerpts translated by van der Schyff, D.

Charef, M. *Le Harki de Merem*. Paris: Galimard, 1992.

Jasserson, G. *Les Harkis en France*. Paris: Editions du Fuseau, 1965.

Kerchouche, D. *Mon Pére Ce Harki*. Paris: Éditions du Seuil, 2003. Excerpts translated by van der Schyff, D.

Kymlicka, W. *Multicultural Odysseys: Navigating the New International Politics of Diversity*. Oxford: Oxford University Press, 2007.

Phillips, J. and Evans, M. *Algeria: Anger of the Dispossessed*. New Haven and London: Yale University Press, 2007.

Stankiewicz, W. J. *In Search of a Political Philosophy: Ideologies at the Close of the Twentieth Century*. London and New York: Routledge, 1993.

Other Sources
http://www.harkis.info/portail/
http://www.coalition-harkis.com
http://www.harkis.org
http://www.harki.net
Harkis (2006), téléfilm by Alain Tasma for France 2, on a scenario by Dalila Kerchouche and Arnaud Malherbe.
Caché (2005), a film by Michael Haneke.

Chapter 6

Ascherson, Neal. *Spanish Civil War.* Granada Television, 1983. Director David Hart.
Beevor, Anthony. *The Battle for Spain: The Spanish Civil War 1936–1939.* Weidenfeld and Nicholson, 2006.
———. *The Spanish Civil War.* Penguin Books, 2001.
BBC News. 3 May 2003. http://news.bbc.co.uk/2/hi/europe/2997767.stm.
Cobb, James T., LaCour, Christopher A., Hight, William H. *Field Artillery.* US Field Artillery Association, March–April 2005. http://www.globalsecurity.org/military/library/report/2005/2-2AARlow.pdf.
Hemingway, Ernest. *By-Line: Ernest Hemingway.* Bantam Books, 1967.
Instituto Opina. *Encuesta España.* Flash 18 July 2006. http://www.opina.es/web/pdfs/90066e.pdf.
Jamail, Dahr. "What Is the US Trying to Hide in Fallujah?" 19 January 2005. http://www.antiwar.com/jamail/?articleid=4470.
———. "IRAQ: 800 Civilians Feared Dead in Fallujah." *Inter Press Service.* 16 November 2004. http://ipsnews.net/interna.asp?idnews= 26296.
Kisch, Richard. *Franco.* Wayland Publishers Ltd, 1976.
Langdon-Davies, John. *Behind the Spanish Barricades: The Classic Eye-witness Account of Spain's Civil War.* McBride, 1937 (reprinted in 2007 by Reportage Press).
Orwell, George. *Homage to Catalonia.* http://ebooks.adelaide.edu.au/
Sempere, Joaquim. "Memoria histórica y consolidación democrática." *El País,* 2 February, 2007. http://www.nodo50.org/unidadcivicaporlarepublica/Memoria%20historiaca%202007/mem%20hist%20y%20cons%20democr.htm.
Spindler, William. Press briefing. UNHCR, The UN Refugee Agency, Palais des Nations, Geneva. 22 January, 2008. http://www.unhcr.org/cgi-bin/texis/vtx/iraq?page=briefing&id=4795e6222.
Tyson, Ann Scott. *Washington Post,* 19 April, 2005. http://www.washingtonpost.com/wp-dyn/articles/A64292-2005Apr18.html.

Whitaker, John T. *We Cannot Escape History*. The Macmillan Company, 1943.

Chapter 7

"Bombing of Dresden in World War II." *German Notes*, 04 November, 2008. http://www.germannotes com/hist_ww2_dresden shtml.
Ferguson, Niall. *The War of the World*. New York: Penguin, 2006.
Gooderham, Mary. "I Never Thought I Would Go Back." *The Globe and Mail*, 08 November, 2008, sec F5.
Hansen, Randall. *Fire and Fury: The Allied Bombings of Germany 1942–45*. Toronto: Doubleday, 2008.
Harris, Arthur and Robert Saundby. "Bombing of Dresden." www.spartacusschoolnet.co.uk/2WWdresden.htm. 28 October, 2008.
Judt, Tony. *Postwar: A History of Europe since 1945*. New York: Penguin, 2005.
Kitchen, Martin. *A World in Flames*. London: Longman, 1990.
Paris, Erma. *Long Shadows: Truth, Lies and History*. New York: Bloomsbury, 2001.
Salewski, Michael. *Deutschland, Eine Politische Geschichte*. Muenchen: Beck'she Reihe, 1993.
Samuel, Wolfgang. *German Boy: A Child in War*. New York: Broadway Books, 2000.
Willmot, H. P. *The Great Crusade*. London: Pimlico, 1989.

Chapter 8

de Zayas, Alfred-Maurice. *The German Expellees: Victims of War and Peace*. New York: St. Martin's Press, 1986.
Naimark, Norman N. *Fires of Hatred: Ethnic Cleansing in Twentieth-Century Europe*. Cambridge, Massachusetts: Harvard University Press, 2001.
Ther, Philipp and Ana Siljak (eds.). *Redrawing Nations: Ethnic Cleansing in Europe, 1944–1948*. Lanham, Maryland: Rowman and Littlefield Publishers, Inc., 2001.
Várdy, Steven Béla and T. Hunt Tooly (eds.). *Ethnic Cleansing in Twentieth-Century Europe*. Duquesne: Duquesne University, 2000.

Chapter 9

Amis, Martin. *Koba the Dread: Laughter and the Twenty Million*. New York: Random House, Inc., 2002.
Conquest, Robert. *The Harvest of Sorrow*. Oxford: Oxford University Press, 1986.

Courtois, Stephane, et al. *The Black Book of Communism: Crimes, Terror, Repression.* Cambridge, Massachusetts: Harvard University Press, 1999.

Grigorenko, Petro. *Memoirs.* New York: W. W. Norton and Company, 1982.

Hryshko, Wasyl. *The Ukrainian Holocaust of 1933.* Toronto: Bahriany Foundation, 1983.

Khrushchev, Nikita. *Khrushchev Remembers.* Boston: Little, Brown and Company, 1970.

Kravchenko, Victor. *I Chose Freedom.* New York: Garden City Publishing Co. Ltd., 1946.

Mace, James E. *Communism and the Dilemmas of National Liberation: National Communism in Soviet Ukraine, 1918–1933.* Cambridge, Massachusetts: Harvard University Press, 1983.

Magocsi, Paul Robert. *Ukraine: An Illustrated History.* Toronto: University of Toronto Press, 2007.

Martin, Terry. *The Affirmative Action Empire: Nations and Nationalism in the Soviet Union, 1923–1939.* Ithaca and London: Cornell University Press, 2001.

Overy, Richard. *The Dictators: Hitler's Germany and Stalin's Russia.* London: Allen Lane, 2004.

Solzhenitsyn, Aleksandr I. *The Gulag Archipelago: 1918–1956, An Experiment in Literary Investigation.* New York: Harper and Row, Publishers, 1973.

Stalin, J. V. *Works.* Moscow: Foreign Languages Publishing House, 1955.

Subtelny, Orest. *Ukraine: A History.* Toronto: University of Toronto Press, 1988.

Chapter 10

Adam, Heribert and Kogila Moodley. *Seeking Mandela: Peacemaking between Israelis and Palestinians.* Philadelphia: Temple University Press, 2005.

Akcam, Taner. *From Empire to Republic: Turkish Nationalism and the Armenian Genocide.* London and New York: Zed Books, Ltd., 2004.

Akcam, Taner. *Dialogue Across an International Divide: Essays Towards a Turkish-Armenian Dialogue.* Cambridge, MA: The Zorayan Institute, 2001.

Balakian, Peter. *The Burning Tigris: The Armenian Genocide and America's Response.* New York: Harper Collins, 2003.

Dadrian, Vahkan N. *The Key Elements in the Turkish Denial of the Armenian Genocide: A Case Study of Distortion and Falsification.* Cambridge, MA: The Zorayan Institute, 1999.

Hovannisian, Richard (ed.), *The Armenian Genocide: Cultural and Ethical Legacies.* New Brunswick, NJ: Transaction Publishers, 2007.

Lewy, Guenter. *The Armenian Massacres in Ottoman Turkey: A Disputed Genocide*. Salt Lake City: University of Utah Press, 2005.

Nussbaum, Martha C. *Upheavals of Thought: The Intelligence of Emotions*. Cambridge, UK: Cambridge University Press, 2001.

Pamuk, Orhan. *Snow*. tr. Maureen Freely. New York: Alfred A. Knopf, 2005.

Phillips, David L. *Unsilencing the Past: Track Two Diplomacy and Turkish-Armenian Reconciliation*. New York: Berghan Books, 2005.

Power, Samantha. *A Problem from Hell: America and the Age of Genocide*. New York: Harper Perennial, 2007.

Chapter 11

Abd-Allah, Umar F. *The Islamic Struggle in Syria*. Berkeley: Mizen, 1983.

Amnesty International Report 1982. London: Amnesty International Publications, 1982.

Amnesty International Report 1983. London: Amnesty International Publications, 1983.

Fisk, Robert. *Pity the Nation: The Abduction of Lebanon*. New York: Thunder's Mouth Press, 2002.

———*The Great War for Civilisation: The Conquest of the Middle East*. London: Fourth Estate, 2005.

Friedman, Thomas L. *From Beirut to Jerusalem*. New York: Farrar Straus Giroux, 1989.

Haklai, Oded. "A Minority Rule Over a Hostile Majority: The Case of Syria." *Nationalism & Ethnic Politics*, Vol. 6 Issue 3 (Autumn 2000). http://proxy.lib.sfu.ca/login?url=http://search.ebscohost.com/login.aspx?direct=true&db=aph&AN=6904235&site=ehost-live.

Leverett, Flynt. *Inheriting Syria: Bashar's Trial by Fire*. Washington: Brookings, 2005.

Mo'az, Moshe. *Asad: Sphinx of Damascus: A Political Biography*. London: Weiden & Nicolson, 1988.

Wedeen, Lisa. *Ambiguities of Domination: Politics, Rhetoric, and Symbols in Contemporary Syria*. Chicago: University of Chicago Press, 1999.

Wiedl, Kathrin Nina. *The Hama Massacre – Reasons, Supporters of the Rebellion, Consequences*. http://books.google.ca/books?hl=en&lr=&id=-2jCN5Ur6yUC&oi=fnd&pg=PA3&dq=hamah+massacre&ots=eT9mF2ylYB&sig=95u-KiJYSXL7_kIIJsyN1bkYmKE.

Wieland, Carstan. *Syria at Bay: Secularism, Islamism and 'Pax Americana'*. London: Hurst, 2006.

Chapter 12

Abu-Lughod, Lila. "My Father's Return to Palestine." *Jerusalem Quarterly File*, 11–12 (2001). www.jaf-jerusalem.org/journal/2001/jqf11-12/.

Bardenstein, Carol B. "Raped Brides and Steadfast Mothers." In Alexis Jetter, Annelise Orleck, and Diane Taylor (eds.). *The Politics of Motherhood: Activist Voices From Left to Right.* Hanover: University Press of New England, 1997, pp. 170–181.

_____. "Trees, Forests, and the Shaping of Palestinian and Israeli Collective Memory." In Mieke L. Bal, Jonathan Crewe and Leo Spitzer (eds.). *Acts of Memory: Cultural Recall in the Present.* Hanover: University of New England, 1999, pp. 148–68.

Barthes, Roland. *Mythologies.* London: Vintage, 2000.

Busaileah, Reja-e. "The Fall of Lydda." *Arab Studies Quarterly* 3, no. 2 (Spring 1981): pp. 123–51.

Caruth, Cathy. *Trauma: Explorations in Memory.* Baltimore: John Hopkins University Press, 1995.

Connerton, Paul. *How Societies Remember.* Cambridge: Cambridge University Press, 1989.

Dershowitz, Alan. *The Case for Israel.* Hoboken, N.J.: John Wiley and Sons, 2003.

Hammami, Rema. "Gender, *Nakbe* and Nation: Palestinian Women's Presence and Absence in the Narration of 1948 Memories." In Robin Robin and Bo Stråth (eds.). *Homelands: Poetic Power and the Politics of Space.* Brussels: P.I.E. Peter Lang, 2003.

Herzl, Theodor. *The Complete Diaries of Theodor Herzl.* Vol. 1 (edited by Raphael Patai). New York: Herzl Press and Thomas Yoseloff, 1960.

Kanaana, Sharif. "Methodology in The Destroyed Palestinian Villages Project." Paper delivered at the Carleton-Bir Zeit Workshop. Carleton University. Ottawa, Ontario: March 8–9, 1989.

Khalidi, Walid. "Why Did the Palestinians Leave? An Examination of the Zionist Version of the Exodus of 48." *Middle East Forum* 34 (July 1959): pp. 21–24.

_____. "Why did the Palestinians Leave, Revisited." *Journal of Palestinian Studies* 34, no. 2 (2005), pp. 42–54.

Misztal, Barbara. *Theories of Social Remembering.* Philadelphia: Open University Press, 2003.

Morris, Benny. *The Birth of the Palestinian Refugee Problem, 1947–1949.* Cambridge: Cambridge University Press, 1987.

_____. *The Birth of the Palestinian Refugee Problem Revisited.* Cambridge: Cambridge University Press, 2004.

Palumbo, Michael. *The Palestinian Catastrophe: the 1948 Expulsion of a People from Their Homeland.* London, Boston: Faber and Faber, 1987.

Pappé, Ilan. *A History of Modern Palestine: One Land, Two Peoples.* Cambridge: Cambridge University Press, 2004.

Said, Edward and Christopher Hitchins (eds.). *Blaming the Victims: Spurious Scholarship and the Palestinian Question.* New York: Verso, 2001.

Slyomovics, Susan. *The Object of Memory: Arab and Jew Narrate the Palestinian Village.* Philadelphia: University of Pennsylvania Press, 1998.

Whitelam, Keith W. *The Invention of Ancient Israel: The Silencing of Palestinian History.* London: Routledge, 1996.

Chapter 13

Behavioral Science Centre on Behalf of Citizen's Initiative. *Humanity at Crossroads in Gujarat, 2002.* Noida: Rainbow Publishing, 2003.

Brass, Paul R. *The Production of Hindu-Muslim Violence in Contemporary India.* Seattle: University of Washington Press, 2003.

Dayal, John (ed.). *Gujarat 2002: Untold and Retold Stories of the Hindutva Lab.* Delhi: Justice and Peace Commission & All India Christian Council; Distributed by Media House, 2002.

Engineer, Asghar Ali (ed.). *The Gujarat Carnage.* New Delhi: Orient Longman, 2003.

Luce, Edward. *In Spite of the Gods: The Rise of Modern India.* New York: Anchor Books, 2008.

Mander, Harsh. *Cry My Beloved Country: Reflections on the Gujarat Carnage.* Noida: Rainbow Publishing, 2004.

Mishra, Pankaj. *Temptations of the West: How to Be Modern in India, Pakistan, Tibet and Beyond.* New York: Picador, 2007.

Chapter 14

Budiardjo, Carmel. *Surviving Indonesia's Gulag.* U.K: Cassell, 1996.

Chomsky, Noam and Herman, Edward S. *The Washington Connection and Third World Fascism.* Boston: Southend Press, 1979.

Cribb, Robert. *The Indonesian Killings 1965–66: Studies from Java and Bali.* Australia: Center for Southeast Asian Studies, Monash University, 1990.

Roosa, John. *Pretext for Mass Murder.* The University of Wisconsin Press, 2006.

Scharfe, Sharon. *Complicity: Human Rights and Canadian Foreign Policy.* Montreal, Canada: Black Rose Books, 1996.

Scott, Peter Dale. "The United States and the Overthrow of Sukarno, 1965–1967." *Pacific Affairs*, 58, Summer 1985.

Scott, Peter Dale. *Coming to Jakarta: a Poem about Terror.* Toronto: McClelland and Stewart, 1988.
TAPOL, *The British Campaign for Political Prisoners in Indonesia.* United Kingdom.
"Indonesian Communism Since the 1965 Coup." *Pacific Affairs*, Spring 1970.

Chapter 15

Hicks, George. *The Comfort Women: Japan's Brutal Regime of Enforced Prostitution in the Second World War.* New York: W.W. Norton & Company, 1995.
Howard, Keith (ed.). *True Stories of the Korean Comfort Women: Testimonies Compiled by the Korean Council for Women Drafted for Military Sexual Slavery by Japan and the Research Association on the Women Drafted for Military Sexual Slavery by Japan.* New York: Cassell, 1995.
Schellsted, Sangmie Choi (ed.). *Comfort Women Speak: Testimony by Sex Slaves of the Japanese Military.* New York: Holmes & Meier Science and Human Rights, 2000.
Ui, Jun (ed.). *Industrial Pollution in Japan.* Tokyo: United Nations University Press, 1992.
Warren, Karen J. *Ecofeminist Philosophy: a Western Perspective on What it is and Why it Matters.* Maryland, USA: Rowman & Littlefield Publishers, Inc., 2000.
Yin, James and Dorfman, S. Young (eds.). *The Rape of Nanking: an Undeniable History in Photographs.* Chicago: Innovative Publishing Group, 1996.
Yoshiaki, Yoshim and O'Brien, S. (tr.). *Comfort Women: Sexual Slavery in the Japanese Military during World War II.* New York: Columbia University Press, 2000.

Conclusions

Adam, Heribert and Kogila Moodley. *South Africa Without Apartheid: Dismantling Racial Domination.* Berkeley: University of California Press, 1986.
Adam, Heribert and Kogila Moodley. *The Opening of the Apartheid Mind.* Berkeley: University of California Press, 1993.
Adam, Heribert, Kogila Moodley, F. Van Zyl Slabbert. *Comrades in Business. Post-Liberation Politics in South Africa.* Cape Town: Tafelberg and Leiden: International Books, 1997.
Adam, Heribert and Kogila Moodley. *Seeking Mandela. Peacemaking Between Israelis and Palestinians.* Philadelphia: Temple University Press, 2006.

Buchanan, Allen. *Secession: The Morality of Political Divorce from Fort Sunter to Lithuania and Quebec.* Boulder, Colorado: Westview Press, 1991.

Crush, J. (ed.). *The Perfect Storm: The Realities of Xenophobia in Contemporary South Africa.* Johannesburg: The Southern African Migration Project, No. 50, 2008.

Fredrickson, G. M. "Mosaics and Melting Pots". *Dissent*, Summer 1999, pp. 36–42.

Hassim, Shireen et al. *South Africa: Go Home or Die Here – Violence, Xenophobia and the Reinvention of Difference in SA.* Johannesburg: Wits University Press, 2009.

Kakar, Sudhir. *The Colors of Violence.* Chicago: Chicago University Press, 1996.

Koenigsberg, Richard. *Nations Have the Right to Kill.* New York: Library of Social Sciences, 1999.

Marchak, Patricia. *No Easy Fix: Global Responses to Internal Wars and Crimes Against Humanity.* Montreal and Kingston: McGill-Queens University Press, 2008.

Nyamnjoh, F. *Insiders and Outsiders: Citizenship and Xenophobia in Contemporary Southern Africa.* London: Zed Books, 2006.

Van den Berghe, Pierre L. *The Ethnic Phenomenon.* New York: Praeger, 1987.

Volkan, Vamic. *Large Groups and their Leaders.* New York: National Book Network, 2004.

Volkan, Vamic. *Killing in the Name of Identity.* Ingram, 2006.

Zaslavsky, Victor. *Class Cleansing: The Massacre at Katyn.* New York: Telos P, 2008.

Index

Abu Ghraib 69
Abu-Lughod, Lila 147
Adam, Heribert 187
Adorno, Th. W. 197
Advani, L. K. 150
African National Congress (ANC) 70, 71
Akcam, Taner 117, 122
Alawites, 126–32
Albright, Madeline 173
Alexander, Jocelyn 11
Algeria 51–61
Ali, Agha Shahid 27
Amnesty International 9, 167
Anderson, Benedict 196
Anderson, David 38–39
Angola xx
Anti Semitism xviii, 196
Asad, Bashar 134
Asad, Hafiz 136
Asherson, Neal 72
Atatürk, Mustafa Kemal 115, 116, 123
Australia viii
Ayodhya 150
Ba'ath Party 126–31
Bajrangi, Babu 153
Balfour 138
Bang, Anne 26
Barthes, Roland 148
Bashir, Omar 189, 200
Bauer, Yehuda xvii
Beevor, Antony 64
Benes, Eduard 91
Ben-Gurion, David 138–39
Berger, Joseph 109
Biafra 41–52
Blakian, Peter 124
Boraine, Alex ix
Bosnia v
Boualam, Bachaga 52
Brandt, Willy vii, 97
Brass, Paul 196
Brecht, Bertold 89
Briere, Elaine xix, 175
Buchanan 190
Budiardjo, Carmel 164
Bush, G. W. 68
Byron 118
Cambodia vi
CARITAS 47
Carney, Mike 174
Chatham House 11
Chechnya vii, xix
China vi
Chomsky, Noam 175
Churchill, Winston 83
Clayton, Anthony 16
Clough, Marshall S. 36, 39
Cobb, James T. 73
Cohen, John 26
Congo, Democratic Republic xix, xx
Conquest, Robert 108
Courtois, Stephane 109
Coventry 79
Crossman, Vasily 101, 104
Crush, Jonathan 193, 195
Cumming-Bruce, F. 45
Czechoslovakia 89–95
Dalits 158
Darfur xv
De Zayas, Alfred-Maurice 95
DeVito, Karen xix
Dink, Hrant 122
Du Toit, Andre ix
Dugger, Celia 161
Dundar, Cam 123
Dunlap, Charles 199
Duranty, Walter 107
East Prussia 92
East Timor v, 171
Edward, Herman 175
Eisenhower, General 94
Elkins, Caroline 35
Erdogan 116
Evans, Martin 60
Evian Accord 55
Falange 64
Ferguson 81
Fisk, Robert 128, 132
Flapan, Simha 148
Ford, Gerald vii
Franco, General 63–73
Fredrickson, George 196
Friedman, Robert 130
Friedman, Thomas 132
Gandhi, Mahatma 158
Garzon, Baltasar 68
Gaza 199–200
Geffen, Nathan xxiii
Geneva Convention 194
Genocide, UN Convention xv
Giliomee, Hermann ix
Goebbels 82
Goering 82
Goldstone, Richard 200
Gönül 117
Gorbachev xix
Govender, Pregs xxiii
Gowon 44
Greenberg Research 49
Grigorenko, Petro 106
Guatemala xx
Guernica xix, 65, 69
Gukurahundi 1–10
Hadawi, Sami 147
Haganah 139
Haile Selassie 11
Haklae, Odette 135
Hamid, Abdul 114
Hansen, Randall 80
Harris, Arthur 75
Hassim, Shireen 193, 195
Havel, Vaclav 96
Hemmingway 65
Hereroes xix
Herzl, Theodor 147
Hesse, Herman 125
Hicks, George 185
Hill, Geoff 11
Himmler 82
Hindutva 150
Hiroshima-Nagasaki 81
Hitler 65, 91
HIV/AIDS xx, xxiii
Ho Chi Minh 54
Holocaust xvii, 85, 153
Holodomor 101–11
Hope, Christopher 11
Hoshino, Yoshiro 186
Hovannisian, Richard 124
Howard, John vii
Howard, Keith 185
Hryshko, Vasyl 111
Hughes, John 166
Human Rights Watch 48
Hunter, Helen 26
Hussain, Sadam 24
International Center for Transitional Justice (ICTJ) ix, 188, 119
International Criminal Court (ICC) v, 199
International Red Cross 47
Iraq viii, 68
Irgun 140
Ironsi 44
Jacopetti, Gualtiero 23

Jaffa 148
Japan 177–87
Jawad, Saleh Abdel 140
Kadane, Kathy 167
Kahlidi, Walid 139
Kakar, Sudhir 198
Kako, Senda 178
Karume, Abeid 23
Katyn xix
Kennedy, Dane 33
Kenya 27–37
Kenyatta, Jomo 37
Kerchouche, Dalila 51
Khosla, Vinit xix
Kibaki, Myai 37
Kikuyu 27–37
Kipande 29
Kirk-Greene, A. H. M. 49
Kish, Richard 72
Koenigsberg, Richard 194
Komsomol 103
Korea 178–85
Kravchenko, Victor 104, 107
Kristof, Nicholas D. xxi
Krupskaya 105
Kubler-Ross, Elizabeth 148
Kulak 104
Kundera, Milan 137
Kymlicka, Will 42
Langdon-Davies, John 72
Lawfare 199
Lemkin, Rafael 115
Lenin 102
Leverett, Flynt 135
Levy, Norman ix
Lockwood, Sandra xix
Lofchie, Michael 18
Lorca, Frederico Garcia 61
Luce, Edward 156, 157, 160
Lyttleton, Oliver 32
MacArthur, Douglas 180
Mace, James 111
Maloba, W. O. 39
Mandela 171
Mao, Zedong xix, 54
Marchak, P. 190
Martin, E. B. 26
Mathews, Elbert 45
Mau Mau 27–37
Mbeki, Thabo xx, 188
McArthur, George 168
McDougall, Gay J. 182
Mishra Pankaj 150, 157, 158
Mkuu, Mwinye 15
Moaz, Moshe 135
Modi, Narendra 151–52
Mola, General 65
Moliner, Juan 66
Molotov Ribbentrop Pact 91
Montseny, Frederica 64
Morgenthau, Henry 115
Morris, Benny 141–42
Mozambique 188
Mugabe, Robert 1–10, 193
Muslim Brotherhood 137–40
Myburg, James xxiii
Nagengast, Emile 98
Naimark, Norman 92
Nakba 137–47
Namas xix
Namibia xix
Nanavati Commission 156
Nazi Germany xv, 77
Ndebele 1–10
Nigeria 41–52
Nixon, Richard 169
Nkomo, Joshua 2
North Korea 4
Nottingham, John 38
Obama, Barack 121
Obasanjo, Olusegun 48
Odinga, Raila 37
Ojukwu 44
Okello, John 21–23
Oputa Panel Report 47–48
Orwell George 63
Pact of Forgetting 66
Pamuk, Orhan 113
Pappe, Ilan 148
Parlange, R. 51
Pearl Harbour vii
Petterson, Don 26
Pettigrew, T. 198
Phillips, David L. 119
Phillips, John 60
Poland, 89–95
Portal, Charles 81
Potsdam Conference 92
Power, Samantha 124
Prosperi, Franco 23
Quebec 190
Robbins, Richard H. 38
Rogan, Eugene 147
Roosa, John 169
Roosevelt 83
Rosberg, Carl G. Jnr 31, 38
Roy, Arundhati 152, 158
Russell, Bertrand 94
Russia vi
Rwanda v, 192
Sadi, Ahmad 147
Sanbar, Elias 143
Sane, Pierre 9
Santayana, George vii, 72
Sarkozy, Nicholas 59
Saroyan, William 122
Savage, Michael ix
Scharfe, Sharon 172
Seale, Patrick 135
Sempere, Joachim 73
Shain, Milton ix
Shaplen, Robert 168
Shevchenko, Taras 101
Shlaim, Avi 147
Sholokov, Mikhail 108
Sierra Leone Special Court v
Slavery 16–18
Smith, Charles 147
Smith, Ian 2
Snider, T. xxiii
Spaatz, Carl 81
Spindler, William 73
Srebrenica 201
Sri Lanka vii
Stalin 83, 92, 102–05
Stasek, Bohumil 92
Stokes, Richard Rapier 78
Stovel, Laura ix
Stremlau, John J. 50
Sudan vii
Sudeten Germans 90–93
Suharto, 163–73
Sukarno 163
Sulzberger, C. L. 168
Syria, 125–35
Taylor, Richard 80
Teeple, Gary ix
Ther, Philipp 98
Thom, Anso xxiii
Tiannamen Square xv
Tibet xix
Tooly, T. Hunt 98
Torpey, John ix
Trudeau, Pierre 172
Truth Commission vi, xix, 37, 188
Tsvangirai, Morgan 9
Ukraine 101–11
Unguja 15
Uys, Stanley ix
Uzokwe, Alfred 46
Van den Berghe, Pierre ix, 197
Vardy, Steven Bela 98
Vatican 47
Versailles 90
Volkan, Vamik 198
Vollmer, Antje 96
Warnock, Kitti 148
Warren, Karen 186
Webb, Sidney and Beatrice 110
Wedeen, Lisa 131
Weinstein, Harvey ix, 192
Werth, Nicholas 105
Whitaker, John T. 72
Wiedl, Katherine 136
Wieland, Carstan 136
Williams, Rowan 25
World Council of Churches 47
Yad Vachem 146
Yin, James 177
Yoshiaki, Yoshimi 185
Young, Shi 177
Yugoslavia vi
ZANU 1–10
Zanzibar 13–26
ZAPU 1–10
Zaslavsky, Victor 191
Zaslove, Jerry ix
Zinn, Howard xvii
Zionism 137–40
Zuma, Jacob xx